American Canvas

RON TYLER

American Canvas

THE ART, EYE, AND SPIRIT OF PIONEER ARTISTS

Quotations compiled by Fred Erisman

PORTLAND HOUSE
NEW YORK

Frontispiece
JASPER F. CROPSEY *Niagara Falls*, 1860. (Collection of Jo Ann and Julian Ganz, Jr.)

This 1990 edition published by Portland House, a division of
dilithium Press Ltd., distributed by Crown Publishers, Inc.,
225 Park Avenue South, New York, New York 10003

Printed and bound in Japan by Dai Nippon

ISBN 0-517-01736-9

hgfedcba

Contents

Preface and acknowledgments 7

Introduction
Visions of paradise 9
Depicting the colonies 19
Opening the West 29
The painters' vision 46

A journey in time from the Atlantic to the Pacific 61

PRELUDE: Artist and writer, "Kindred Spirits" in the American wilderness 64

The East 66
Colonial cities – A nation emerges – Cities of the Federal
age – Boston – Development of the country – The new capital:
Washington – The painters' state: New York – The farmers'
paradise – Niagara Falls – The railroad transforms the
countryside – The gathering storm – The face of commerce –
"Dark Satanic mills" – Improvement by education – Artists in
the landscape

The South 98
Exploration and settlement – The naturalist's world – Early
towns – The age of steam – Cities of the South – Plantation
economy – Scenes exotic and sublime – A divided
nation – The defeated South – The Crescent City

The Midwest 118
A frontier fort – From fort to city – A pioneer settlement –
Evidence of the Ancients – St Louis, gateway to the
West – Along the rivers – Across the country – Farming on
the prairie – Chicago – Midwestern metropolises

The West   136

American ventures – Rivers of the West – The native sons –
Hunting the bison – Noble Savages – The Mormon
migrations – Miller and the route West – The Gold Rush –
The Overland Trail – The urban West – Yosemite –
The transcontinental railroad is complete – Thomas Moran's
West – The cowboy conquers the Plains – The bountiful land

The Southwest   166

The Mexican Southwest – Texas and the war with Mexico –
Trade and exploration – Richard Kern in New Mexico –
The Southwestern surveys – Santa Fe – The Colorado
River of the West

The Northwest   182

Spanish explorers in Alaska – The Colville Indians –
Disputed territory: Washington State – Explorer artists –
Towns of the Willamette Valley

POSTLUDE: After the explorers, tourists discover America   192

Bibliography   193

Annotated catalogue of the illustrations   195

Index   206

Map of America   62

Preface and acknowledgments

The earliest eye-witness picture of America to survive, a scene of Florida
Indians by the French cartographer Jacques Le Moyne de Morgues, dates
from 1564. It was the first of a host of documentary pictures that were to be
made over the next three hundred years, capturing the country's original
inhabitants, its landscapes, and its towns. The gradual discovery and
depiction of America is the story with which this book is concerned. Its form
is not a continuous narrative, but a series of rapid impressions of the new
land as it revealed itself to observers, recorded in images and in words.

Some artists were individual explorers, like Mark Catesby, who got as far
west as the Appalachians in the 1720s, George Catlin, who painted the
Mandan Indians of North Dakota in the 1830s, and Paul Kane, who
investigated the Pacific Northwest in the 1840s. Others took part in journeys
of record or discovery: Karl Bodmer accompanied the scholarly German Prince
Maximilian of Wied-Neuwied to northern Montana in 1833, and the mid-
century explorations of the Southwest and of possible routes for a
transcontinental railroad resulted in a wealth of images by various hands,
chief among them John Mix Stanley and John Russell Bartlett. Yet other
artists set up to produce views of specific places to be engraved and sold
commercially, from William Burgis's New York and Boston prints of the 1720s
through the lithographed townscapes of such firms as Sachse & Co. of
Baltimore and Kuchel & Dresel of California.

In addition to the documentary, there was another mode in which artists
approached the new land. Starting in the 1820s with young Thomas Cole, a
school of American painters grew up for whom the depiction of a scene was
no less important than the scene itself. The men of the Hudson River School
came to see in the American wilderness a manifestation of God. The
Luminists, of the next generation, used art to conceal art, contriving in their
wide canvases to bring the viewer directly into the landscape. Both traditions,
the documentary and the painterly, merged when the artist Thomas Moran
accompanied scientific expeditions into the Yellowstone and then into the
Grand Canyon. Two vast and stunning paintings, one of each of those
spectacular landscapes, were purchased by the United States government not
long before the nation's first centennial in 1876.

By then the mood of America was changing, with the rising aesthetic and
philosophical tide of the machine age; and photographers, exploiting the
brilliance and popularity of a new machine, could produce handsome scenes
of town and country that the public immediately accepted as truthful (as
indeed they were). Their achievements dealt the *coup de grace* to landscape
and view painting – a human activity which could, at its best, convey more
than bare facts.

The main problem in writing about a complex nation over a long period of
time is that genuine complications are rendered over-simple, and unrelated
and distant events, by force of space, are joined and burdened with meaning

that careful analysis might not bear out. The sense of time and place can be enhanced, however, by going to written records – travelers' books, diaries, even fiction based on first-hand knowledge – and juxtaposing them to the surviving pictures. In making up this book, we have been constantly surprised at the degree of agreement between writers and artists, and at the extra depth that each medium lends the other, building up an almost three-dimensional sense of "being there." Artists and writers show the same sensitivity, the same quirks of perception, and the same awed realization that they were experiencing something that few generations *could* experience: how the American continent looked as it gradually revealed its secrets to discovery, and as it grew to adulthood.

An undertaking of this nature simply is not possible without the willing assistance of dozens of curators and scholars. The search for and acquisition of photographs and transparencies of pictures means that librarians and curators must lay aside their normal duties to provide reproductions of works in their collections. For many this is routine, but others have gone far beyond the normal response in assisting with this book. I would especially like to thank David Hunt of the Joslyn Art Museum and Bernard Reilly of the Prints and Photographs Division of the Library of Congress for their many favors. Also of great assistance were Parrott Bacot of the Anglo-American Art Museum, Louisiana State University; Steven W. Plattner of the Cincinnati Historical Society; Rebecca Tiger of the Corcoran Gallery of Art; John Lawrence and Dode Platou of the Historic New Orleans Collection; J. B. Harter of the Louisiana State Museum; Sarah E. Boehme of the Stark Museum of Art; and William Cuffe of the Yale University Art Gallery.

Several members of the Amon Carter Museum staff have been especially helpful and supportive. Jan Keene Muhlert, the Director, has been most encouraging in the use of materials from the museum collection. Carol Clark, William Howze, and Martha A. Sandweiss read the introductory essay and offered valuable suggestions for its improvement, and Linda Lorenz and her staff, Rynda White and Earl C. Moore, provided quality photographic reproductions. Anne Adams and Melissa Thompson made information from the Registrar's office instantly available, while Librarian Nancy Graves Wynne and Assistant Librarian Milan Ross Hughston provided great assistance in my research and last-minute questions.

I would like to thank, finally, my wife, Paula Eyrich Tyler, who talked with me frequently during the development of the idea behind the book and proofread and edited every version of the manuscript. The mistakes and oversights that have crept in are, of course, my responsibility, but they would have been far greater in their number without the conscientious assistance that I have received.

RON TYLER *Fort Worth, Texas*

Introduction

A garden paradise to the west was but a figment of the imagination of dreamers and the subject of ancient myths when Christopher Columbus sailed out of the Spanish port of Palos with his tiny fleet of three ships in August 1492. Seventy days and some three thousand miles later, he walked ashore on one of the small islands in what is today the Bahamas and claimed San Salvador for the Spanish Crown, mistaken in the belief that he had reached the Orient. Columbus did not know that a New World blocked his path to the east, and in his letter reporting to Isabella and Ferdinand of Spain, he claimed that he had reached the islands near the Great Khan.

The demand for information about Columbus's adventure was so great that his letter was quickly translated and published throughout southern Europe. Skilled engravers designed images to illustrate it, although no artist had accompanied the expedition. Working from what the Mexican historian Edmundo O'Gorman has described as Europe's preconceptions of this tropical garden, the artists relied on the centuries of literature and legends of paradise to form their images. The Classics are rife with descriptions of idyllic garden spots, such as Plato's mythical continent of Atlantis, the Islands of the Blessed, and the Elysian Fields, all offering a pristine environment with extraordinary vegetation and awe-inspiring landscapes. With the passage of centuries, inquisitive men did not give up hope of finding such an earthly paradise, but the names changed and the myths grew even more glamorous. By the mid-fifteenth century, explorers searched not for mythical abodes of the soul, but for fountains of youth, the land of the Amazon women, the Seven Cities of Cíbola, and El Dorado. Because no one really knew what Columbus had discovered, a rather familiar image began to emerge as artists combined these vague and Classically inspired concepts of a garden with Columbus's eye-witness accounts.

Columbus had landed on islands that he believed were just off the coast of Cathay, near the gold mines and in the "best position" to take advantage of trade with the Great Khan. Cuba he described as a "most beautiful" land with "wide fertile plains . . . filled with trees of a thousand kinds." His friend Peter Martyr, a learned member of the Spanish court as well as one of the first historians of the New World, agreed, declaring in his *Decades de Orbe Novo* (1511) that this "golden world" was the paradise "of which old writers speak so much" and where naked dancing girls recalled "those splendid naiads or nymphs of the fountains, so much celebrated by the ancients."

pp.10, 11   The small and cramped woodcuts that accompanied various editions of Columbus's letter were hardly equal to that vision. To the painfully overdressed Europeans of the fifteenth century who knew of few primitive peoples, one of the most interesting aspects of his description was the nakedness of the Indians. Both the Swiss artist who designed the illustration for the Basel edition (1493) and the Italian who in the same year engraved the

Insula Hyspana, from the first illustrated edition of Christopher Columbus's "Letter to Sánchez," Basel, 1493. (The New York Public Library, Astor, Lenox and Tilden Foundations)

cover for the Florence edition were careful to include easily recognizable drawings of the natives.

As interesting as these woodcuts are historically, they are in reality little more than decoration for Columbus's narrative. The scene from the Basel edition, probably the first picture representing an American incident, shows a figure (supposedly Columbus) trading with the Indians. Some of the natives come forward to exchange goods with him, while others shyly retreat toward a forest, exhibiting none of the exuberance that Peter Martyr would have expected. Vertical mountains and rolling hills and valleys beyond indicate the fertility and lushness of what is evidently an Eden-like setting. The second picture, on the cover of the Florence edition of the letter, depicts Columbus's arrival in the Indies. The Spanish King, in the left foreground, directs the explorer's three ships toward the island, which is inhabited by giants who need little clothing and only tabernacle-like structures to live in. In fact, the images evoked by Columbus's descriptions were so similar to the European concept of a virgin land that printers who published his letter simply used woodcuts prepared for books that had nothing to do with Columbus or his discovery, rather than go to the trouble and expense of preparing new illustrations.

The idea of America as the garden paradise of literature flourished despite the fact that further exploration revealed numerous thorns on the roses of this garden. Columbus himself was disappointed to learn during his second voyage that the cannibalism he had noted during his first trip seemed more prevalent, and that some of the tempting fruits he had so enthusiastically described in his letter turned out to be deadly poisons. During his last two voyages Columbus charted several more Caribbean islands and explored along the coasts of Central and South America, but he brought back no additional riches and never realized that the sea route to the Orient that he so urgently sought had been discovered by the Portuguese Vasco da Gama sailing around the tip of Africa in 1498.

pp.12–13 Initial Spanish forays on the North American mainland were even less fortunate, yet the first picture to come out of the Spanish conquest of the American Southwest also confirmed the image of a pastoral, though hardly peaceful, garden. With additional explorations, the Spaniards soon realized that they were dealing not with the Orient but with a New World, and turned to the business of conquering and looting what they considered to be an unclaimed land. Following on the heels of Hernán Cortés's brutal conquest of Mexico in 1519–21 and Francisco Pizarro's rape of the Inca empire in Peru, Pánfilo de Narváez set sail with an ill-fated expedition of six hundred prospective settlers in 1528. In Florida they became separated from their ships, and tried to reach Mexico by sailing along the Gulf coast in crudely-constructed rafts. Among them Alvar Núñez Cabeza de Vaca and three companions, whose raft was wrecked on the coast of Texas, finally reached Mexico in 1536 after surviving seven and a half years as slaves, traders, and medicine men among the Indians of the Southwest. Even though he had no first-hand knowledge of precious metals or wealthy cities, Cabeza de Vaca described the Southwest in terms that kept alive the *conquistadores'* hope for "another Mexico" and led them to conclude that the heralded Seven Cities of Cíbola lay within their grasp.

The King of Spain directs Columbus's landing in the Indies: illustration from *La lettera dellisole che ha trouato nuouamente il Re dispagna*, Florence, 1493. (British Library, London)

A scout's reports erroneously confirmed the rumors of a city of gold, and Antonio de Mendoza, Viceroy of New Spain, mounted one of the largest expeditions the New World had ever known, under twenty-nine-year-old Francisco Vásquez de Coronado. More than three hundred Spanish soldiers, some with their wives, children, and slaves, along with more than eight hundred Indian allies, and thousands of cattle, mules, and sheep proceeded northward from Mexico, expecting a larger empire where the inhabitants used gold for utilitarian tools. Instead, they found the modest adobe pueblo of Háwikuh, full of Zuñis already apprehensive of the Spaniards because of the reconnaissance and unwilling to surrender. Coronado had to protect his careless scout from frustrated troops, while informing Mendoza that the man had "in reality . . . not told the truth in a single thing that he said . . ." Still, the encounter led to perhaps the most significant imaginary picture of America done in the sixteenth century.

pp.12–13

The Zuñis laid down lines of sacred corn meal, forbidding the Spaniards to cross them. Coronado's announcement that he had come in peace had no effect, and when the Spaniards put down their arms, inviting the Zuñis to do the same, the Indians attacked. This brief battle on June 24, 1540, in which perhaps a dozen Indians died and Coronado was wounded before the Zuñis were routed, seems to be the subject of a mysterious picture by the Dutch artist Jan Mostaert, painted about 1542. This shows a fantasy landscape with naked natives on the left, rallying to fight invaders who have just come from the sea on the right. Beyond the extraordinary rocky village, the landscape recedes past lakes and a forested area to mountains in the upper left-hand corner.

It is probable that Mostaert worked from a now unknown – and perhaps irrevocably lost – description of the event, but Pedro de Castañeda's history of the Coronado expedition, published after Mostaert's death, provides an

JAN MOSTAERT *"An Episode in the Conquest of America,"* or *"West Indian Landscape,"* c. 1542. (State-Owned Art Collections Department, The Hague (Dienst Verspreide Rijkskollekties te den Haag))

account to which the painting can be compared. Castañeda, for example, describes in detail Coronado's advance against the village, with the Indians hurling rocks down the cliffs, and Coronado's rescue by two of his officers, a scene depicted in the right center of the painting. "They knocked me down to the ground twice with countless great stones which they threw down from above," Coronado later wrote, "and if I had not been protected by the very good headpiece which I wore, I think that the outcome would have been bad for me." Castañeda also describes the peculiar cliffs and the ladders leading to the dwellings in the mountains, and verifies that these villages were ruled by elders – who can be seen, with their long beards, leading the natives against the invaders.

The overwhelming impression to be drawn from the painting, however, is that Mostaert sympathizes with this pastoral and idyllic people in the face of invasion by foreigners. Although the battle scene is presented in an apparently unbiased and historically plausible manner, the perspective of the spectator is tilted toward the Indians, so that the viewer finds himself behind the Indians – in their camp – and opposing the Spaniards, who are relegated

to the right-hand third of the picture. In the lower left-hand corner, natives with what appear to be shepherd's staffs rush to defend their village, while cattle, sheep, and other animals peacefully graze across the foreground. Is the bias anti-Spanish because Mostaert knew of the Spanish atrocities in the New World that had been so eloquently condemned by Friar Bartolomé de las Casas, or had he had some personal experience of Spanish troops in the Low Countries? Or is Mostaert simply illustrating the conflict between unspoiled nature and aggressive civilization? Whatever the answer, his painting clearly shows a New World paradise that has been molded by European experience. The fact that it depicts the desert Southwest filled with trees and grazing livestock shows how persuasive – and wrong – the legends of paradise could be. Nevertheless, these visions, literal as well as figurative, inspired the subsequent exploratory expeditions by virtually all the competing powers of Europe, intent on breaking the Spanish monopoly on North America.

The tug-of-war began shortly after Columbus's discoveries. John Cabot had given the English a claim to the continent when he landed, probably on the Newfoundland or Nova Scotia coast, in 1497. The French claim was entered in

1524 when Giovanni Verrazano, an Italian in the service of Francis I, sailed up the eastern coast from the Carolinas to Nova Scotia, and strengthened in 1562 when Jean Ribault established a colony at the mouth of the St Johns River in Florida with the twofold intention of providing a refuge for French Huguenots and a base from which to attack Spanish treasure fleets navigating the Florida straits.

p.14

It is to an artist associated with that French settlement in Florida that we owe the first eye-witness depictions of America. Jacques Le Moyne de Morgues, probably trained in the great French map-making school in his home town of Dieppe, served as cartographer and artist on an expedition led by René de Laudonnière in 1564 to reinforce Ribault's nearly extinct colony. Le Moyne recorded a crucial scene in what is his only painting to survive: the chief showing Laudonnière the stone column that Ribault had erected as proof of France's claim to Florida. Not only was it still intact, the chief pointed out, but it was now an object of worship by the Indians. Le Moyne depicts not only the harvest of the land, but a sampling of the Indians' preparations, their utensils, and their weapons.

After JACQUES LE MOYNE DE MORGUES Map-view of part of Florida, showing ''Cedar Island'' and the pillar erected by the French commander bearing the arms of the King of France (F; see p. 15), and also (top right) vines and round Indian huts, from Theodor de Bry, *Indorum Floridam provinciam inhabitantium eicones*, Frankfurt, 1591. (British Library, London)

14

JACQUES LE MOYNE DE MORGUES
*René de Laudonnière and Chief
Athore*, 1564. (The New York
Public Library, Astor, Lenox and
Tilden Foundations)

Gathering the tattered remains of Ribault's settlement, Laudonnière established Fort Caroline on the south bank of the St Johns River. By the time Ribault returned in late summer, 1565, however, he found the settlement again in ruins. Racked by quarreling and mutiny and in a frenzy to find gold, the French had neglected to plant corn. Subsequent attempts to obtain food from the Indians had involved them in intertribal wars that left most of them sick and disillusioned, many of them on the high seas in mutiny, and dozens of them dead. They thought Ribault's return signaled their salvation, but in fact it coincided with the arrival of a Spanish expedition which completely destroyed Fort Caroline and most of the French contingent. Le Moyne was lucky to escape with his life, let alone his drawings.

Back in France, it is likely that Le Moyne began to work up his sketches into paintings. Considering the devastation of the French colony and his own hardships, it is ironic that his one known painting shows friendship and harmony in a land of plenty. Had it been used to recruit emigrants for the French colonies, as it was doubtless intended to be, it would have been misleading indeed. Following the massacre of Protestants in Paris on St Bartholomew's Day, 1572, Le Moyne emigrated to England, and continued his work there. He specialized in gouache painting and made some of the earliest studies directly from fruits and flowers, a tendency which is evident in his American picture.

England half-heartedly entered the contest for North America in 1583 and 1584 when Sir Humphrey Gilbert sent an ill-financed group of colonists to Newfoundland, and Sir Walter Raleigh attempted to settle Roanoke Island off the coast of North Carolina. With all available ships engaged in a war with Spain, however, none could be spared for resupplying the colonies. Gilbert's effort collapsed, but Raleigh's, located in a more hospitable climate, offered every hope of success. Judging from the initial accounts, Virginia (as the new region was named, in honor of Queen Elizabeth I) was the equal of any mythical paradise. As he approached Roanoke Island in 1584, Captain Arthur Barlowe, in command of one of Raleigh's ships, described the "shole water . . . where we smelt so sweet, and so strong a smell, as if we had bene in the midst of some delicate garden abounding with all kinde of odoriferous flowers." The lushness of the land impressed him more once he had landed: the country was "so full of grapes . . . I thinke in all the world the like abundance is not to be found," and he concluded that these natives lived "after the manner of the golden age."

The artist John White clearly agreed. A draughtsman and cartographer for Raleigh's colony who fared little better than Le Moyne, White painted lively and informative watercolors which, coupled with the narrative of Thomas Hariot, the expedition's mathematician and astronomer, also emphasized the friendly natives and the rich land. Hoping to attract settlers, White and Hariot did not dwell on the excessive primitivism they found among the Virginia Indians, but described their domestic life and unusual customs instead. White painted them in their ceremonial and hunting attire, and Pl.36 showed their lodges and their villages. He also recorded, with the skill of a naturalist, the plants and animals that made up their world.

Little is known of White. He could have been any one of the dozens of John Whites recorded in the parish registers of mid-sixteenth-century Britain. He probably went to Roanoke in 1584 or 1585, and although his name does not appear on the list of settlers, it is likely that he remained in Virginia and returned in 1586 with all the other members of the colony. During his time in Roanoke, White produced a record of the *"sondry things collected and counterfeited according to the truth."* One of his most informative paintings shows the Indian village of Secoton, an unenclosed compound consisting of thirteen pole-and-mat houses. The picture is full of detail for the historian — the nine natives dancing around the seven poles carved in the form of human heads, for example. "The fayrest Virgins" dance around "posts carved with heads like to the faces of Nonnes," Hariot wrote, making "the strangest gestures that they can possibly devise." The most reassuring elements of the picture to potential immigrants, however, would have been the three cornfields, each with the corn at a different stage of maturity, indicating fertile land and a long growing season.

p.17 White's watercolor of Indians fishing is even clearer in its suggestion of a bountiful Eden. No doubt a combination of several sketches, set probably in the area near Cape Hatteras, North Carolina, it shows the various implements that the natives used in fishing, including lances and a multi-pronged spear,

The manner of their fishing.

nets, and traps. The small fire in the middle of the dug-out canoe suggests that they also hunted at night. The Indians are surrounded by the other occupants of their paradise: a king crab or horseshoe crab in the right foreground and a hammerhead shark beyond; shad in the boat; and catfish, burrfish, and sturgeon all about the canoe. Overhead a brown pelican, two swans, and several ducks seem to be undisturbed by the fishermen. The

After JACQUES LE MOYNE DE
MORGUES "A council of state
between the chiefs and principal
councillors," from Theodor de
Bry, *Indorum Floridam
provinciam inhabitantium eicones*,
Frankfurt, 1591. (British Library,
London)

rivers were "full of divers sorts of fishe," Hariot claimed. The natives "take muche pleasure in huntinge . . . ther is great store in the contrye, for yt is fruit full, pleasant, and full of Goodly woods."

Evidently greatly esteemed by Raleigh, White returned as governor of the Virginia colony in 1587, no doubt much in agreement with Hariot that "yt is a pleasant sighte to see the people . . . free from all care of heapinge opp Riches for their posteritie, content with their state, and livinge friendlye together of those thinges which god of his bountie hath given unto them." After unloading supplies at Roanoke, White returned to England, confidently leaving behind his daughter, her husband, and their daughter Virginia, the first child born to English parents in North America. The colorful and exotic scenes that White painted could in no way have prepared him for the shock he received upon his return in 1590. He found the colony devastated and all the inhabitants, including his daughter and granddaughter, missing and apparently dead. He had no doubt what had happened. "We saw in the sand the print of the Salvages feet of 2 or 3 sorts troaden that night," he recalled. "We found the houses taken down . . . Wee found five chests . . . three were my owne, and about the place many of my things spoyled and broken, and my bookes torn from the covers, the frames of some of my pictures and Mappes rotten and spoyled with rayne, and my armour almost eaten through with rust." He pleaded with the ships' captains to stay and search for possible survivors, but a storm blew in, and they departed. Historians have been hesitant to accept White's judgment against the Indians, pointing out that the settlers might have feared starvation and moved to another site. The fate of the Roanoke colony remains an enigma.

During an earlier stay in London, perhaps after his first or second voyage to Virginia, White may have met Le Moyne, who died in 1588; certainly he appears to have made watercolor copies of some of Le Moyne's Florida drawings – either the originals or the engravings which were, as we shall see, made after them. So far both men were unsuccessful in their attempts to colonize in the New World and unknown as artists. They likely would have remained obscure had it not been for a Flemish publisher and engraver named Theodor de Bry.

A Protestant driven by Spanish persecution to seek refuge in Germany, de Bry wanted to publish a book on the New World: he had probably read Laudonnière's report, published in Paris in 1586 (which mentioned Le Moyne), and it may be that his own sufferings impelled him to tell the story of the Huguenots in Florida. At any rate, he traveled to London in 1587 or early in 1588 and sought out Le Moyne, hoping to purchase his paintings. Le Moyne did not want to sell – he may well have intended to publish his own account – but he died a few months later, and his widow sold de Bry both his pictures and his narrative. Elated at his success, de Bry is likely to have mentioned his purchase to the geographer Richard Hakluyt, then in the process of finishing his great work, *The Principal Navigations . . . of the English Nation*, and it may have been Hakluyt who told de Bry of John White. Before he returned home, he had also purchased White's paintings.

pp. 14, 18 De Bry's book on Virginia, with engravings after White, came out in 1590; his book on Florida, with engravings after Le Moyne, was published in 1591. Their first-hand illustrations of North America, the earliest to be published, were shown to an audience larger than they could ever have anticipated. Despite the reality of the artists' sufferings and failures, their pictures told of a paradise to the west where a naive people occupied a bountiful land and waited to embrace civilization.

Depicting the colonies

When William Bradford stepped off the deck of the *Mayflower* and onto the bleak New England shore in December, 1620, he did not expect to find a New World paradise, but to create it. His notion of paradise had nothing to do with a virgin continent or mineral wealth, but with human behavior and community and a firm belief in a heavenly paradise after death. No artist accompanied the Pilgrims to document the country, for they considered paintings material objects and shunned them as evil.

Instead of paradise, Bradford, who was to serve thirty terms as governor of the future Plymouth colony, saw all around him a "hideous and desolate wilderness." He failed even to find a vantage point from which "to view . . . a more goodly country" and settled down with his people to till the thin New England soil, confident that their "errand into the wilderness" was worthy of the sacrifice. "Wilderness" was a stage, Cotton Mather, the great Puritan preacher, later wrote, "thro' which we are passing to the Promised Land." They intended for their "city set on a hill" in America to form a moral pattern by which England itself would be redeemed, and would have considered any suggestion of an earthly paradise blasphemy.

With the restoration of Charles II to the throne in 1660, however, the New England Puritans became an increasingly peculiar and isolated people, even among their own sect. The complete triumph of Anglicanism in the Restoration settlement left them no hope of having an impact on England and no purpose other than to save the remnant of God's people that had sought refuge with them in the New World. It has been suggested that this realization was the first step in turning these Englishmen into Americans; it certainly changed their attitude toward their place of refuge.

Having hitherto merely held the wilderness at bay, the colonists became aggressive. The happiest scene imaginable was one that showed the hand of man — a clearing in a forest, a plowed meadow, giant trees trimmed and cut and stacked to form houses. This was not a natural paradise: this was a paradise created by man. The Puritans' ideal, after all, was a "city set on a hill," and for that the wilderness must make way. Combined over the generations with the early Virginians' feeling that America was a garden awaiting the gardener, the Puritan morality led Americans to conclude that the virgin land that lay before them was theirs to possess.

In contrast to the Spanish search for treasure in the Southwest, virtually the entire movement westward from the Atlantic coast can, without doing great injustice to historical fact or to personal motive, be seen as morally inspired. Settling the land was not wrong: it was an opportunity to be welcomed by responsible citizens. And, although colonial America was more than three thousand miles from Europe — perhaps seventy-five days away by fast sailing ship, and light years away in attitude — America, with the assistance of European entrepreneurs, grew rapidly. It is true that the initial efforts failed or faltered badly, but by the end of the seventeenth century, British settlements extended from Maine to the Carolinas, with perhaps as many as 22,000 of the 250,000 inhabitants concentrated in the new cities of Boston, Newport, New York (acquired from the Dutch in 1664), Philadelphia, and Charleston, and the rest settled in one of the towns or plantations clustered along the coast. Few Englishmen knew the land beyond the mountains.

Pls.2,3

Unlike the English, the French pressed overland to explore the interior, using the waterways to investigate and map the Midwest. In the summer of 1673 Louis Joliet and the Jesuit missionary Father Jacques Marquette floated down the Mississippi as far as its confluence with the Arkansas. Inspired by their effort, in 1679 René Robert Cavelier, Sieur de la Salle, set out from Fort Frontenac at the mouth of Lake Ontario, hoping to establish a great French empire in America. With him was Father Louis Hennepin, the first European to report on Niagara Falls. La Salle left fortifications at strategic points along the way and, finally reaching the mouth of the Mississippi, claimed all of the land that it drained for France and named it Louisiana, in honor of King Louis XIV. La Salle did not live to implement his dream; the settlement of the Mississippi was left to other Frenchmen.

p.21

The first European depiction of the ''horrible Precipice'' of Niagara Falls, from Father Louis Hennepin's *Voyage curieux*, The Hague, 1704. (British Library, London)

The French founded Port Biloxi on the Gulf coast in 1699, and by 1717 John Law, the energetic Scottish financial genius then in the service of the French King, had established the Company of the West to oversee the settlement and development of the Mississippi Valley. In 1718, eight hundred settlers left France for Louisiana. Under the leadership of young Antoine Simon Le Page du Pratz, they landed on Mobile Bay, then moved over to the crescent of land at the mouth of the Mississippi where the town of New Orleans was in the process of being laid out. Hearing of better land upriver, Le Page du Pratz moved his group to the Natchez Bluffs, and soon the route from New Orleans past Baton Rouge, the mouth of the Red River, and Natchez to the Arkansas was well known. The French also fanned out upriver, exploring the St Francis, the Missouri, and other tributaries of the Mississippi. The ''Mississippi Bubble,'' as Law's endeavor was known, burst in 1720, but not before Jean-Baptiste Michel Le Bouteaux, the assistant Pl.37 director of Law's concession, had recorded the headquarters camp at New Biloxi in an excellent drawing and the French had established themselves as dominant in the region.

The visual record of these early years of French and British settlement is scant, for few artists were among the first immigrants to the colonies. As the historian Frederick Jackson Turner pointed out in his analysis of the American character, the colonists had a ''coarseness and strength combined with acuteness and inquisitiveness'' that gave them a ''masterful grasp of material things,'' but left them ''lacking in the artistic.'' The trans-Atlantic crossing was still too rough to attract frivolous travelers, and not many artists chose to settle in a region so far from aesthetic amenities and likely patrons.

One of the first to rise above the ordinary and gain a reputation, perhaps earn a part of his income, with his art was William Burgis, who drew a large four-part view of New York and had it engraved in 1719–21. We know little

about Burgis. He was presumably an educated Englishman who sought his fortune in the colonies. Whether he made any money is unknown, but he did offer his New York view for sale and evidently was successful enough to move to Boston in 1722 to repeat the effort. A view of that city made about 1723, which includes the figure of a draughtsman seated sketching in the foreground, is probably by him, and he definitely engraved a large three-part panorama of Boston in 1725. These prints and the New York view are among Pl.3 the earliest depictions of American cities.

Burgis's views of New York and Boston, with the skylines punctuated by handsome church spires and the harbors full of ships, probably prompted Thomas Penn, the London-based proprietor of Pennsylvania, to ask his agent in the colony to commission a view of Philadelphia. Such pictures were often used to recruit prospective colonists, and Penn did not want to fall behind his two main rivals. The agent discouragingly replied that there were no artists in the city and, besides, the city would "make a most miserable Perspective for want of Steeples." But Penn pressed the matter. Two artists failed before George Heap, a local map-maker, succeeded with a striking perspective of the city viewed from the shore of the Delaware River.

p.22 Published on four large sheets of paper in 1754, and in a single-sheet version two years later, the panorama proved to be quite popular, although comparison with later views of Philadelphia suggests that Heap might have exaggerated the steeples a bit.

One of the rare Englishmen to take an interest in the interior of the country was Mark Catesby (1679–1749). After a stay of seven years in Virginia he returned to England, and then set out again in 1722 to continue his study of natural history, exploring the area around Charleston and up the Savannah and Ashley rivers. He withstood the difficulties of a raw and uncivilized frontier, thunderstorms fiercer and louder than those he had experienced in Europe, and various debilitating and potentially fatal illnesses as he collected his specimens and made his sketches. In less than four years he was back in London, where he spent the best part of the next twenty years preparing his monumental two-volume *Natural History of Carolina, Florida, and the Bahama Islands.* When funds could not be raised to employ printmakers, Catesby taught himself how to engrave. (The first 100 copies of the first volume alone required that 10,000 engravings be pulled from his carefully made copper plates, then hand-colored.) When a publisher could not be found, he obtained a loan to pay the expenses.

The work, which appeared in 1731–48, was a triumph. The magnificently illustrated folio volumes catalogued the flora and fauna of the areas Catesby

PL 38 had visited, often combining objects strikingly different in scale. The *Natural History* went through two more English editions and several spurious printings on the Continent, and stands today as an unparalleled aesthetic and scientific document of eighteenth-century America. The project earned Catesby a much-deserved membership of the Royal Society.

The first English views of the Midwest are due to Captain Jonathan Carver, of Massachusetts, who set out from Boston in 1760 intending to reach Mackinac on the Great Lakes. He criss-crossed the north country, later telling in his book, *Jonathan Carver's Travels Through the Interior Parts of North America in the Years 1766, 1767, and 1768* (1778), of such beautiful sights as
p.23 the Falls of St Anthony and the Falls of Ste Marie. His handsome illustrations, engraved by the English landscape artist Michael Angelo Rooker, are detailed enough to be convincing, and it is not unlikely that the engraver was working from rough sketches by Carver. His highly popular book went through more than twenty-three editions in London, Dublin, and Paris.

By the time Carver's views were published, the political scene had undergone two radical changes. The first was France's loss of her North American empire; and out of that grew the second, Britain's loss of the United States. Things began in a small way. The French controlled the Mississippi Valley, and extended their claim further eastward as well. First Pennsylvania fur traders, then Virginia settlers, made their way over the Appalachian Mountains, and the French, realizing that the prize was dominance in North America, reacted vigorously. In 1748 they swept down on an English fur trading post at Pickawillany, in western Ohio, and completely destroyed it. Then they established a line of forts from Lake Erie south along the Pennsylvania line. The pacifist authorities of Pennsylvania chose to ignore the intrusion, but in 1753 the Governor of Virginia, citing his colony's virtually open-ended royal charter as authority, sent twenty-one-year-old George Washington to advise the French that they were trespassing on his territory. Washington's force was defeated and captured, and the contest was under way.

"The falls of St. Anthony in the River Mississippi, near 2400 Miles from its entrance into the Gulf of Mexico," from Jonathan Carver, *Travels Through the Interior Parts of North America in the Years 1766, 1767, and 1768*, London, 1778. (Courtesy Amon Carter Museum, Fort Worth, Texas)

UnhappyBoston! fee thy Sons deplore,
Thy hallow'd Walks befmear'd with guiltlefs Gore:
While faithlefs P——n and his favage Bands,
With murd'rous Rancour ftretch their bloody Hands;
Like fierce Barbarians grinning o'er their Prey,
Approve the Carnage, and enjoy the Day.

If fcalding drops from Rage from Anguifh Wrung,
If fpeechlefs Sorrows lab'ring for a Tongue,
Or if a weeping World can ought appeafe
The plaintive Ghofts of Victims fuch as thefe:
The Patriot's copious Tears for each are fhed,
A glorious Tribute which embalms the Dead.

But know, Fate fummons to that awful Goal,
Where Justice ftrips the Mud'rer of his Soul:
Should venal C——ts the fcandal of the Land,
Snatch the relentlefs Villain from her Hand,
Keen Execrations on this Plate inferib'd,
Shall reach a JUDGE who never can be brib'd.

The unhappy Sufferers were Meſſ.ᵣˢ SAMᴸ GRAY SAMᴸ MAVERICK, JAMˢ CALDWELL, CRISPUS ATTUCKS & PATᴷ CARR
Killed. Six wounded; two of them (CHRISTᴿ MONK & JOHN CLARK) Mortally

PAUL REVERE *The Bloody Massacre perpetrated in King Street, Boston on March 5th 1770.* (The Metropolitan Museum of Art, New York, Gift of Mrs Russell Sage, 1910)

Ultimately, the overwhelming numbers of British colonists in America – 500,000 by mid-century, as against only 90,000 French – doomed the French effort, but this was not immediately apparent as they pressed their temporary advantages: they already held the territory in question, and they sent well-trained and disciplined troops to face the disorganized and ill-managed colonials. They also armed anti-British Indians, eager to avenge a century and a half of frustration at the hands of the relentlessly advancing settlers.

The French and Indian War, as it became known (part of a worldwide conflict known as the Seven Years War), took a different turn when the British Prime Minister William Pitt, recognizing the potential value of America, stopped relying on the parsimonious colonial assemblies to defend themselves and increased the British commitment to the war. He promoted talented young officers – two of them became Generals Wolfe and Amherst – and used the navy to isolate New France. Soon his grand strategy paid off. French forts began to fall in 1758, and after the British captured Montreal in 1760 the French abandoned Canada. In 1762 France gave to Spain, her ally,

New Orleans and the Louisiana Territory. Finally, in the settlement confirmed by the Treaty of Paris in 1763, France gave up all claims to North America: Britain kept Canada, and further acquired from Spain the eastern half of the Mississippi Valley and Florida. (Later, in 1800, France briefly got Louisiana back when Napoleon conquered Spain.)

The euphoria was short-lived. There was an initial outburst of goodwill toward the Crown, but this victory, which seemed to insure the stability of the British Empire in America, in fact contained the seeds of its destruction. No honest colonial could deny that British troops and money had won the war, but the taxes imposed by Parliament to recover some of the costs (the Sugar Act in 1764, the Stamp Act in 1765), and the Proclamation of 1763 prohibiting settlement beyond the Appalachian divide – initially designed to stabilize the frontier and lessen conflicts with the Indians, then extended to discourage the growth of competitive local manufacturing – made it seem that the fruits of a victory which they were now being asked to pay for had slipped from their grasp. Subsequent Parliamentary efforts to force compliance led to radical opposition in America, marked by such well-known incidents as the Boston Massacre in 1770 (when Redcoats fired into an angry crowd, killing five) and the "Tea Party" in 1773.

p.24

The convening of the Continental Congress in 1774 led King George III to conclude: "The New England governments are in a state of rebellion. Blows must decide whether they are to be subject to this country or independent." Much to the surprise of the British, the blows struck by those colonials who only a few years earlier had earned General Wolfe's contempt proved sufficient, with the aid of the vengeful French, to win their independence.

The American Revolution and the accompanying demand for military information brought many artists and cartographers to the continent. British, French and Americans produced hundreds of views, recording every significant port, river and strategic location from Canada to Savannah, and many campaigns in the war. Two of the most detailed pictures are gouaches by Louis Nicolas van Blarenberghe, the battle-painter of the French war department, recording the last major engagement of the Revolution, at Yorktown: working probably from both written and pictorial accounts, van Blarenberghe depicted with almost microscopic precision of the chief events of the siege and surrender of Lord Cornwallis's army. Most of this material was consigned to the "top secret" files of the British and French war departments, in effect sealing in a time capsule a record of the emerging nation for future generations. Today these documents provide us with delightful and seemingly stolen glances at the birth pangs of the United States.

pp.26–27

In addition, certain events, such as the Boston Massacre and the destruction of the equestrian statue of George III in New York City, proved popular enough to induce artists and publishers to collaborate in the production of an image intended to be sold as an eye-witness report of the event, much as the news magazines offer today. These images reinforced the realization that Americans were finally free to pursue their paradise westward, aware that foreign troops, hostile Indians, and the wilderness itself stood in their way, but confident that the Almighty had preserved it for them alone.

Pierre L'Enfant *Panorama of West Point, New York* (detail), 1778? (Library of Congress)

Louis Nicolas van Blarenberghe *The Siege of Yorktown in Virginia, October 18, 1781* (detail), 1784. (Musée National du Château de Versailles)

28

The artists of the Revolution provided an abundance of documentation along the eastern seaboard, but no accurate images of the interior by trained draughtsmen yet existed. As Americans poured into the previously forbidden territory, the need for information was acute. Many maps were published, and a few pictures – such as Carver's of the Falls of St Anthony – achieved notoriety, but perhaps the most striking example of the demand for information was the success accorded a slim volume that was intended as little more than a real estate tract. John Filson's honeyed description of the land in the Great Bend of the Ohio River included an account of a settler called Colonel Daniel Boone only as an afterthought; but as a result of Filson's story, Boone soon became a national hero and the stereotypical American pioneer.

p.28

Filson, a former schoolteacher, surveyor, and land speculator, published his book, *The Discovery, Settlement and present State of Kentucke*, in 1784 in an effort to attract settlers to land that had only recently been cleared of Redcoats and still sheltered a number of potentially hostile Indians. Addressing these dangers directly in an appendix entitled "The Adventures of Col. Daniel Boon; containing a Narrative of the Wars of Kentucke," Filson told the heroic story of Boone, who had moved from his home in North Carolina to the "dark and bloody ground" of Kentucky, losing two sons and a brother to the Indians in the process. He had successfully founded Boonesboro in a wilderness of pristine beauty and had shown that the white man could adapt to the frontier lifestyle. The invitation was clear. "Now the scene is changed," Boone says. "Peace crowns the sylvan shade." Settlers could move west in safety.

Filson's book was spectacularly successful, going through dozens of editions in the United States and being translated into several different languages. It was pirated and plagiarized in both Europe and America and was touted as the sequel to *Letters from an American Farmer*, the discerning book published in 1782 by Michel Guillaume Jean de Crèvecoeur, a French veteran who had settled on a New York farm after travelling through the Great Lakes and Ohio Valley country. In France, Boone was described as a natural philosopher and his image ultimately encompassed all the characteristics of Crèvecoeur's "new man": hunter and woodsman, farmer, frontiersman, entrepreneur. The real Daniel Boone was a brave and talented man, to be sure, but he was not the storybook hero that Filson described.

Filson's boosterism and exaggerations almost surely offended the sensitivities of one who had been interested in reliable information on the western lands for years. In 1782, Thomas Jefferson had written his own book, describing in a much more accurate and organized way some of the same territory that Filson had discussed. The *Notes on the State of Virginia* (published 1785, 1787), which included a great deal more than present-day Virginia because of the colony's undefined western boundaries, were based largely on Jefferson's own observations. He researched each of the major rivers: width, distance, high and low waters, and navigational information. He catalogued the plants and animals in some detail and ventured speculatively into geology, using common sense to raise logical questions about the nature of the convulsions that had created the land masses. He eloquently described such natural marvels as the confluence of the Potomac

After CHESTER HARDING *Col. Daniel Boon* [*sic*], 1820. (The St Louis Art Museum)

and the Shenandoah rivers and the Natural Bridge of Virginia. He, more than Boone, fitted the French concept of a natural philosopher.

All this publicity led to unprecedented growth west of the Appalachian Mountains and along the Ohio River Valley. In the decade before 1800, the population of Kentucky rose from 73,677 to 220,955. Pittsburgh, Cincinnati, and Louisville received thousands of new residents, who looked to the Ohio and the Mississippi as the natural outlet for their goods and trade. The line of settlement had reached the Mississippi, but it would not wait there long.

It was no doubt with great satisfaction that Jefferson, after he became President, prepared orders for Captains Meriwether Lewis, his friend and private secretary, and William Clark to lead the first American reconnaissance into the West. In a secret message to Congress in January, 1803, Jefferson requested $2,500 for an expedition that would determine the feasibility of using the Missouri and Columbia rivers as a link to the Pacific and oriental trade. This would require crossing lands claimed by France, Spain, and Great Britain, but Jefferson explained that he hoped the scientific purposes of the expedition would persuade the other governments to issue the necessary passports.

Before Captain Lewis left Pittsburgh, he learned that he would need no French or Spanish passport. France had regained Louisiana, but now Napoleon, realizing that could no longer defend it against the British navy, had sold it to the United States.

Lewis and Clark spent the winter of 1803–04 on the Mississippi River opposite the mouth of the Missouri. By November, 1804, they had reached the Upper Missouri villages of the Mandans and the Minnetarees or Hidatsas, where they encountered a Shoshone Indian from the Rocky Mountains who proved immensely valuable as an interpreter and guide during the remainder of the trip. Sacajawea's assistance was a good omen for the journey. Of the thirty-one crew members who headed up the Missouri that spring, only one died during the expedition, and that was probably from natural causes.

They boated as far upriver as they could. As they neared the continental divide, they abandoned the canoes and set out in search of Indians who would trade them horses for the overland portion of the journey. The first Indian they saw fled, but they finally found Sacajawea's people, negotiated a trade, and crossed the mountains, where they fashioned five canoes Indian-style and floated down the Snake and Columbia rivers to the Pacific. They returned to St Louis in September, 1806. During the more than two years of their expedition, Lewis and Clark had traveled over eight thousand miles and had only one violent encounter with the Indians.

Survival was news enough, but as soon as their hundreds of specimens and their map and journal were studied, the expedition was declared a scientific success as well. Lewis had gathered immense amounts of material on the language and customs of the Indians, on the rivers, and on potential mineral sources. His description of the bountiful northwestern waters and the abundant game, written at Jefferson's behest on waterproof birchbark, sharpened American interest in Oregon, and a population not yet well apprised of its most recently acquired possession, Louisiana, now began thinking in terms of spanning the entire continent.

Unfortunately there was no documentary artist on the Lewis and Clark expedition, nor on the two expeditions that Lieutenant Zebulon Montgomery Pike led to the West and Southwest between 1805 and 1807. His "Geographical, Statistical, and General Observations . . . on the Interior Provinces of New Spain," published as a part of his official report in 1810, included pertinent information on a section of the country that would soon be a part of the United States, and together with Lewis and Clark, Pike provided maps and accurate descriptions of large sections of the West. Operating under the aegis of the farsighted Jefferson, they had laid the groundwork for the armies of artists, scientists, and explorers to follow.

In an age that was rapidly becoming accustomed to handsome prints produced by hand-engraving and aquatint, Americans developed an insatiable thirst for pictorial images, and the next government expedition, led by Major Stephen H. Long in 1819–20, included two artists: Samuel Seymour and Titian Ramsay Peale. Seymour (whose dates of birth and death are unknown) had come from England in 1796 and had been apprenticed to William Birch in Pl.7 Philadelphia, where he earned his reputation assisting Birch on his extremely fine set of views of the city. He was well acquainted with other artists there, such as Thomas Sully and James Wesley Jarvis, and was a member of the well-known local natural history circle. As official artist on the Long expedition, Seymour was to "furnish sketches of landscapes, whenever we meet with any distinguished for their beauty and grandeur," and to "paint miniature likenesses . . . of distinguished Indians, and exhibit groups of savages engaged in celebrating their festivals, or sitting in council."

CHARLES WILLSON PEALE *Stephen H. Long* (detail), 1819. (Independence National Historical Park Collection, Philadelphia)

SAMUEL SEYMOUR *Pawnee Council.* (Courtesy Beinecke Rare Book and Manuscript Library, Yale University)

Titian Ramsay Peale (1800–1885) was the son of the famous Philadelphia painter and museum proprietor, Charles Willson Peale. Already an acceptable artist by 1819, he had gained considerable expertise in his father's natural history museum, surrounded by the relics of the Lewis and Clark expedition. At the age of seventeen he had been elected to membership in the Academy of Natural Sciences in Philadelphia and the following winter had traveled with the distinguished naturalist Thomas Say to Georgia and Florida, later producing fine illustrations for the prospectus of Say's *American Entomology.* Peale was named assistant naturalist for the Long expedition.

The expedition left Pittsburgh in May, 1819. Descending the Ohio, they reached the Mississippi and turned upriver, passing through St Louis. They then headed northwestward up the Missouri to Council Bluffs, Iowa, where they spent the winter. In early June, 1820, the expedition marched overland along the Platte River until they reached the Rocky Mountains. There they turned southward to the Arkansas River, where the party split into two groups. They joined up again at Fort Smith, Arkansas, then returned to the East.

Pl.72 Although Seymour was an adequate documentary artist, his views of the Rocky Mountains do not convey a real sense of their geological structure, and none of his pictures – at least none of those that survive – reflects what Colonel Long called the "Great American Desert." Perhaps Seymour, too, was so convinced of the garden paradise in the West that he could not bring himself to paint it as it really was. Of the perhaps 150 sketches that he produced in the field, he finished sixty; as few as a dozen are known to
p.33 survive and, unfortunately, even fewer were engraved for Long's report: six for the American edition, five others for the English edition, making a total of eleven.

Naive as they are, Seymour's pictures stand as eye-witness images of the West, and their uniqueness drew the attention reviewers at the time. The London *Monthly Review* called the reproductions "plain and unadorned," but American publications were (as might be expected) more charitable: the *Niles*

After SAMUEL SEYMOUR *View of the Rocky Mountains on the Platte 50 miles from their Base*, from Edwin James, *Account of an Expedition from Pittsburgh to the Rocky Mountains . . . under Maj. S. H. Long*, 1821–23. (Courtesy Amon Carter Museum, Fort Worth, Texas)

Weekly Register found the illustrations "elegantly executed," and for the Washington *Daily National Intelligencer* they contributed to an awesome idea of "the magnificent extent of the domain of the Republic." No-one mentioned that Titian Peale had brought back the first picture of an Indian tipi.

The dawning fashion for open-air sketching and the thirst for scientific knowledge soon led other painters into the wilderness on their own. Peter Rindisbacher (1806–34), who had come from Switzerland with his family in 1821 to the Earl of Selkirk's Red River Colony in Canada, was perhaps the first artist to portray the life of Plains Indians such as Chippeways, Assiniboins and Sioux. No-one before him had recorded the inside of a tipi, and he may have been the first to document the Indians' use of the A-shaped travois, snowshoes, and toboggans.

Pl.56

p.33

PETER RINDISBACHER *Assiniboin hunting on Snowshoes* (detail), 1833. The snowshoes kept the Indians mobile on the surface of the snow; the buffalo eventually fell through the crust and could not escape. (Courtesy Amon Carter Museum, Fort Worth, Texas)

It was probably the demand for pictures for the newly-emerging illustrated magazines that led Rindisbacher to establish a studio in St Louis in 1829. He would earn his living by painting miniature portraits and landscapes and supplement it by selling his illustrations to Eastern journals. A set of six colored lithographs after his paintings had been published in London in 1825, and in December, 1829, he began an association with the young *American Turf Register and Sporting Magazine* that lasted until his early death. Ten of his pictures were used in that publication, causing the *Missouri Republican* to comment, upon his death, that his "talents . . . gave every assurance of future celebrity." A number of journals went on using his well-designed, detailed scenes, one even appearing on a Republic of Texas bank note in 1838. As one who knew him put it, Rindisbacher was an artist who had spent most of his youth "in our *western wilds*. He is perfectly acquainted with the subject of his very successful effort; and has . . . views of many of the finest scenes in that part of the country, whose *untamed wilderness* has never before furnished subjects for the pencil or the burin."

While Rindisbacher painted delicate and compelling miniatures of Indian life, George Catlin (1794–1872) caught some of the natives' drama and exoticism with his passionate and colorful portraits. Catlin, born in Wilkes Barre, Pennsylvania, was a self-trained painter whose trip up the Missouri River in 1832 helped answer a popular concern about the American Indian that had been building for more than fifty years. Ever since 1762, when Jean Jacques Rousseau argued in *Emile* that man should free himself from corrupted, civilized life in order that his innate goodness should prevail, intellectuals had seized upon each new revelation about the American Indians to reason that these "noble savages" were the last people on earth living as nature had intended. When the young Catlin saw "a delegation of some ten or fifteen noble and dignified-looking Indians, from the wilds of the 'Far West' passing through Philadelphia on their way to Washington," the thought that they still existed in their original state persuaded him to give up a potentially profitable legal career and a firmly established portrait business in order to travel west and become their historian: he set out alone, he later wrote, "unaided and unadvised, resolved, (if my life should be spared), by the aid of my brush and my pen, to rescue from oblivion so much of their primitive looks and customs as the industry and ardent enthusiasm of one lifetime could accomplish."

Catlin covered some of the same ground that Seymour and Peale had, but rather than capture an impression of the country, he intended to preserve the image of a people he felt were doomed by the white man's whiskey, disease, and bayonet. His first call in St Louis was on General William Clark, the old explorer, who had settled there as Superintendent of Indian Affairs and had assembled his own museum of native materials. Catlin painted Indians in and around the city and traveled with Clark to Prairie du Chien, Wisconsin, in 1830. By 1832 he was prepared.

Boarding the American Fur Company steamboat *Yellowstone* in March, he set out up the Missouri River. Bound for Fort Union at the mouth of the Yellowstone River, the steamboat stopped at each post and village along the way. Catlin took these opportunities to acquaint himself with the local Indians and painted portraits of as many of them as possible. The work of

p.34

Pl.73

Above GEORGE CATLIN *Little Bear, A Hunkpapa Brave*, 1832. (National Museum of American Art (formerly National Collection of Fine Arts), Smithsonian Institution, Washington, D.C., Gift of Mrs Joseph Harrison)

Above left GEORGE CATLIN *Catlin painting the Portrait of Mah-to-toh-pa – Mandan* (detail), 1857–69. "Four Bears" was also painted by Bodmer: see p. 38. (Courtesy National Gallery of Art, Washington, D.C.)

that summer is awesome. During an eighty-six-day period he rode with the Indians in buffalo hunts, sat in their councils, and watched their games, dances, and religious ceremonies. He kept a journal that would later become his popular *Letters and Notes* (1866), and painted more than 135 pictures: 66 portraits, 36 domestic scenes, 26 landscapes, and 8 hunting scenes.

p.35 Catlin worked through situations that lesser men would have shunned. As he finished a portrait of the Hunkpapa Sioux warrior Little Bear during his last day at Fort Pierre in South Dakota, The Dog, chief of a rival band, insultingly observed of the three-quarter-profile portrait that Little Bear was only half a man. Little Bear answered the challenge, and in the ensuing fight he was killed. (Catlin specifically noted that the side of his face not painted was shot away.) Confusion reigned as the rival bands massed. The "great medicine painter" was relieved to pack his paints, brushes, and canvases aboard the *Yellowstone* the next morning to continue up the river.

On his return trip down the river, Catlin stopped at the Mandan villages below Fort Clark, North Dakota. He befriended one of the chiefs and was permitted, along with the white trader James Kipp, to watch the Mandans' most elaborate religious ceremony, the O-kee-pa, by which they explained the creation of the earth and all their traditions. Catlin was the first white man to record this sequence of rituals, spread over a number of days, which included Pl.77 a Bull Dance to ensure the coming of buffaloes and culminated in a gruesome p.36 trial of endurance. The young men were skewered with splints of wood under the skin of their back or breast, and were suspended from the roof timbers of the ceremonial lodge until they became unconscious. They were then lowered to the ground, the little fingers of their left hands were chopped off as a sacrifice to the Great Spirit, and they were sent out to participate in the Last Race. With buffalo skulls and other weights attached to the splints,

GEORGE CATLIN *The Cutting Scene*, 1832. (Harmsen Collection, Denver)

Opposite After KARL BODMER *Fort Mackenzie* [sic], *August 28th, 1833*, 1840. (Courtesy Amon Carter Museum, Fort Worth, Texas)

the young men ran, or were dragged, around a great circle in front of the entire village. When the weights pulled out of a warrior's flesh, he was taken to his lodge where his friends and family revived him.

With several more trips, Catlin ultimately completed a staggering 470 paintings for his Indian Gallery, which he showed in New York, Boston, Washington, and Philadelphia beginning in 1837. The powerful portraits and the astonishing series of pictures of the O-kee-pa drew large crowds. In New York he had to move to a larger hall to accommodate all the spectators. He sailed for London in 1839 and exhibited the Gallery at the Egyptian Hall, Piccadilly, for nearly five years. The climax of Catlin's European tour was an invitation in 1845 to display his pictures at the Louvre for King Louis Philippe and his guests.

Catlin's career did not end happily, for the crowds eventually dwindled until he could no longer afford to rent a hall, and in 1852 he sold his Gallery to Joseph Harrison, an American locomotive manufacturer. Fortunately, it fell into the hands of the Smithsonian Institution, where he spent his remaining days elaborating on his first-hand observations.

Meanwhile, the same curiosity that had lured Catlin westward resulted in one of the most dramatic pictures in the whole of nineteenth-century American art. While Catlin was in Cincinnati in the summer of 1833 working the sketches from his first trip into finished paintings, another artist boarded the *Yellowstone* at St Louis for a trip up the Missouri. Karl Bodmer (1809–93), a young Swiss painter, traveled in the employ of Maximilian, Prince of Wied-Neuwied, a small German principality on the Rhine. Maximilian (1782–1867) was a scholar and scientist who, following in the footsteps of his mentor Alexander von Humboldt, had already visited South America and had published a book of his findings. He planned a similar publication on North America and brought Bodmer along to provide the illustrations.

p.37 They had gotten as far as Fort McKenzie, in Montana, when gunfire startled them from their sleep at daybreak on August 28. Bodmer and Maximilian climbed the elevated platform inside the palisade and saw hundreds of Indians charging across the prairie. They first thought the fort was under attack, but soon realized that a group of some six hundred Assiniboins and Crees had attacked the eighteen to twenty Piegan lodges outside the fort. The dazed Piegans retreated inside the walls, while the whites in the fort covered their flight. Some trappers reported that Maximilian – a veteran of the Napoleonic wars – even fired a few rifleballs at the attackers. The Piegans regrouped and, with reinforcements from some of the other Blackfeet villages, drove the aggressors back to the Marias River, where the fight continued until evening.

Bodmer's print of the conflict is one of the few eye-witness pictures of Plains Indian intertribal battle, and none of the others is as convincing. He successfully captured the intensity of the scene as deadly enemies charged each other with a variety of weapons: rifles, lances, knives, clubs, and bows and arrows. Wounded braves were carried from the field in the midst of battle, while the Americans fired a few shots from over the wall of the fort. Several Indians were killed or wounded, but one old chief later boasted that he had escaped unscathed because of the magical power in the portrait that Bodmer had done of him a few days before.

After KARL BODMER *The Travellers . . . Near Fort Clark* (detail), 1840. Prince Maximilian is on the left, with Dreidoppel behind him; Bodmer is the stylish figure on the right. (Courtesy Amon Carter Museum, Fort Worth, Texas)

After KARL BODMER *Mato-Topé, the Mandan Chief, in his State Dress*, 1840. Mato-Topé (Four Bears) was a distinguished warrior, and one of the Indians Maximilian and Bodmer got to know best. In April 1834 at Fort Clark, Maximilian writes, "Mr. Bodmer painted the chief, Mato-Topé, at full length, in his grandest dress. The vanity which is characteristic of the Indians induced this chief to stand stock-still for several days, so that his portrait succeeded admirably. He wore on this occasion a handsome new shirt of bighorn leather, the large feather cap, and, in his hand, a long lance with scalps and feathers." Mato-Topé was also painted by Catlin (p. 35). He died in the great smallpox epidemic of 1837.

Not all of Bodmer's sitters were so pleased. To make as thorough a record as possible for Maximilian's book, Bodmer painted portraits of different Indians in a variety of dress. After he pictured several Mandans and Hidatsas in their finest attire, however, one who had posed in something less than his best costume returned, claiming that he had been insulted, and demanded that his portrait be destroyed. Having endured sweltering earth-lodges in summer and frozen paints in winter to get his pictures, Bodmer was not willing to give one up so easily. He left the room for a few moments on the pretense of searching for the controversial portrait and made a quick copy of it. He returned and destroyed the copy in front of the offended brave, settling the matter satisfactorily.

Bodmer's paintings, made for the demanding Maximilian, are as beautiful as they are accurate. Whereas Catlin was self-taught, Bodmer was a trained artist from a family of artists. Catlin's prodigious output probably required that he sometimes paint as many as six canvases per day, while Bodmer often worked on a single picture for two or three days. Bodmer also saw more of the Upper Missouri than Catlin: Maximilian refused to stop at Fort Union, where Catlin had turned back the previous summer, proceeding upriver to Fort McKenzie and beyond.

There is surprisingly little duplication in their work, considering that they covered much of the same territory and met many of the same Indians. This is probably due to Maximilian's careful preparation. He, Bodmer, and Dreidoppel, his hunter, had visited museums and bookstores along the east coast as they gathered background material on the American West. There was much to learn from the reports of Lewis and Clark, Pike, and Long, which had been published several years before. They had visited the Peale Museum in Philadelphia to study the artifacts that Lewis and Clark had deposited there and had talked with Titian Peale, who showed them Seymour's pictures and told them of his own Western experiences. And one of their first calls in St Louis, of course, was on General Clark. Although Bodmer and Catlin did not meet, Bodmer did see several of Catlin's paintings in the home of Benjamin O'Fallon, General Clark's nephew in St Louis, and had the opportunity to study the artifacts in the General's museum.

Together Catlin's and Bodmer's records of the Upper Missouri constitute a vivid and comprehensive document without parallel. Both visited the Mandan villages near Fort Clark and painted numerous portraits as well as domestic scenes. No other artist had the chance, for a smallpox epidemic virtually exterminated the Mandans in 1837. Both men's paintings were engraved – Bodmer's about 1840, Catlin's in 1844 – and the prints were widely distributed and shamelessly copied by later artists who were not fortunate enough to see the Indians of the Great Plains while they were still in their unspoiled state.

Neither Catlin nor Bodmer, however, got as far as the Rocky Mountains. The Prince had hoped to spend the winter there, but friends at Fort McKenzie convinced him that the threat of hostile Indians made it too dangerous. (Bodmer did one picture which the Prince titled "The Rocky Mountains," but it was probably what Bodmer saw as he climbed the heights near Fort McKenzie. In reality, he was several days' journey from the mountains.) The first images of the mountains of the Far West, therefore, came a few years later, after Catlin and Bodmer had returned to civilization.

In 1837 Alfred Jacob Miller (1810–74), a Baltimore artist trained in Paris and Rome, accompanied Captain William Drummond Stewart to the annual rendezvous of fur traders and trappers in the Wind River Mountains of western Wyoming. He spent several weeks in the mountains and returned with a portfolio of delicate and highly romantic watercolors of Indians, fur trappers, and the mysterious Rockies, which the fur trappers had known for years but Easterners had never seen.

Captain Stewart was the second son of a noble family that lived in Murthly Castle in Perthshire, Scotland. After his return from the Napoleonic wars, he had fought bitterly with his older brother, who had inherited all the family estates and titles, and made an unhappy marriage to a farmgirl. Perhaps to escape, in 1832 he sailed for the United States, that new land of democracy, as was fashionable among many of the nobility. After visiting Niagara Falls, he journeyed to New Orleans to spend the winter in a warmer climate.

It was probably in this international, commercial port city at the mouth of the Mississippi that he heard of the annual rendezvous between the fur trappers and traders. Established by a St Louis fur trader in 1825, the rendezvous was a perfect capitalistic solution to the problem of how to get the trappers' pelts to market without the men having to travel to St Louis each year. Instead of spending six months en route, they gathered at a predetermined spot in the mountains to meet a supply train from the city. During this three- to four-week "saturnalia," as one visitor described it, the trappers exchanged their pelts for the goods and supplies the merchants had brought.

Stewart, in St Louis in the spring of 1833 en route to the rendezvous, met Prince Maximilian and Bodmer. Perhaps it was this encounter that led him, four seasons later, to take an artist with him. At any rate, the Captain happened into Miller's second-floor studio on Chartres Street in New Orleans

Above ALFRED JACOB MILLER *Self-Portrait*, c. 1837. (The InterNorth Art Foundation, Joslyn Art Museum, Omaha, Nebraska)

Left ALFRED JACOB MILLER *Indian Encampment near the Wind River Mountains*. Captain Stewart is reclining on the left while an Indian fills his pipe. (Courtesy Buffalo Bill Historical Center, Cody, Wyoming)

ALFRED JACOB MILLER *The Trapper's Bride*, 1845. (The Harrison Eiteljorg Collection)

some time in the spring of 1837. He liked the mistiness and romanticism of Miller's work and, during a second visit, invited the twenty-seven-year-old artist to accompany him to the Rockies that summer.

Miller was the first artist to travel the route that became known as the Oregon Trail. Following the Kansas River to its confluence with the Little Blue, the expedition turned northwestward until they reached the Platte. They then followed that river, taking the north fork and passing by such landmarks as Chimney Rock, Scott's Bluff, and Fort Laramie en route to the rendezvous site near Horse Creek on the western slope of the Wind River Mountains. Miller was thus the first to document the landmarks along the trail which within a few years would bear thousands of emigrants westward. His pictures of Fort Laramie are unique, for the post was destroyed and reconstructed at a nearby site before another artist visited it.

Miller is best known for his pictures of the trappers and Indians at the rendezvous. His are the only paintings of trappers at work, heading out on the hunt and setting traps in a stream, and frolicking at the rendezvous. His Indians at times recall ancient Greek and Roman figures, and indeed he noted in his journal that these Indians were the physical equal of any sculpture he had seen in Europe. In his pictures of Indian domestic life Miller evokes Rousseau's ideal of the noble savage, and in them his debt to the Romantic artist Eugène Delacroix, whose work he studied in Paris, is apparent. His p.40 painting of *The Trapper's Bride* clearly suggests the combination of civilized and savage life that Rousseau might have applauded. No wonder that Miller's large oils caused such a sensation in New York, even though they were exhibited two years after Catlin's. They show the noble savages happily relaxing in their wilderness sanctuary – although Miller confided to his journal that the Indians were filthy, employed crude manners at best, and commonly ate dog meat. (Such beliefs, probably unfounded, kept the artist from sharing many meals with them.) Miller continued to make studio Pls.86–88 pictures from his sketches all his life.

ALFRED JACOB MILLER *Trapping Beaver* (detail), 1858–60. (Courtesy the Walters Art Gallery, Baltimore)

Other vast and empty sections on the national map were filled in by scientists, naturalists, and artists traveling as members of U.S. Government expeditions. One of the most important of these expeditions followed virtually in Miller's footprints. Senator Thomas Hart Benton of Missouri had called for a transcontinental road, and, unable to get his expansionist measures passed in Congress, he arranged for his explorer son-in-law, John C. Frémont, to be appointed head of an expedition to the Rocky Mountains with instructions to provide information that would prove the economic and scientific value of the West. Thousands of pioneers would, he hoped, then settle in the Western lands, putting the question of expansion beyond argument.

Frémont's 1842 expedition received such good notice that the following year Benton asked him to survey a route between the Sweetwater River and the Columbia, which Commander Charles Wilkes had documented in 1841. This would give the United States a firmer claim to the rich Oregon Territory in the heightening competition with the British. The two countries had agreed in 1827 that Oregon would be considered "open land," with each hoping that it could gain ultimate control through occupation by its mountain men and pioneers. (The two countries eventually compromised, in 1846, and agreed on the 49th parallel as the boundary.) After he reached Oregon, Frémont considered his assignment complete and turned south to investigate the territory of California, which belonged to Mexico. His first glimpse of northern California was important, for he immediately recognized it as the pastoral paradise that many travelers had sought for so long.

By 1845 the expansionist spirit – what a New York journalist christened the Americans' "Manifest Destiny" to settle the West and Southwest – had reached its zenith. Texas had won its independence from Mexico in 1836 and now appeared certain to join the Union. As politicians began thinking of adding further territory to the United States, at the expense of Mexico, other expeditions marched into little-known regions of the soon-to-be-contested land. In February, 1845, Frémont surveyed the Red and Arkansas rivers. Once he had reached the Upper Arkansas, he divided his command, sending Lieutenant James W. Abert to complete the mission and himself returning to

California. There he arrived in time to participate in the "Bear Flag" revolt, when a group of Americans in the Sacramento Valley seized Sonoma and raised the flag of independence.

Pl.106   The anticipated war began when a Mexican force attacked one of General Zachary Taylor's advance guards in disputed territory north of the Rio Grande. General Taylor led his force into northern Mexico, while Colonel Stephen Watts Kearny, already in the field with his Army of the West, captured Santa Fe in August, 1846, then headed on to California. In his party were Lieutenant William H. Emory and the artist John Mix Stanley. Their route took them through the Santa Rita del Cobre copper mines in southwestern New Mexico and the Pima and Maricopa villages along the Gila to the Pacific, which one of the mountain men dubbed "a great prairie without a tree." Eventually, on December 6, they managed a Pyrrhic victory at San Pascual, and marched home. In September of the following year the U.S. army occupied Mexico City, and the Treaty of Guadalupe Hidalgo, formally ending the war, was signed on February 2, 1848.

The amount of information gathered on Kearny's expedition, and published
Pl.109   in Emory's *Notes of a Military Reconnoissance* (1848), was enormous. Stanley (1814–72), a native of New York State, was a very good artist, though this could scarcely be guessed from the somewhat inept lithographs after his drawings that illustrate Emory's book. These are nevertheless of great interest, for Stanley was the first to portray the Southwest. Emory himself, during the expedition, began his inquiries into the origins of the Pueblo tribes, collected geological and botanical specimens, and produced a map that was for years the best cartographic document available on the region. More important for the future of American occupation of the region, however, he observed that the southwestern boundary between the United States and Mexico should be drawn south of the Gila River, since that was the only land through which he thought a railroad could be built. The boundary did, in fact, prove a problem in negotiating the peace, and a joint survey was set up in 1849.

Everyone agreed that the acquisition of Oregon, California and the Southwest called for the building of a transcontinental railroad, but the route it should take remained in question. While Congress debated the different options – a debate exacerbated by the sectional and moral and racial issues that were quickly building to the Civil War – Senator Benton gathered funds to finance an exploration of a proposed route from St Louis to San Francisco. It was to be led, of course, by Frémont, who had been court-martialed because of his unauthorized actions in California and was anxious to vindicate himself.

The party headed west in October, 1848, Frémont hopeful of proving that it was feasible to cross the mountains in winter. With Charles Preuss, a veteran of his previous expeditions, as cartographer, Old Bill Williams as guide, and Benjamin, Richard, and Edward Kern as scientists and artists, Frémont reached the San Juan Mountains in Colorado by mid-December. Williams lost his way, and the expedition was soon in serious trouble. By December 17 they were at 12,327 feet (3,757 meters), and the temperature had dropped to −20 °F (−29°C). The mules were dying from the cold, and "that old fool Bill," Preuss noted in his diary, "lay down and wanted to die, just at

the summit." In desperation, Frémont turned back. He divided his command in the hope of finding aid. One party, blinded and insensible from the snow and cold, got only a few miles from camp before the leader died. Frémont found them, tragically huddled around a campfire and in a starving condition. The dead man could not be found. Preuss baldly stated in his diary that they "had eaten part of his body." The leader of the main party, Lorenzo Vincenthaler, decreed that only the strong should survive, and left his dying men scattered along the trail as he headed for Taos. The Kern brothers, in another group, escaped the ordeal by agreeing to proceed as rapidly as possible, but to share their food and to leave no one behind.

Frémont tried to pretend that he had gathered valuable information, but the expedition was a complete failure, with ten men dead and the unprovable charge of cannibalism hanging over the heads of many of the survivors. The railroad would have to wait.

The next major exploration began in July, 1849, when commissioners representing Mexico and the United States met in San Diego to start the survey to establish the boundary between the two countries. At first progress was hampered by technical and diplomatic disagreements, then the Americans found it almost impossible to proceed because they were overwhelmed by prospectors – the famous "Forty-Niners" – headed for the goldfields of Pls.89–91 northern California. The discovery of gold in the American River near Sacramento had brought gold fever to the West, and prices rose dramatically. Hopeful men and women set off for California by whichever route they could, including the Oregon Trail, a southern route through northern Mexico and the American Southwest, and the Isthmus of Panama. The surprised boundary surveyors frequently had to share their meager supplies with destitute Forty-Niners who had lost all their goods in crossing the desert.

The boundary survey was essentially finished in 1853, and material on the history, natural history, geography, geology, and resources of the region was catalogued in the official report, published by Emory in 1857. Artists among the scientific corps had produced a stunning visual record of the entire length of the boundary. The best of them all was the Boundary Survey Commissioner himself, John Russell Bartlett (1805–86), whose watercolors and

Above left JOHN RUSSELL BARTLETT *Crossing the Pecos,* *c.* 1851. William Henry Chase Whiting wrote of the Pecos in his *Journal* (1849), "it rolls its discolored and rushing waters in a bed rarely in any place over forty feet in width, and winds from one side of the narrow valley to the other in abrupt turns. It is generally so deep as to be unpassable by fording – a pocket edition of the lower Rio Grande." (Courtesy John Carter Brown Library, Providence, Rhode Island)

Above JOHN RUSSELL BARTLETT *Guadalupe Mountain, Texas,* *c.* 1852. (Courtesy John Carter Brown Library, Providence, Rhode Island)

p.43; Pls.114,115 drawings document his trip from the coast of Texas through the Southwest to California, and into northern Mexico. Bartlett, a bookseller and bibliophile from New York City, probably thought of himself as a scientist rather than an artist, but his pictures and the book that he later wrote, *Personal Narrative of Explorations and Incidents in Texas, New Mexico, California, Sonora and Chihuahua* (1854), remain the most popular and easily accessible documents of all the material gathered on the survey.

After Frémont's disastrous expedition, a number of other explorers had attempted to survey possible routes for a transcontinental railroad. In the end, Congress took charge of the project, and in March, 1853, Secretary of War Jefferson Davis was requested to present the necessary information by the following January. It seemed an impossible task, because all of the surveys had to be carried out and the reports written in less than a year, but Davis, naming his old friend William H. Emory to direct the surveys, quickly Pl.78 organized four separate expeditions. The first was to explore the 49th and pp.44–45 47th parallels, from St Paul westward to Puget Sound, and was led by Isaac I. Stevens. The second group was to proceed along the 38th parallel westward from St Louis, under the direction of Captain John W. Gunnison. The third team advanced along the 35th parallel from Fort Smith, Arkansas, under Pl.116 Lieutenant Amiel W. Whipple. The fourth, documenting the 32nd parallel, consisted of Captain John Pope's reconnaissance westward from Fort Washita, Oklahoma, and Lieutenant John G. Parke's march eastward from Fort Yuma, Arizona.

Davis instructed the explorers not only to determine the feasibility of their route for a railroad but to gather material on the nature of the country, climate, geology, plants and animals, and the degree of sophistication of the natives. Specialists, including artists, were assigned to each team. Each had a

Is.111–113 military escort, although it proved tragically insufficient when Captain Gunnison led his expedition, which included the artist Richard Kern, into Mormon country near Manti, Utah, in October, 1853. Hostile Paiutes attacked the camp and killed all but four members of the party. Kern was among the dead. It was the worst disaster that the army had yet suffered in the West.

Besides Kern there were ten other artists attached to the railroad surveys. The results of their efforts were published between 1855 and 1861 in the twelve-volume octavo set entitled *Reports of Explorations and Surveys to Ascertain the Most Practicable and Economic Route for a Railroad from the Mississippi River to the Pacific Ocean*. These books, which required five different lithographic firms to complete and cost more than $1 million (almost double the expense of all the explorations combined), are probably the most important single contemporary source on Western geography and history.

The *Reports* dealt a severe blow to those who still harbored hopes that all the West was a garden. Long in 1821 had described the Great Plains as the American desert, and Colonel Randolph B. Marcy, who led an expedition in 1849 from Fort Smith, Arkansas, to Albuquerque, New Mexico, christened the area the "American Zahara"; but some had disagreed. Now the surveys as a whole upheld the notion. "Before the accession of California," commented a writer for *The North American Review*, one of the leading intellectual magazines of the day, "the western possessions of the United States were looked upon as a sort of fairy land basking under the influence of a most delightful climate, and enriched by the choicest gifts of nature." Now, he concluded, "we may as well admit that [most of these territories] . . . are perfect deserts . . . and that, whatever route is selected . . . must wind the greater part of its length through a country destined to remain for ever an uninhabited and dreary waste."

Ironically, the knowledge gained in the surveys only increased the confusion in Congress. The explorers had found not one route, but several. Secretary of War Davis in his report to the Senate in 1858 recommended the southern route, along the 32nd parallel. It offered the best prospect — but the choice left the southerner Davis, who would shortly forsake the Union and serve the Confederacy as its President, open to the charge of sectional prejudice. Because Congress could make no decision, the Pacific Railroad Surveys, which had been intended as a unifying and strengthening factor, further divided the country north and south and the transcontinental railroad was not completed until after the Civil War had run its course. When the rails did meet, in 1869, the route was none of those proposed. The Central Pacific Railroad was built eastward from Sacramento, California, to Promontory Point, Utah, on the Great Salt Lake, just north of the 41st parallel, and the Union Pacific Railroad was built westward to join it from Omaha, Nebraska, along the Platte River and through Cheyenne, Wyoming.

Pl.99

The painters' vision

"In the Forest scenery of the United States we have that which occupies the greatest space, and is not the least remarkable; being primitive, it differs widely from the European. In the American forest we find trees in every stage of vegetable life and decay. . . . Trees are like men, differing widely in character; in sheltered spots, or under the influence of culture, they show few contrasting points; peculiarities are pruned and trained away, until there is a general resemblance. But in exposed situations, wild and uncultivated, battling with the elements and with one another for the possession of a morsel of soil, or a favoring rock to which they may cling — they exhibit striking peculiarities, and sometimes grand originality."

Thomas Cole, "Essay on American Scenery" (1836)

In the fall of 1825 the elderly John Trumbull, beloved as the painter of the American Revolution, happened by a New York frame shop and saw three paintings of the Hudson River by a young English artist named Thomas Cole. Excited by the raw and powerful qualities of his realistic renderings of the wilderness, Trumbull hurried to the studio of his friend, the artist William Dunlap. "This youth has done what I have all my life attempted in vain," said Trumbull. They returned to the shop, where the shy and tongue-tied Cole soon stood before them.

Cole (1801–48), born in Lancashire, had arrived in the United States with his family in 1818. First working in Philadelphia as a wood engraver, he then offered his services as a portrait painter to residents in small towns in Ohio. Discouraged and kept from a debtor's cell only by charity, he returned to Philadelphia and sought guidance for his real love of laadscape painting in the galleries of the Pennsylvania Academy. There the pictures of Thomas Doughty and Thomas Birch encouraged him to try sketching out of doors. Cole headed up the Hudson in the summer of 1825, just as the Erie Canal was turning that waterway into a vast commercial thoroughfare. The valleys, mountain vistas, and river itself — nature in its "magnificence and grandeur" — inspired him to draw until his hands cramped and his eyes grew tired. Back in his rented attic room in New York, he hurried to put down the "perfect beauty" of what he had sketched. These were the paintings that Trumbull and Dunlap praised, and they marked the first clear break that American painters had made from the popular views of Birch and others.

The twenty-four-year-old Cole, infusing his landscapes with more than the documentary detail of his contemporaries, helped welcome the idea of "wilderness" to America. For years the pioneers had used military metaphors when talking of the wilderness. It was an "enemy" to be "conquered" by the "army of settlers" as they "marched" westward. That attitude had begun to change in eighteenth-century Virginia as men like William Byrd II and William Bartram, who admittedly did not face the life-or-death struggle with nature that the frontiersmen did, subscribed to the essentials of Romantic

primitivism propounded by Rousseau. Influential and charming visitors like the French writer François-René de Chateaubriand, who sought out the American wilderness in 1791, popularized the pleasures of unspoiled nature among their friends and acquaintances in the cities along the eastern seaboard. American intellectuals were influenced by the writings of British Romantics such as Shelley and Byron, both of whom dealt with themes of civilized man escaping into nature. "Man is naturally a wild animal," observed the noted Philadelphia physician Benjamin Rush in his autobiography (1800), "and . . . taken from the woods, he is never happy . . . 'till he returns to them again."

Early in the nineteenth century, patriotic writers searching for something unique about America seized on its wilderness. They realized that it was fiercer, harsher, and larger than any to be found in Europe. Thomas Jefferson in his *Notes on the State of Virginia* had claimed that a glimpse of the

THOMAS COLE *Landscape*, 1825. (Courtesy Museum of Art, Rhode Island School of Design, Providence, Walter H. Kimball Fund)

confluence of the Potomac and Shenandoah rivers in the Allegheny Mountains, near present-day Harper's Ferry, West Virginia, was "worth a voyage across the Atlantic." In a grander statement, the patriot Philip Freneau declared that the Mississippi was a "prince of rivers in comparison of whom the *Nile* is but a small rivulet, and the *Danube* a ditch."

Pl.52

Pl.1   To Cole, however, the wilderness offered more than visual or sensual pleasure: it had religious connotations as well. "Those scenes of solitude from which the hand of nature has never been lifted . . . are his [God's] undefiled works, and the mind is cast into the contemplation of eternal things." He never came to agree fully with the swelling New England intellectual and religious movement known as Transcendentalism, which held that each element of nature was an expression of a higher, corresponding or parallel truth, but he did reach an accommodation that permitted him to combine his mystical Romanticism with the more sophisticated aesthetic qualities of the European masters. Following a personally challenging and maturing trip to Europe in 1829–32, he concluded that wilderness must yield to man's civilizing influence and subdued the primitive wild that he had featured in his earlier works. This attitude is embodied in a painting made more than ten

Pl.19 years after his return from Europe, *Home in the Woods*, and there, it has been suggested, Cole reminds us by the shape of a cross formed of sticks at the left of the log cabin that the pioneer's life has more than a material dimension.

Cole's work represents the beginning of a different strand in American topographical art, over a century after William Burgis's first views of New York and Boston. In the tradition represented by artists such as Thomas Birch and William J. Bennett, and continued after Cole's time by the host of expeditionary limners who documented marches into the great West, the subject was usually more important than the overall effect: pictures, often intended to be engraved or lithographed, were made in a highly detailed manner. The ability of the potential client to recognize his city or a particular landmark was of the utmost importance and an obvious test of the "truth" of a painting.

Cole's contribution was to enrich the realism of the view painter with an artist's creative imagination: it was this combination that had attracted Trumbull, and led to some of Cole's greatest works. After arguing with the Baltimore collector and patron Robert Gilmor, Jr, that pictures should not be "mere imitations of nature" and that the imagination must be free in order to produce "anything truly great," Cole painted a "view" that he hoped would prove his point. "I have already commenced a view from Mount Holyoke,"

p.49 he wrote of *The Oxbow* in March, 1836. "It is about the finest scene I have in my sketchbook, and is well known." The huge canvas more than fulfilled his concept of art. Cole's trademark, the gnarled tree, dominates the scene at the left, yet the intimacy and freshness obtained by working directly from nature pull the viewer's eye toward the Connecticut River, the neat cultivated fields, and the storm clouds and mountains in the background. The painting has an immediacy sought by all the nature painters, but which was rare, even in Cole's work, at this time.

Perhaps the best combination of Cole's new-found talents, however, is his

Pl.17 famous picture, *Genesee Scenery (Mountain Landscape with Waterfall)*, which he completed in 1847 shortly before his untimely death. It seems the perfect

synthesis of nature and civilization, imagination and reality. Here his budding awareness of the appearance of "things" is apparent (it was about this time that he criticized the English artist Turner, comparing his rocks to "sugar candy"). Yet the picture, as a product of Cole's developing imagination, is clearly more than the "mere imitation of nature." As one art historian noted, it clearly established Cole's leadership among American artists of the day. It also showed subsequent painters of the ever-popular views how to infuse their images with a spiritual strength that many chauvinists associated with America itself.

While admitting the power and logic of Cole's work, artists who followed him into the wilderness developed a more rigid view of its relationship to God that was closer to Transcendentalism. The New Jersey-born painter Asher B. Durand (1796–1886) and the other members of what a New York critic derisively called the "Hudson River School" came to believe that God's truth revealed in untrammeled nature could be transmitted to the viewer by reproducing exactly the wild scene. The "legitimate and holy task of the scenic limner," wrote the contemporary critic Henry T. Tuckerman, was to interpret nature, and therefore God, because God had imbued nature with his spirit. Durand advised the host of young painters who looked to him for

intellectual and creative leadership "not to transcribe whole pages [of nature] indiscriminately 'verbatim ad literature'; but such texts as most clearly and simply declare her great truths"; landscape painting, he concluded, "will be great in proportion as it declares the glory of God, by representation of his works, and not of the works of man."

Art never had a higher calling or a more devoted and eager following. By painting the wilderness, artists both honored America in its uniqueness and communicated God's will to man. Durand, to whom Cole's mantle of America's outstanding landscape artist fell, imparted such wisdom to all the younger painters who gathered around him, and his sixteen years as president of the National Academy of Design and frequent articles in a short-lived but influential art periodical called *The Crayon* further insured the dissemination of his ideas.

Durand paid more attention to detail in nature than did Cole. Geology, meteorology, botany – all the developing sciences were at the disposal of artists who followed the English critic John Ruskin in emphasizing observation and truth to detail rather than imagination. During the 1850s p.51 Durand executed a series of open-air nature studies which seemed to epitomize his approach to painting, but his comments on the pictures in the "Letters on Landscape Painting," which he published in *The Crayon*, reveal that he fell short of objectivity. The landscapes themselves might have been accurate reproductions of what he had seen, but Durand could not consider them apart from a sacred presence. Following the logic of Jonathan Edwards, the eighteenth-century Puritan theologian who considered even the sun a manifestation of God's Son, Durand still conceived of the atmosphere as divinely inspired and commented with special significance on the "cheerful sentiment" that a wash of sunlight added to a picture.

Durand's most popular picture, which ranks with Cole's *Genesee Scenery* as Pl.1 a superb combination of the real and the ideal, is his homage to Cole. He painted *Kindred Spirits* the year after Cole's death, and in it he depicted the artist with the poet William Cullen Bryant, standing on a rocky ledge and talking together under the protective arch of a large tree limb and shrouded by a golden haze that has settled over the entire valley. The "Kindred Spirits" of the title refers to more than just the intimacy between the two friends; it includes the Catskill Mountains wilderness around them as well.

A number of younger artists surpassed Durand in their quest for realism by seeming to bring the viewer closer to the landscape. The paintings of Fitz Hugh Lane (1804–65), John F. Kensett (1816–72), Martin Johnson Heade (1819–1904), and Frederic Church (1826–1900), and in some cases those of William Sidney Mount (1807–68), George Caleb Bingham (1811–79), Thomas Worthington Whittredge (1820–1910), Sanford R. Gifford (1823–80), Albert Bierstadt (1830–1902), and Samuel Colman (1832–1920), seem to be devoid of any foreground, or obvious place for the artist to stand. The effect is that of admitting the viewer directly into the scene, the pictorial equivalent of Transcendentalist thinker Ralph Waldo Emerson's comment that when truly stirred by nature, he became "a transparent eye-ball; I am nothing; I see all."

Known today under the all-inclusive term of "Luminists," these artists painted tonal, realistic views that were subdued in mood and almost invariably horizontal in form. Their response was more objective than that of the spiritually-inspired Cole and Durand, and the light in their pictures is cool and plainly evident rather than diffused and atmospheric. Turning away from the scenes of raw and untamed nature so popular before, they preferred

Pl.25
Pl.21
Pl.63
Pls.117, 34
Pl.51

FITZ HUGH LANE *Brace's Rock, Eastern Point, Gloucester*, 1863. (Private collection)

disciplined, quiet compositions, which, if not always "quite divested of human association," as the critic James Jackson Jarves put it, place man and his activities in a very minor role. (One can believe that the dominant sounds in Colman's *Storm King on the Hudson*, despite the steamboats in the background, were the oars slapping the water, or in Whittredge's *Indian Encampment on the Platte River* the barking of the dog.) The surfaces of Luminist paintings are smooth: by minimizing brush strokes, the artists minimized their own presence, and stood aside to let the viewer become, in Emerson's phrase, "a transparent eyeball."

Pl.24

Pl.75

The characteristics of Luminism are perhaps best seen in the work of Fitz Hugh Lane, a Boston lithographer turned painter known for his beach and harbor scenes. His Civil War-era pictures of Brace's Rock near Gloucester, Massachusetts, show unpeopled scenes, poignant in their quiet loneliness and melancholy, with the deserted sailboat perhaps a troubled reference to the ship of state, wrecked and abandoned on the beach of war.

p.50

A figure better known for his grandiose Rocky Mountain vistas than for his Luminist views is Albert Bierstadt, who was born in Germany, grew up in the Connecticut whaling town of New Bedford, and returned briefly to Germany to gain his technical competence as a landscapist in Düsseldorf – a not unusual training for an American artist. He exhibited a number of pictures in New Bedford upon his return in 1857, but soon grew restless and arranged to accompany Colonel Frederick West Lander on his 1859 expedition along the Overland Trail. Perhaps it was the clarity and intensity of the Western light that led Bierstadt toward his first Luminist paintings, made during this trip. The characteristically vacant or non-existent foreground, the horizontalness, the smooth, flat surface, and the dominant light are all present. Now, however, the light is not a benevolent expression of God as it was in the paintings of Durand, but unemotional evidence of the brilliant Western sky.

Pl.51

The Bombardment of Fort Sumter, painted after Bierstadt had returned to the East, depicts the opening battle of the Civil War. Its Luminist qualities are so strong, particularly its quiet impersonalness, that they completely subdue the narrative portion of the picture in the background. One hardly notices that the bombardment of the fort is in progress.

By the close of the Civil War the same lure of the West that had enticed Bierstadt had captured other intellectuals and artists. Bierstadt himself returned on several occasions and soon earned a reputation as a master of the grand Rocky Mountain landscape. John Frederick Kensett, who had made an unsuccessful trip in 1854, journeyed west on three subsequent occasions, but p.53 found it unsuited to his style. He painted a somber picture of the upper Mississippi River that is much in keeping with his treatment of Eastern subjects, but hardly what one expected of the American West after Bierstadt. Kensett finally concluded, as noted in *The Crayon*, that "we should not report very favorably on the picturesqueness of the West in comparison with the East."

Schooled in the same tradition as Bierstadt and more enthusiastic about the West than Kensett, Thomas Worthington Whittredge made his first trip in 1866 with an army expedition. Leaving Fort Leavenworth, Kansas, in the summer, he journeyed to Denver, then turned southward to Santa Fe. "Nothing could be more like an Arcadian landscape," he wrote of the mountains, "than what was here presented to our view." Whittredge's exuberance at being in the wilderness was heightened when in Santa Fe he met an authentic hero, Kit Carson, the famous scout who had accompanied Frémont on his 1845–46 march to California. "I had all my life wanted to meet a man who had been born with some gentle instincts and who had lived a solitary life, either in the woods or somewhere where society had not affected him and where primitive nature had full swing of his sensibilities," he wrote. "The nearest approach to such a character I ever met . . . was Kit Carson." Whittredge came up against a different kind of Western character Pl.117 when he set out to depict the town of Santa Fe, but triumphed, and he was justifiably proud of the fine painting that resulted.

What that large view did for Santa Fe, in terms of atmosphere and ambiance, Whittredge's masterful oils, made during his second trip west in Pl.75 1870, did for the Plains, truthfully depicting the vacant land and vast space that overwhelmed many a traveler. Arriving by train in Denver and sheathing his paint brushes until he had gotten out of the mountains, Whittredge rendered quiet, serene scenes along the banks of the "thousand miles long and six inches deep" Platte River. "I had never seen the plains or anything like them," he recalled. "They impressed me deeply. I cared more for them than for the mountains, and . . . [most] of my western pictures have been produced from sketches made . . . on the plains with mountains in the distance. Whoever crossed the plains . . . could hardly fail to be impressed with its vastness and silence and the appearance everywhere of an innocent, primitive existence." His eloquent paintings are still evocative of the atmosphere and feeling of the flatlands, through which the river meanders toward its confluence with its North Fork in Nebraska.

Traveling with Whittredge in 1870 were Kensett and Sanford R. Gifford. Leaving Kensett and Whittredge in Colorado, Gifford accepted the invitation of Dr Ferdinand V. Hayden, a medical doctor who had given up his practice to study geology, to accompany his U.S. Geological Survey team on its

summer expedition into Utah and Wyoming Territory. Along with Hayden were the artist Henry Wood Elliott and photographer William Henry Jackson. Spending two months in the field, the party traveled up the Lodgepole, down the Chugwater, up the Platte and the Sweetwater rivers, through South Pass, and down parts of the Green River through the Uinta Mountains back to Cheyenne. Only eight of Gifford's paintings survive from the trip. Whittredge commented on the small output, observing that Gifford was unused to the great distances and had spent most of his time traveling rather than painting.

p.55 Notable among the eight, however, is a small and delicate study, *Valley of the Chug Water*, which, like Whittredge's pictures of the West, is accurate in its portrayal of a scene, yet possesses a painterly beauty of almost abstract design.

The painter who followed Gifford into Wyoming Territory, Thomas Moran (1837–1926), was to find in the West his greatest inspiration. Born in Lancashire, like Thomas Cole, Moran considered himself an "impressionist" in the mold of Ruskin, who urged artists to give a "true impression" of the scene as well as its higher symbolic and artistic truth. All of the Hudson River School artists would have agreed with that statement, but Moran went a step further. "I place no value upon literal transcripts from Nature," he said in one of his most quoted statements. "My general scope is not realistic, all my tendencies are toward idealization." Of one of his most famous

p.57 paintings, *Grand Canyon of the Yellowstone*, he said, "Topography in art is valueless . . . while I desired to tell truly of Nature, I did not wish to realize the scene literally, but to preserve and to convey its true impression." Still, Moran boasted that the details of his completed pictures were "so carefully

SANFORD R. GIFFORD *Valley of the Chug Water, Wyoming Ter., Aug. 9th 1870.* (Courtesy Amon Carter Museum, Fort Worth, Texas)

drawn that a geologist could determine their precise nature," and he made no effort to hide the fact that he consulted scientists in an effort to lend authenticity to his paintings. Perhaps Moran overstated his feelings to distinguish himself, as a proponent of "fine art," from illustrators and photographers, both of whom could produce literal copies of nature.

Moran's first field experience in the West came when Hayden organized his expedition to the Yellowstone in the summer of 1871. The artist Elliott and the photographer Jackson, previous Hayden crew members, were scheduled to go, and Hayden had asked Gifford to accompany them, but as Gifford's previous summer in Wyoming had not been very productive he had declined, and Hayden gratefully accepted Moran's request to come along. Few would have held out any great hope for the "frail, almost cadaverous" painter's success in the field. Jackson, a seasoned frontiersman, later noted that "Moran had never known a true wilderness, and he was as poorly equipped for rough life as anyone I have ever known. . . . He seemed incapable of surviving the rigors of camp life and camp food." But the plucky artist surprised them all. "He had a solution for every problem," Jackson recalled. "Never had he mounted a horse before we left the Botelers' [Ranch]. And then he did so with a pillow tucked in over the cantle of his saddle . . ."

The hardships were abundantly rewarded. From Fort Ellis, north of what is today Yellowstone National Park, they caught their first sight of the

WILLIAM H. HOLMES *William H. Holmes and George B. Chittenden measuring a High Mountain Station*, 1874. One of the best topographical artists to work in the West, Holmes was with Hayden in the Yellowstone, then accompanied him to Colorado, where this dramatic wash drawing was made – perhaps after a photograph by W. H. Jackson. (National Museum of American Art (formerly National Collection of Fine Arts), Smithsonian Institution, Washington, D.C.)

THOMAS MORAN *The Grand Canyon of the Yellowstone*, 1872. (U.S. Department of the Interior)

Yellowstone country. "The view from the mountains south east of our Camp . . . [is] glorious," Moran noted in his diary, "and I do not expect any finer general view of the Rocky Mountains." Heading south into the Yellowstone, the party passed the Devil's Slide on Cinnabar Mountain, Mammoth Hot

p.57 Springs, Tower Falls, and the Grand Canyon of the Yellowstone River, which Jackson called "pictorially the climax of the expedition." Hayden remembered that Moran had despaired, "with a sort of regretful enthusiasm, that these beautiful tints were beyond the reach of human art"; yet he tried, and the result is memorable. On their way out of the region, Moran and

Pl.101 Jackson visited the geyser basins on the Fire Hole River, where they saw Old Faithful, which Nathaniel Langford had named the previous year, and Castle Geyser. It was also on this trip that Moran first saw the magnificent cliffs of

Pl.100 the Green River, which he was to paint many times. A reporter for the Denver *Rocky Mountain News* confirmed that Moran had seen some of "the most remarkable scenery" that the West had to offer.

The significance of Moran's watercolors became apparent the following year, 1872, when Hayden joined the effort to have the Yellowstone declared the country's first national park and submitted Jackson's photographs and Moran's paintings as evidence of its uniqueness. Congress established the park that spring. A writer for the *Nation*, who saw Moran's watercolors in New York before they were shipped to their purchaser, the English collector William Blackmore, delighted in them: "They are abundantly finer works than the painting we have been admiring. They are rapid, racy, powerful, romantic specimens of water-color sketching, showing in each example faculties any artist ought to glory in." A reviewer for *Scribner's Monthly* declared them "the most brilliant and poetic pictures that have been done in America thus far."

Moran's pictures reached an even larger audience when the Boston chromolithographer Louis Prang produced a portfolio of fifteen prints after his Yellowstone watercolors in 1876. It was an ideal time – the centennial of the Declaration of Independence from Britain – to celebrate the wonders of America. Prang printed 1,000 sets that sold for $60 each. *The Times* of London was enthusiastic: "No finer specimens of chromo-lithographic work have been produced anywhere."

Moran had intended to spend the summer of 1872 finishing the orders that he had received for Yellowstone paintings, and he had turned down invitations to join both Hayden's and Colonel John Wesley Powell's summer expeditions, but by August the urge to travel and see new territory had become too strong to resist. He set out for Yosemite, which the painters Pl.97; p.59 Bierstadt and Thomas A. Ayres and the photographers Eadweard Muybridge and Carleton Watkins had made famous. The Governor of California had designated the spectacular country as a state recreation area in 1864. But Half Dome, the sheer granite cliff that dominates Yosemite Valley, did not inspire Moran, as it had visitors before him, and he returned with only a few pencil sketches and four watercolors. Perhaps Moran's indifference reflected Yosemite's already established popularity as well as its close association with Bierstadt and the photographers.

In search of new and more congenial scenery, Moran accepted Colonel John Wesley Powell's invitation the following summer to float down the Colorado River through Utah and Arizona, including the Grand Canyon. Powell had already explored the region twice. In 1869, following up Lieutenant Joseph C. Pls.118,119 Ives's 1858 expedition to the floor of the canyon, he had traveled down the Green and Colorado rivers, and he and his crew had been the first to float through the Grand Canyon. His second expedition, in 1871–72, involved a more elaborate documentation of the canyon, helped by the work of the artist Frederick S. Dellenbaugh and of John K. Hillers, a boatman on a previous expedition who had assumed the position of photographer. Still, Powell was in need of an artist of Moran's stature to paint the scenes that he admitted were "too vast, too complex, too grand for verbal description."

Moran departed from Salt Lake City and arrived in camp, near the fork of the Rio Virgin, late in July, 1873. While Powell was away dealing with the same Indians who twenty years before had massacred the Gunnison party, the crew passed through the Zion Valley. Moran happily discovered that the colors along the Rio Virgin suited his brilliant palette much better than had Yosemite, and when he reached the Grand Canyon of the Colorado, he realized that he had found another site, like Yellowstone two years before, that only he could render in its full beauty and majesty. "I was completely carried away by its magnificence," he wrote his wife. "I will not attempt to say anything about it as no words can express the faintest notion of it." The result of the trip, in addition to numerous watercolors, was a vast and Pl.120 spectacular oil painting entitled *The Chasm of the Colorado*. The government p.57 purchased it for $10,000 as a companion to Moran's *Grand Canyon of the Yellowstone*, acquired the previous year.

As the nation moved toward a giant celebration in honor of the centennial

of its independence, Moran's huge canvases seemed appropriate monuments to the faith that Americans had placed in the land. The wilderness and its wealth had attracted immigrants since the sixteenth century. It had fueled the greatest transcontinental migration in our history as the West was settled, and, even as Moran painted, it inspired the greatest exodus from one continent to another that the world has ever known. These "uprooted," as the European immigrants became known, numbered more than a million annually by 1874. They settled on the vast farmlands of the Midwest and West and in the burgeoning cities, where they found work as a result of the unprecedented industrial expansion following the Civil War. By 1870 New York, Brooklyn, Philadelphia, Chicago, and St Louis each had between 250,000 and 500,000 inhabitants, and three industrial workers out of every four in America were foreign-born.

Pls.67, 104

Pls.61, 68

Some of Moran's more talented contemporaries did not share his optimism and belief in the future. The internecine rivalry of the Civil War was a profound shock to national sensibilities, and its impact can be detected in the sensitive and lonely landscapes of the Luminists. Ominous thunderstorms overwhelming small boats and even smaller people, helpless in the elements, suggest the artists' despair at the fate of the nation, tossed about in a world that some felt was no longer watched over by a benevolent God. Cadmium red, a vivid color only recently made available, permitted artists to paint unnatural and eerie sunsets, suggesting an unknown and now less optimistic future.

Pl.24

After T.A. AYRES *General View of the Great Yo-semite Valley, Mariposa County, California,* 1859. (Courtesy Amon Carter Museum, Fort Worth, Texas)

59

THOMAS EAKINS *Pushing for Rail*, 1874. (The Metropolitan Museum of Art, New York, Arthur H. Hearn Fund, 1916)

By 1870 Luminism had run its course. As an artistic movement, it formed a transition between two very different visions of the relationship between man and the world around him: that of the Hudson River School painters, for whom nature was the physical manifestation of a higher spiritual being and man a special creature; and that of a later generation, led by Winslow Homer (1836–1910) and Thomas Eakins (1844–1916), who were deeply affected by Darwin's theories and by the social developments they saw around them. The American Republic itself had moved from youthful optimism and faith to its inevitable position as a maturing nation with complex psychological and aesthetic needs.

After painting several pictures with Luminist attributes, Homer established himself as an independent figure. Inspired by Darwin, he saw man as part of nature and engaged in a profound struggle to survive – against the forces of nature itself, often represented by the sea, or those of society, as in *The Morning Bell*, where a solitary girl, her face hidden by her broad-brimmed bonnet, walking through a sunlit landscape to spend the day working in a dark, cramped mill, assumes heroic proportions.

Pl.30

No longer is the immense land itself, or God's communication with man through its unsullied state, the subject of paintings. Thomas Eakins's *Pushing for Rail* shows hunters, a ''higher'' element of nature, as they walk through the marshes looking for birds. The picture is a quiet and subtle reminder of the validity of nature's law of the survival of the fittest and man's own mortality. As the nation rushed toward its centennial, the era of the view painter and landscape artist closed almost unnoticed. Changing intellectual and aesthetic philosophies had stripped the landscapist of his purpose, while the photographer rendered the view painter obsolete.

p.60

60

A journey in time
from the Atlantic to the Pacific

As the storm is now subsiding, and the horizon becoming serene, it is pleasant to consider the phenomenon with attention. We can no longer say there is nothing new under the sun. For this whole chapter in the history of man is new. The great extent of our republic is new. Its sparse habitation is new. The mighty wave of public opinion which has rolled over it is new.

Thomas Jefferson to Dr Joseph Priestly, March 21, 1801

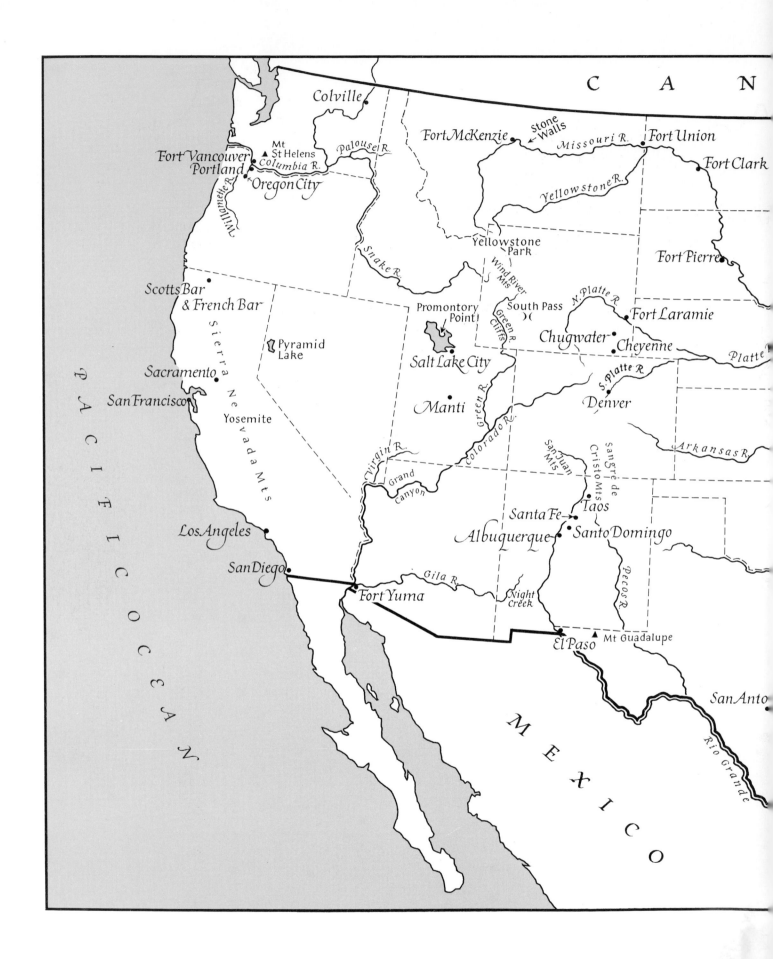

C A N A D A

Falls of
t Anthony
St Paul
Mississippi R.
Prairie
du Chien
Omaha
Council Bluffs
Bellevue
Missouri R.
ort
eavenworth
StLouis
Ohio R.
Louisville
Fort Smith
d R.
Mississippi R.
Biloxi
New Orleans

Chicago
Detroit
Cleveland
Cincinnati
Pittsburgh
Marietta

Niagara
Falls
Genesee
Falls
Erie Canal
Scranton
Philadelphia
Washington
Richmond
Alleghen
Mts
Natural Bridge
of Virginia

Hudson R.
Catskill
West Point
New York
Harper's Ferry

MT DESERT I.
Boston

ROANOKE I.

Savannah R.
Charleston
Savannah
Fort Caroline
St.Augustine

A T L A N T I C   O C E A N

G U L F   O F   M E X I C O

0   500 MIs
0   800 Kms

Artist and writer, "Kindred Spirits" in the American wilderness

Asher B. Durand's "Kindred Spirits" is one of the most famous and best loved American paintings. In it the artist's two friends, the painter Thomas Cole and the poet William Cullen Bryant, stand amid a wild mountain landscape, on a ledge above the Kaaterskill Clove in the Catskills, both moved to Wordsworthian emotions by the presence of untamed nature. But both, too, feel something more than the conventional romantic response – for this is America, *their own vast, untraveled, virtually unknown land, holding secrets and resources that can barely be imagined. It is therefore fitting that the picture is almost a national icon, and fitting that it should stand at the beginning of this book, which will explore exactly that theme through more than two centuries: the sense of discovering a new world, embodied in the two arts of painting and writing.*

To Cole, the painter, departing for Europe

Thine eyes shall see the light of distant skies;
  Yet, Cole! thy heart shall bear to Europe's strand
  A living image of our own bright land,
Such as upon thy glorious canvas lies;
Lone lakes – savannas where the bison roves –
  Rocks rich with summer garlands – solemn streams –
  Skies, where the desert eagle wheels and screams –
Spring bloom and autumn blaze of boundless groves.
Fair scenes shall greet thee where thou goest – fair,
  But different – everywhere the trace of men,
  Paths, homes, graves, ruins, from the lowest glen
To where life shrinks from the fierce Alpine air.
  Gaze on them, till the tears shall dim thy sight,
  But keep that earlier, wilder image bright.

William Cullen Bryant, 1829

In the woods, is perpetual youth. Within these plantations of God, a decorum and sanctity reign, a perennial festival is dressed, and the guest sees not how he should tire of them in a thousand years. In the woods, we return to reason and faith. There I feel that nothing can befall me in life – no disgrace, no calamity, (leaving me my eyes,) which nature cannot repair. Standing on the bare ground – my head bathed by the blithe air, and uplifted into infinite space – all mean egotism vanishes. I become a transparent eye-ball. I am nothing. I see all. The currents of the Universal Being circulate through me; I am part or particle of God.

Ralph Waldo Emerson, *Nature*, 1836

1 Asher B. Durand *Kindred Spirits*, 1849. (Art and Architecture Division, The New York Public Library, Astor, Lenox and Tilden Foundations)

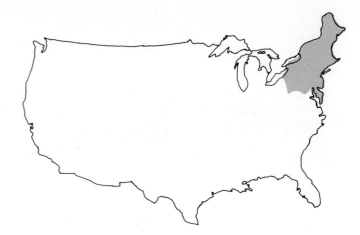

The East

Colonial cities

Although colonial America is usually thought of as rural and agricultural, several seacoast towns developed immediately into cities. New Amsterdam, which enjoys the finest natural harbor on the continent, was founded in 1625 as a trading post for the Dutch West India Company, and fell in 1664 to the English, who renamed it New York. Boston, ideally situated at the mouth of the Charles River, took advantage of the nearby New England forests to support a thriving shipbuilding industry and dominated the West Indian trade. Along with Philadelphia, these were the largest and best known cities in the colonies.

Around this fort a progeny of little Dutch-built houses, with tiled roofs and weathercocks, soon sprang up, nestling themselves under its walls for protection. . . . Outside of these extended the cornfields and cabbage-gardens of the community, with here and there an attempt at a tobacco-plantation; all covering those tracts of country at present called Broadway, Wall Street, William Street, and Pearl Street.

Washington Irving, *A History of New York, by Diedrich Knickerbocker*, 1809

The Houses are for the most part raised on the Sea-Banks, and wharfed out with great Industry and Cost; many of them standing upon Piles, close together, on each side the streets, as in London, and furnished with many fair Shops; where all sorts of Commodities are sold. Their streets are many and large, paved with Pebbles; the Materials of their Houses are Brick, Stone, Lime, handsomely contrived, and when any New Houses are built, they are made comfortable to our New Buildings in London since the fire.

John Dunton, *Letters Written from New-England*, 1686

2 JAN VINCKEBOONS *New Amsterdam or now New York on the Island of Man[hattan]* (detail), sketched probably c.1650–53, but painted, as an inscription indicates, after the city had been taken by the English. (Algemeen Rijksarchief, The Hague)

3 After WILLIAM BURGIS *A South East View of the Great Town of Boston in New England in America* (detail), 1725 and 1736. (British Library, London)

A nation emerges

Increasing conflict with the British Parliament and George III led the colonists to convene the First Continental Congress in Philadelphia. Their actions were construed as rebellion, and in April, 1775, troops were dispatched to capture the arms and munitions the colonists had been accumulating at Concord.

Boston and New York, as the two major ports, were obvious targets for the British in their effort to subdue the rebels. In March, 1776, General Washington ousted the British from Boston by placing his troops and artillery on Dorchester Heights, commanding the narrow neck between the city and the mainland. Soon afterwards, however, the British General Sir William Howe took advantage of Washington's inexperience and easily outflanked him to win the battle for New York. Washington had pulled back to Long Island; the British landed on Staten Island and then, on July 12, 1776, the "Phoenix" and the "Rose" forced their way up the North or Hudson River between the Americans' batteries, and effectively cut off the rebels' provisions from upcountry. Had Howe pressed the advantage, he might have ended the revolution in New York. He did not, and Washington escaped.

4 LIEUTENANT WILLIAM PIERIE of the Royal Regiment of Artillery *Map and views of Boston and the surrounding area, 1773.* (British Library, London)

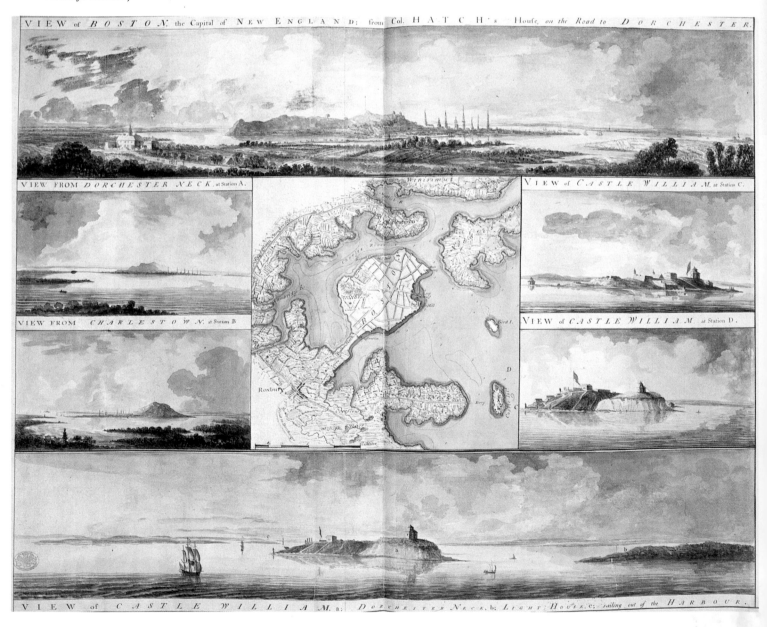

5 DOMINIC SERRES *Capt. Hyde Parker in the Phoenix going up the North River, New York*, 1776. (British Museum, London)

Boston is joined to the continent by a narrow tongue of land, at the two sides of which creeks, or bays run into the land. Over these creeks there are several long wooden bridges, made to draw up in the middle, one of which leads, in a north-west direction, to the neighbouring town of Charlestown; another, more to the south, to Cambridge. . . . We took the road through Charlestown, to the Navy Yard, close to which is the eminence on which the Bunker's Hill monument is erected. . . . Withinside, a convenient stone staircase leads to the top, and from the small windows in the roof, there is an incomparable view over the city of Boston, Charlestown, the two inlets, the long bridges, the Bay of Boston, with its diversified islands, and the ships with their white swelling sails, coming from, and bound to, all parts of the world. Looking into the country, there is an alternation of verdant hills, numerous villages, and dark woods; the whole forming a highly picturesque landscape.

Maximilian of Wied-Neuwied, *Travels in . . . 1832, 1833, and 1834*, 1843

A week or ten days before we were drove from Boston, 'tis impossible to give you an adequate idea of our situation. . . . With astonishing celerity the Provincials had erected batteries at Dorchester Heights, from which they commanded three-fourths of the town, and on their will it depended to destroy it. They gave us an antepast of what we were to expect by the fiery mission of several bombs the day before we quitted; four persons were killed, a soldier and three of the townspeople.

Anonymous letter to the *Morning Chronicle*, March 21, 1776

The Phoenix and Rose men of war have passed up the North River, about 24 miles, where they were attacked by row-gallies and floating batteries, all which they either burnt or sunk, with a vast number of men; it was a dangerous service, and to the honour of Captain Hyde Parker, and Captain James Wallace most intrepidly performed; they are just returned, having expended all their ammunition.

"A gentleman who has escaped from the provincials," letter to *Farley's Bristol Journal*, August 17, 1776

Cities of the Federal age

Philadelphia was the capital of the United States when its leading artist, William Birch, set out with his son Thomas to engrave views of the entire city. Though it lost that eminence to Washington in 1800, it kept its cultural distinction. William Strickland pioneered the Greek Revival in this city of white marble: his Branch Bank of the United States, of 1819–24, was the first in the world to enshrine finance in a Greek Doric temple.

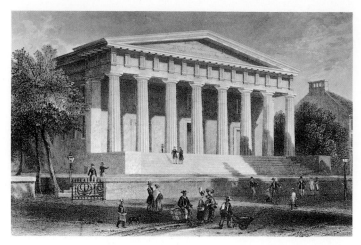

6 After W. H. BARTLETT *Branch Bank of the United States, Philadelphia, c.1840.* (Courtesy The Historical Society of Pennsylvania)

7 WILLIAM BIRCH *High Street [now Market Street], from Ninth Street, Philadelphia* (detail), 1799. (Courtesy The New York State Historical Association, Cooperstown)

70

8 JOHN RUBENS SMITH? *Nos. 168–172 Fulton Street, New York, showing the Shop and Warehouse of Duncan Phyfe*, 1816–17. From left to right the buildings are the workshop, shop, and warehouse. (The Metropolitan Museum of Art, New York, Rogers Fund, 1922)

Philadelphia may be considered the metropolis of the United States. It is certainly the most beautiful and best-built city in the nation, and also the wealthiest, though not the most ostentatious. Here you find more well-educated men, more knowledge of politics and literature, more political and learned societies than anywhere else in the United States.

J. P. Brissot de Warville, *New Travels in the United States of America*, 1788

Philadelphia seemed to me a beautiful city with wide streets; some, lined with trees, crossed one another at right angles in regular order from north to south and east to west. . . .

François-René de Chateaubriand, *Travels in America*, 1791

New York, meanwhile, had become the major commercial center in the nation, and attracted skilled tradesmen and craftsmen such as the Scots-born Duncan Phyfe, who became one of the most distinguished and prosperous cabinetmakers in the country, and is credited with introducing the Greek Revival style in American furniture. In his workshop – which, like his shop, proclaimed his refined taste in design – he employed as many as a hundred people, and on his death in 1854 he left an estate valued at almost half a million dollars.

Boston

Long the most important city in colonial America, Boston maintained its importance as a center of commerce and learning after independence. Here the artist James B. Marston has provided a newcomer's look at the Old State House at the end of State Street – the site of the Boston "Massacre" (see p. 24) – which ran eastward to the Long Wharf.

Boston's situation as a port led to the development of large hotels, whose peculiar customs intrigued foreign visitors such as Prince Maximilian of Wied-Neuwied, who visited the city on the Fourth of July, 1832.

Boston, an extensive city, with above 80,000 inhabitants, reminded me, at first sight, of one of the old English towns; but various differences soon appeared. The streets are partly long and broad, partly narrow and irregular, with good flag pavement for foot passengers; the buildings are of brick or stone; but in a great portion of the old town the houses are of wood; the roofs are, for the most part, covered with shingles; the chimneys resemble those in England, but do not seem to be so lofty; the dark colours of the buildings give the city, on the whole, a gloomy appearance. There are many important buildings and churches. . . .

After we had enjoyed a hasty view of the city, we returned to our inn, where we had an opportunity of making ourselves acquainted with many new customs, differing from those of Europe . . . there is a peculiar arrangement, which many travellers have noticed, and which we do not meet with in ours – I mean the bar-room, where a man stationed behind the bar, mixes compounds, and sells all sorts of beverages, in which a quantity of ice and of freshly gathered peppermint leaves are employed. Very agreeable cooling liquors are here prepared, which the heat of the climate calls for.

Maximilian of Wied-Neuwied, *Travels in . . . 1832, 1833, and 1834,* 1843

9 J.B. MARSTON *State Street, Boston* (detail), 1801. (Courtesy The Massachusetts Historical Society, Boston)

10 GEORGE TATTERSALL *Highways and Byways of the Forest, a Scene on "the Road"*, 1838. (Courtesy Museum of Fine Arts, Boston, M. and M. Karolik Collection)

The road we went over that day, was certainly enough to have shaken tempers that were not resolutely at Set Fair, down to some inches below Stormy. At one time we were all flung together in a heap at the bottom of the coach, and at another we were crushing our heads against the roof. Now, one side was down deep in the mire, and we were holding to the other. Now, the coach was lying on the tails of the two wheelers; and now it was rearing up in the air, in a frantic state, with all four horses standing on the top of an insurmountable eminence, looking cooly back at it, as though they would say "Unharness us. It can't be done."
. . . A great portion of the way was over what is called a corduroy road, which is made by throwing trunks of trees into a marsh, and leaving them to settle there. The very slightest of the jolts with which the ponderous carriage fell from log to log, was enough, it seemed, to have dislocated all the bones in the human body. It would be impossible to experience a similar set of sensations, in any other circumstances, unless perhaps in attempting to go up to the top of St. Paul's in an omnibus.

Charles Dickens, *American Notes*, 1842

Development of the country

Roads were often no more than rough trails carved out of the virgin forest, and the rutted and potholed highways between the larger towns became the subject of many travellers' accounts of America. Water transportation, by comparison, was fairly easy and quick. The Hudson River proved to be an economic lifeline, especially after the Erie Canal connected it with Buffalo, on Lake Erie, in 1825.

Allowing boats to pass all the way from the Great Lakes to the Atlantic, the canal increased New York City's dominance over the rest of the country. Its prosperity was reflected in its main street, Broadway.

12 After WILLIAM GUY WALL *Palisades* (detail), c.1820. (Courtesy Amon Carter Museum, Fort Worth, Texas)

11 After W. WILSON *View of the Upper Village of Lockport, New York [on the Erie Canal]* (detail), 1836. (Courtesy of The New-York Historical Society, New York City)

At Lockport, an extensive place, situated on the eminence, the canal is conducted, by means of five sluices, down a slope of at least sixty feet. The prospect from the eminence is very beautiful.

Maximilian of Wied-Neuwied, *Travels in . . . 1832, 1833, and 1834*, 1843

OVERLEAF

. . . the splendid Broadway . . . runs through the whole city. This noble street may vie with any I ever saw, for its length and breadth, its handsome shops, neat awnings, excellent *trottoir*, and well-dressed pedestrians. It has not the crowded glitter of Bond-street equipages, nor the gorgeous fronted palaces of Regent-street; but it is magnificent in its extent.

Mrs Trollope, *Domestic Manners of the Americans*, 1832

13 After T. HORNOR *Broadway, New-York. Shewing each Building from the Hygeian Depot corner of Canal Street to beyond Niblo's Garden* (detail), drawn in 1834 and published in 1836. (The New York Public Library)

The new capital: Washington

In 1800 the Government moved to Washington, D.C., on the bank of the Potomac River. The French engineer Major Pierre L'Enfant designed great Neo-classical boulevards and circles that were only muddy streets to the 3,000 residents who lived in the new capital, but the city gradually began to grow into L'Enfant's plan. The president's mansion was built by James Hoban and modified by Benjamin Latrobe after the British had burned it in 1814.

By 1852, when this view of Washington looking west was published, Thomas Ustick Walter's enlargement of the Capitol was underway (though not finished, as shown here; and the great dome would not be added until later). In the background to the left is the Washington Monument, with the turreted Smithsonian Institution in front of it. The wide street in the center of the view is Pennsylvania Avenue, leading to the White House.

14 BENJAMIN LATROBE *Elevation of the South front of the President's house*, 1817. (Library of Congress)

15 EDWARD SACHSE *View of Washington*, 1852. (Library of Congress)

From the base of the hill on which the capitol stands extends a street of most magnificent width, planted on each side with trees, and ornamented by many splendid shops. This street, which is called Pennsylvania avenue, is above a mile in length, and at the end of it is the handsome mansion of the president; conveniently near to his residence are the various public offices, all handsome, simple, and commodious; ample areas are left round each, where grass and shrubs refresh the eye.

Mrs Trollope, *Domestic Manners of the Americans*, 1832

It is sometimes called the City of Magnificent Distances, but it might with greater propriety be termed the City of Magnificent Intentions; for it is only on taking a bird's-eye view of it from the top of the Capitol, that one can at all comprehend the vast designs of its projector, an aspiring Frenchman. Spacious avenues, that begin in nothing, and lead nowhere; streets, mile-long, that only want houses, roads and inhabitants . . . are its leading features.

Charles Dickens, *American Notes*, 1842

The painters' state: New York

The artists of the Hudson River School made the Catskill Mountains and upper New York State virtually synonymous with American landscape for over thirty years after Thomas Cole had "discovered" the Hudson with his canvases of 1825 (see p.45).

Cole himself lived in the small town of Catskill, on the Hudson. Towards the end of his relatively short life he turned his attention from the wilderness to scenes revealing the hand of man. "Where the wolf roams, the plough shall glisten", he had written in 1836; and in his view of the Genesee Falls he rejoices in the presence of the mill and homestead.

16 ALBURTIUS DEL ORIENT BROWERE *Catskill*, 1849. (The Brooklyn Museum, Dick S. Ramsay Fund)

. . . the Catskill Mountains [are] a picturesque range, with fine summits, such as are seldom seen in North America. . . . Along the shore, at the foot of this range, lies the village of Catskill, on Catskill Creek, which runs through the village, and flows into the Hudson. Here we landed, and took in some passengers, who, in token of their having come from those more elevated regions, brought in their hands large bunches of the beautiful kalmia blossoms. The village contains about 350 houses and 5000 inhabitants. I would recommend the view of the Catskill Mountains to every landscape painter.

Maximilian of Wied-Neuwied, *Travels in . . . 1832, 1833, and 1834,* 1843

80

17 THOMAS COLE *Genesee Scenery (Mountain Landscape with Waterfall),* 1847. (Museum of Art, Rhode Island School of Design, Jesse Metcalf Fund)

18 Francis Alexander *Ralph Wheelock's Farm*, c.1822. (Courtesy National Gallery of Art, Washington, D.C., Gift of Edgar William and Bernice Chrysler Garbisch 1965)

19 Thomas Cole *Home in the Woods*, c.1846. (Reynolda House Museum of American Art, Winston-Salem, North Carolina)

The farmers' paradise

Farming was the American profession, from President Thomas Jefferson, who invented a plow, to the nine out of every ten Americans who lived and worked on farms in 1800. Proponents of easily accessible public lands succeeded in changing government policy, which was originally designed to produce revenue for the Treasury, to permit easy acquisition of land. In 1800 the minimum amount one could purchase was 360 acres; in 1804 this was reduced to 160 acres, with only a one-fourth down payment required in order to take possession.

He is an American, who leaving behind him all his ancient prejudices and manners, receives new ones from the new mode of life he has embraced, the new government he obeys, and the new rank he holds. . . . Here individuals of all nations are melted into a new race of men, whose labours will one day cause great changes in the world. . . . Here the rewards of his industry follow with equal steps the progress of his labour. . . .Wives and children, who before in vain demanded of him a morsel of bread, now, fat and frolicsome, gladly help their father to clear those fields whence exuberant crops are to arise to feed and to clothe them all. . . . The American is a new man, who acts upon new principles; he must therefore entertain new ideas, and form new opinions.

Michel Guillaume Jean de Crèvecoeur, *Letters from an American Farmer*, 1782

20 EDWARD HICKS *An Indian Summer View of the Farm & Stock of James C. Cornell of Northampton, Bucks county, Pennsylvania, October, 1848.* (Courtesy National Gallery of Art, Washington, D.C., Gift of Edgar William and Bernice Chrysler Garbisch)

Niagara Falls

America had no ancient ruins or magnificent cathedrals like Europe, but it did have natural splendor unexcelled – cathedrals of nature, as one chauvinistic poet put it. The greatest of these was Niagara Falls, whose sheer power and majesty humbled all observers. The early settlers had viewed the falls as devilish and dangerous, and the French explorer, Father Hennepin, recoiled from the "horrible Precipice" when he first viewed it in 1679 (see p. 21). Perhaps no image excels that of Frederic Church. In his stupendous view of the Horseshoe Falls he brings the spectator right up to its brink.

21 Frederic Edwin Church *Niagara Falls*, 1857. (In the Collection of the Corcoran Gallery of Art, Washington, D.C.)

In this moment the sun rose and dispelled the shadows of the night. Its rays . . . gave this great sheet of water the crystal clarity of glass. It was then that we discovered three rainbows: the first, on the waters of the abyss; the second nearer us; and the third above our heads. . . . Finally, after fortifying ourselves with a glass of rum, we followed our guide, and with the aid of ladders, we climbed down.

J. Hector St John de Crèvecoeur, *Journey Into Northern Pennsylvania and the State of New York*, 1801

The railroad transforms the countryside

Railroads came rapidly to the United States and played a crucial role in its expanding industrialism. The Baltimore and Ohio had only thirteen miles of track laid in 1830, but within a few years railroads operated all along the Atlantic seaboard; 3,328 miles of track existed by 1840. Some artists reveled in the sheer power of the locomotive, while others, like George Inness, regretted its impact on the American wilderness.

The Utica railroad is one of the best in America. . . . The locomotive was of great power, and . . . threw out such showers of fire, that we were constantly in danger of conflagration. The weather was too warm to admit of the windows being closed, and the ladies, assisted by the gentlemen, were constantly employed in putting out the sparks which settled on their clothes – the first time I ever heard ladies complain of having too many *sparks* about them. As the evening closed in we actually were whirled along through a stream of fiery threads – a beautiful, although humble imitation of the tail of a comet.

Captain Frederick Marryat, *Diary in America*, 1839

22 CURRIER & IVES after FRANCES F. PALMER *The "Lightning Express" Trains. "Leaving the Junction,"* 1863. (Courtesy Amon Carter Museum, Fort Worth, Texas)

23 GEORGE INNESS *The Lackawanna Valley, or The First Roundhouse of the Delaware, Lackawanna and Western Railroad at Scranton, Pennsylvania*, 1855. (Courtesy National Gallery of Art, Washington, D.C., Gift of Mrs Huttleston Rogers, 1945)

The nation itself . . . lives too fast. Men think that it is essential that the *Nation* have commerce, and export ice, and talk through a telegraph, and ride thirty miles an hour . . ., but whether we should live like baboons or like men, is a little uncertain. If we do not get out sleepers, and forge rails, and devote days and nights to the work, but go to tinkering upon our *lives* to improve *them*, who will build railroads? And if railroads are not built, how shall we get to Heaven in season? But if we stay at home and mind our business, who will want railroads? We do not ride on the railroad; it rides upon us.

Henry David Thoreau, *Walden*, 1854

The gathering storm

24 SAMUEL COLMAN *Storm King on the Hudson* (detail), 1866. (National Museum of American Art (formerly National Collection of Fine Arts), Smithsonian Institution, Washington D.C., Gift of John Gellatly)

25 MARTIN JOHNSON HEADE *Thunderstorm over Narragansett Bay* [*Rhode Island*], 1868. (Courtesy Amon Carter Museum, Fort Worth, Texas)

The Hudson River School painters incorporated light from an evident source in their landscapes, as the physical representation of a superior being; to later painters such as Colman and Heade, however, it was a secular light that reflected from every part of their canvas. The moody and brooding qualities of these taut and stunning paintings also force one to wonder if the artists were not commenting on the country's painful maturing process of Civil War, Reconstruction, and industrial upheaval.

The title of Colman's painting refers to the mountain, which always attracted storms because of its height and, therefore, served as a weather signal to the local residents.

About forty miles from New-York you enter upon the Highlands, as a series of mountains which then flank the river on both sides, are called. The beauty of this scenery can only be conceived when it is seen. One might fancy that these capricious masses, with all their countless varieties of light and shade, were thrown together to show how passing lovely rocks, and woods, and water could be. Sometimes a lofty peak shoots suddenly up into the heavens, showing in bold relief against the sky; and then a deep ravine sinks in solemn shadow, and draws the imagination into its leafy recesses.

Mrs Trollope, *Domestic Manners of the Americans*, 1832

The face of commerce

The railroad improved transportation and distribution, increasing business all along the coast and beyond, and new inventions created new businesses. Architecture in turn evolved new forms to serve the new commerce. The Grover & Baker Company in New York, makers of sewing machines, boasted a prefabricated cast iron front – an American specialty – of unusual Gothic design. (Packages on the van indicate that Grover & Baker shipped to Havana, Hamburg, Madrid and Valparaiso, as well as

Nashville, Tennessee.) L. J. Levy & Company of Philadelphia carried on a more traditional trade, in handsomely panelled showrooms made light and spacious by the use of iron columns. But perhaps the symbol of the new age was the Western Union Building in New York, designed by G. B. Post and built in 1873–75. It was one of the first skyscrapers, enabling the Western Union Telegraph Company to lead the way momentarily in construction as well as in communications technology.

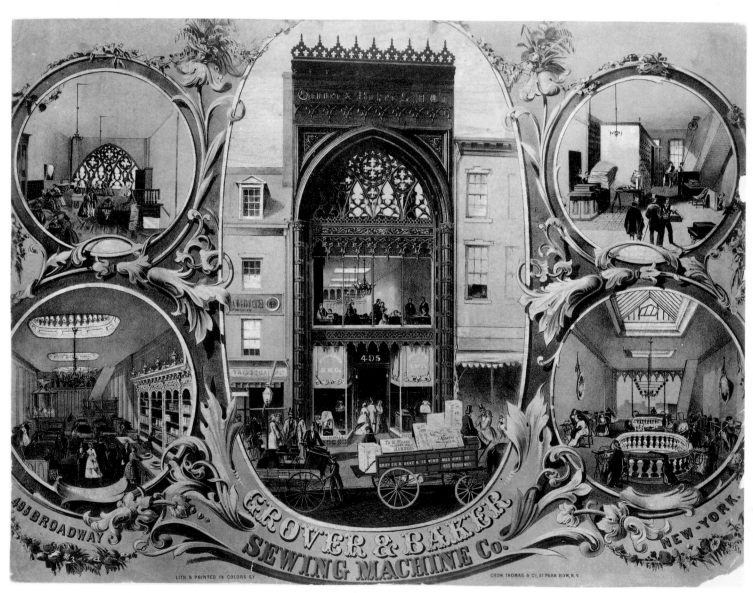

26 *Grover & Baker Sewing Machine Co., 495 Broadway, New York, c.1860.* (Library of Congress)

It is well known that Iron has been used in
England and other European countries for *interior*
supports in various kinds of edifices, in the form of
columns, beams, etc.; but its introduction for the
exterior of buildings is believed to be of purely
American invention . . .

Daniel D. Badger, *Illustrations of Iron Architecture*, 1865

One of the sights with which the New York people
astonish English visitors is Stewart's dry-goods
store in Broadway, an immense square building of
white marble, six stories high, with a frontage of
300 feet. The business done in it is stated to be
above 1,500,000£ per annum. There are 400 people
employed at this establishment, which has even a
telegraph office on the premises, where a clerk is
for ever flashing dollars and cents along the
trembling wires. There were lace collars 40 guineas
each, and flounces of Valenciennes lace, half a yard
deep, at 120 guineas a flounce.

Isabella L. Bird, *The Englishwoman in America*, 1854

27 *Western Union Telegraph
Company, Broadway, New York*,
c.1875. (Museum of the City of
New York)

28 MAX ROSENTHAL *Interior view
of L.J. Levy & Co.'s Dry Goods
Store, Chestnut St., Phila.*, c.1857.
(The Free Library of Philadelphia)

"Dark Satanic mills"

In 1800 Eli Whitney, a young graduate of Yale College who had already invented the cotton gin, contracted with the government to supply 10,000 rifles and manufactured them with such precision that the parts were interchangeable, a development that made the later assembly-line system of production possible. Shortly after Whitney's third contract with the War Department William Giles Munson recorded the gun factory, which stood near New Haven at a point where power was provided by a waterfall.

By 1860 only Britain was a greater industrial power than the United States. The demands of the Civil War increased American output and set the nation on the road to becoming the world's industrial leader by the end of the century. Artists responded to this change in society with mixed feelings. Winslow Homer shows young women on their way to work in a mill: the landscape is brilliant, the mill dark and uninviting; and Homer invites us to follow the central figure in our imagination, and to ponder on her life and the nature of a society that sends young girls out of the morning sunlight to toil in gloomy factories.

When the first attempt was made [to establish a small arms factory] there were but few persons in the country acquainted with the business; and but one of these (Eli Whitney of Connecticut) who embarked in it succeeded; all the rest were either ruined by the attempt or found the business so unprofitable and hazardous as to induce them to relinquish it.

George Bomford, 1824

30 WINSLOW HOMER *The Morning Bell*, c.1866/70. (Yale University Art Gallery, Bequest of Stephen Carlton Clark, B.A. 1903)

29 WILLIAM GILES MUNSON *The Eli Whitney Gun Factory, Connecticut* (detail), 1826–28. (Yale University Art Gallery, The Mabel Brady Garvan Collection)

"For our factory here, we will not have married women; they are apt to be off-and-on too much. We want none but steady workers: twelve hours to the day, day after day, through the three hundred and sixty-five days, excepting Sundays, Thanksgiving, and Fast-days. That's our rule."

Herman Melville, "The Tartarus of Maids," 1855

We have abundant proof that unremitted toil is not always derogatory to improvement. A factory girl's work is neither hard or complicated; she can go on with perfect regularity in her duties, while her mind may be actively employed on any other subject. There can be no better place for reflection, when there must be toil, than the factory.

W. J. S., *The Lowell Offering*, 1844

Improvement by education

Travelers frequently commented on untutored American society, but many Americans were soon exercising their cultural aspirations in rather traditional ways. Harvard College celebrated its bicentennial anniversary in 1836, and by the time George Catlin sketched this view of West Point, hundreds of cadets had been trained for the nation's armies. By the latter half of the century, privately-funded public institutions, such as the Museum of Fine Arts in Boston, had opened both to accommodate a growing taste for culture and to permit the newly wealthy to show off their treasures.

31 WILLIAM BURGIS *A Prospect of the Colledges in Cambridge in New England*, 1726. (Courtesy The Massachusetts Historical Society)

32 After GEORGE CATLIN *West Point Military Academy*, 1828. (Courtesy Kenneth M. Newman, The Old Print Shop, New York)

33 ENRICO MENEGHELLI *The Lawrence Room, Museum of Fine Arts, Boston,* 1879. (Courtesy Museum of Fine Arts, Boston, Gift of M. Knoedler and Co.)

It pleased God to stir up the heart of one Mr. *Harvard* (a godly Gentleman, and a lover of Learning, there living amongst us) to give the one halfe of his Estate (it being in all about 1700. l.) towards the erecting of a Colledge: and all his Library . . . The Colledge was, by common consent, appointed to be at *Cambridge*, (a place very pleasant and accommodate) and is called (according to the name of the first founder) *Harvard Colledge.*

The Edifice is very faire and comely within and without, having in it a spacious Hall; (where they daily meet at Commons, Lectures) Exercises, and a large Library with some Bookes to it, the gifts of diverse of our friends, their Chambers and studies also fitted for, and possessed by the Students, and all other roomes of Office necessary and convenient, with all needfull Offices thereto belonging.

New Englands First Fruits, 1643

West Point is famous in the short history of this country. It is the key of the Hudson River. . . . At present, a Military College is established here, which turns out about forty officers every year. Although they receive commissions in any regiment of the American army . . . they are all educated as engineers. The democrats have made several attempts to break up this establishment, as savouring too much of *monarchy,* but hitherto have been unsuccessful. It would be a pity if they did succeed, for such has been the demand lately for engineers to superintend railroads and canals, that a large portion of them have resigned their commissions, and found employment in the different States. This consideration alone is quite sufficient to warrant the keeping up of the college, for civil engineers are a *sine quâ non* in a country like America.

Captain Frederick Marryat, *Diary in America,* 1839

One of the prominent characteristics of Boston and its suburbs is the development in many ways of the great public spirit of the people. . . . Its wealthy residents . . . have been continually devoting their fortune to the benefit of the town by giving it statues and fountains, libraries and halls and educational endowments, many of which are of princely character. It has more schools and colleges, libraries, conservatories of music, art and scientific collections, museums, technological institutes and educational establishments than any other American city.

A Visit to the States: A Reprint of Letters from the Special Correspondent of the Times, 1887

Artists in the landscape

By mid-century the figure of an artist, with his paints, his stool, and his umbrella, was familiar to a public which, if not supportive of the painters, was at least tolerant. "What with Artists, Archbishops, Bishops, Priests, Nuns, Deacons and Fathers," a friend of the painter Paul Kane wrote him with tongue in cheek in 1847, "the country will be lost forever." It was no doubt as much awe at their own insignificance in nature as ego that led Gifford and Cropsey to place small self-portraits in these landscapes.

The island of Mount Desert, on the coast of Maine, . . . affords the only instance along our Atlantic coast where mountains stand in close neighborhood to the sea; here in one picture are beetling cliffs with the roar of restless breakers, far stretches of bay dotted with green islands, placid mountain-lakes mirroring the mountain-precipices that tower above them, rugged gorges clothed with primitive forests . . . on the mountains are frightful precipices, wonderful prospects of far-extending sea, and mazes of land and water, and magnificent forests of fir and spruce.

Oliver B. Bunce, in *Picturesque America*, 1872–74

34 SANFORD R. GIFFORD *The Artist sketching at Mount Desert, Maine*, 1864–65. Gifford depicts himself sketching Otter Cove from the summit of Green (Cadillac) Mountain. (Collection of Jo Ann and Julian Ganz, Jr.)

35 JASPER F. CROPSEY *The Narrows from Staten Island*, 1868. (Courtesy Amon Carter Museum, Fort Worth, Texas)

The river and bay scenery, all about New York island, any time of a fine day — the hurrying, splashing sea-tides — the changing panorama of steamers, all sizes, often a string of big ones outward bound to distant ports — the myriads of white-sail'd schooners, sloops, skiffs, and the marvelously beautiful yachts — the majestic sound boats as they rounded the Battery and came along toward five, afternoon, eastward bound — the prospect off toward Staten island, or down the Narrows, or the other way up the Hudson — what refreshment of spirit such sights and experiences gave me.

Walt Whitman, speaking of New York *c.* 1850–60, in *Specimen Days*, 1882

The South

Exploration and settlement

The warm climate and inviting coastline attracted a number of early venturers to the South, among them John White, who was one of the settlers in Sir Walter Raleigh's colony of Roanoke, off the coast of North Carolina. There he gathered material to paint a series of delicate watercolors, including this one of an Indian village with seemingly peaceful natives dancing and "sitting at meals," their fields rich with three crops of corn at differing stages of maturity. (In a little hut amid the ripe corn, top right, an Indian sits to scare off birds.) The promotional nature of White's watercolors could not hide the fate of the colony itself, however, which disappeared without explanation between 1587 and 1590.

The French had little better luck more than a century later on the Gulf of Mexico coast, where the attempted settlement on Biloxi Bay perished from lack of sustenance, either from the land or from France. In this detail of a view of the camp drawn by its Sous-directeur we see the artist himself in the foreground, seated in one of the barges used to unload ships in the harbour. The two huts on the left housed the apothecary and the hospital; behind them is the barn-like stores building; residential tents are scattered among the trees.

36 JOHN WHITE *The Village of
Secoton*, c.1585–87. (British Museum,
London)

37 J.-B. M. LE BOUTEAUX *View of the
Camp of John Law's Concession at
New Biloxi, Louisiana* (detail), 1720.
(Courtesy of the Edward E. Ayer
Collection, The Newberry Library,
Chicago)

The naturalist's world

Scientific explorers like Mark Catesby and John James Audubon devoted their lives to documenting the plants and animals of this "strange new world," then to publishing and disseminating their findings. Both men produced magnificent books: Catesby's "The Natural History of Carolina, Florida, and the Bahama Islands" (first published in 1731–48) and Audubon's "The Birds of America" (1827–38).

Catesby spent years exploring Virginia, then turned in 1722 to the area further south, around Charleston and inland. This image – in which Catesby combines in his distinctive way an animal with a large-scale botanical detail – shows that in the early eighteenth century bison still existed in the south-eastern states. Bison-rubbed trees were a common sight on the frontier, with their bark rubbed smooth and lower branches snapped off. When Audubon settled at Louisville, Kentucky, less than a century later, he noted with regret that the bison had only recently disappeared from that region. He ranged widely throughout the new nation, observing animal behaviour and collecting skins on which his spectacular illustrations were based.

39 After JOHN JAMES AUDUBON *Long-Billed Curlew (City of Charleston)*, 1834, from *The Birds of America*, 1827–38. (Courtesy Amon Carter Museum, Fort Worth, Texas)

38 MARK CATESBY *Bison by Acacia Tree*, from Catesby's *Natural History of Carolina, Florida, and the Bahama Islands*, 1754. (Courtesy Amon Carter Museum, Fort Worth, Texas)

One beautiful November morning I left Charleston with my host the Reverend John Bachman for a visit to Cole's Island, twenty miles distant. . . . We gunners made ready for the arrival of the Long-billed Curlews at sunset. They began to appear in twos, threes, or fives – by no means shy. . . . They would flap regularly for ten or more yards, then sail for a few seconds, their long bills and legs stretched to their full extent, directly toward the "Bird Banks." . . . We followed them to these small sandy islands, but the moment they saw us land, the flock of several thousand rose, performed a few evolutions in silence, and alighted again with one accord on the far edges of the sand bank close to the tremendous breakers. It was not dark, but flocks were still arriving as we left the place.

John James Audubon, *Ornithological Biography*, 1831–39

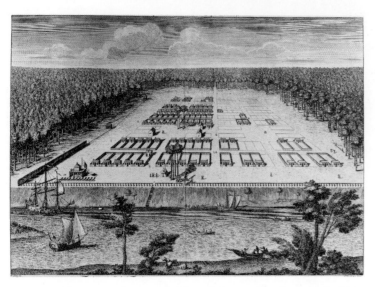

40 After PETER GORDON *A View of Savannah as it stood the 29th of March, 1734,* 1734. (Courtesy Amon Carter Museum, Fort Worth, Texas)

Early towns

New Orleans and Savannah were founded within fifteen years of each other – New Orleans in 1718 on a bend in the Mississippi River about 100 miles from its mouth, and Savannah in 1733 on the river of the same name about eighteen miles from the Atlantic Ocean. Savannah was British from the beginning, laid out according to proprietor James Oglethorpe's plan of combining residential and public buildings into wards around public squares. Firmin Cerveau's view from a similar perspective a century later (looking from the river down the axis of the left-hand street and square in Gordon's view) shows how the town developed along the lines laid out by Oglethorpe. New Orleans, on the other hand, was thrust into the political maelstrom and owned successively by the French, the Spanish, the French, and, finally, the United States, hence the eagle and the banner shown above the city as a celebration of its acquisition in the Louisiana Purchase.

Wednesday the 7th we begane to digg trenches for fixing palisadoes round the place of our intended setlement as a fence in case we should be attacked by the Indians, while others of us were imployed in clearing of the lines and cutting trees to the proper lengths, which was the 14 foot for the palisadoes. . . .

Thursday the 8th each family hade given out of the stores, an iron pott, frying pan, and three wooden bowls, a Bible, Common Prayer Book, and Whole Duty of Man. This day we . . . sett about sawing and splitting boards eight foot long in order to build clapp board houses, to gett us under better cover.

Peter Gordon, *Journal*, February, 1733

I waited upon the Trustees at their office, and gave them the best account I was able, of the situation of affairs in the Colony, and at the same time presented to them a view of the new Town of Savanah, its situation, and manner it was laid out in, as likewise the forme and elevation of all the houses and other publick buildings that were compleated at the time I left it. The Trustees seem'd pleased with it, and order'd me to gett a compleat drawing made of it . . . for which they ordered me a small present.

Peter Gordon, *Journal*, January, 1734

41 J. L. BOQUETA DE WOISERI *A View of New Orleans taken from the Plantation of Marigny*, November, 1803. (Courtesy, The Historic New Orleans Collection)

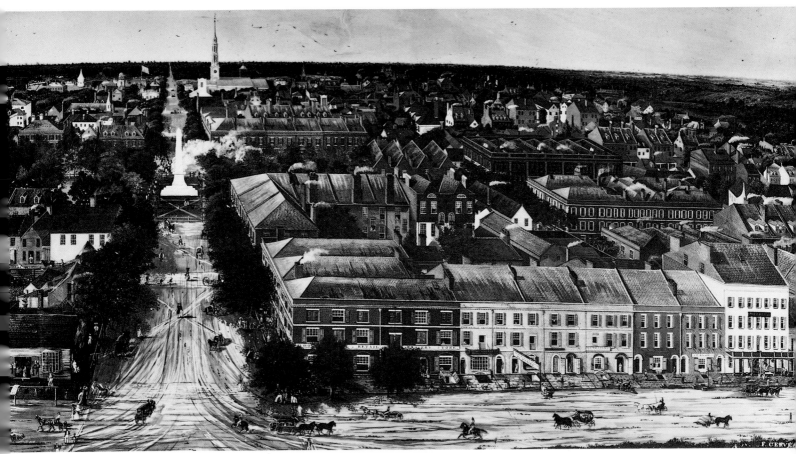

42 FIRMIN CERVEAU *View of Savannah, looking Inland from Bay Street* (detail) , 1837. (Courtesy The Georgia Historical Society, Savannah)

The age of steam

While mechanics linked steam boilers to clumsy land vehicles with varying degrees of success, sleek steamboats began to ply the nation's waterways as early as 1808. By the 1840s, when the "Ouishita" traveled up and down the Red River of Louisiana, steamboats had brought distant parts of the nation closer together. They were also considered the most luxurious method of travel, as Marie Adrien Persac has suggested in this picture of the interior of the "Princess," the boat he honeymooned on in 1851.

We had to keep watch by turns through the night, expecting the boat every moment: at last, we heard her puffing and roaring . . . the night being calm, the noise of the broken-winded, high-pressure steam-engine might be heard distinctly for ten miles. . . .
At daylight, we found ourselves in the Red River; a sullen, sluggish, red ochre-coloured stream. Floods from the Rocky Mountains had caused it to overflow its banks for somewhere about one hundred miles, as we ascended; which gave us the appearance of steering right through the forest — the effect was grand and novel; the stream was rapid, and the great red flood rushed through the trees which extended as far as the eye could reach. On every log or uncovered bank lay numbers of alligators . . . They seldom prove the attacking party, but such instances have occurred: it is said that the best mode of escape is for the attacked to get to a tree, and run constantly round it. The alligators cannot turn quickly; all their strength, when on land, is in the tail, with which they sweep their prey into their mouths . . .

Quantities of the beautiful egret, or lesser egret, together with rose-coloured spoonbills, also appeared on the banks.

R. G. A. Levinge, *Echoes from the Backwoods*, 1846

43 R.G.A. Levinge *The Paddle Steamer "Ouishita" on the Red River, Louisiana Territory, c.1836.* (Courtesy Amon Carter Museum, Fort Worth, Texas)

44 MARIE ADRIEN PERSAC *Interior of the Steamboat "Princess"*, 1861. (Courtesy, Anglo-American Art Museum, Louisiana State University, Baton Rouge, Gift of Mrs Mamie Persac Lusk)

A stranger to this mode of travelling would find it difficult to describe his impressions upon descending the Mississippi for the first time in one of these steam boats. . . . He contemplates the prodigious construction, with its double tiers of cabins, and its separate establishment for the ladies, and its commodious arrangements for the deck passengers and the servants. Over head, about him, and below him, all is life and movement. He contemplates the splendor of the cabin, its beautiful finishings of the richest woods, its rich carpeting, its mirrors and fine furniture, its sliding tables, its bar room, and all its arrangements for the accommodation of eighty cabin passengers. The fare is sumptuous, and every thing in a style of splendor, order, quiet and regularity, far exceeding that of most city taverns.

Timothy Flint, *A Condensed Geography and History of the Western States*, 1828

The moment we were under way I began to prowl about the great steamer and fill myself with joy. She was as clean and as dainty as a drawing-room; when I looked down her long, gilded saloon, it was like gazing through a splendid tunnel; she had an oil-picture, by some gifted sign-painter, on every stateroom door; she glittered with no end of prism-fringed chandeliers; the clerk's office was elegant, the bar was marvelous, and the barkeeper had been barbered and upholstered at incredible cost. . . . This was unutterable pomp.

Mark Twain, *Life on the Mississippi*, 1883

Cities of the South

The Southern states grew almost as rapidly as the North following independence. The cotton-producing sections doubled and quadrupled in population, while the urban areas expanded at a more modest rate. Charleston, with its distinctive houses bordered by verandahs ("piazzas"), was the only true Southern city until early in the nineteenth century, when Richmond and New Orleans joined it as prosperous and festive communities that vibrated with concerts, balls, and parties when the planters came to town for the social season.

Richmond, founded in the 1730s, became the Virginia capital in 1789 because it was considered a safer site than Williamsburg. Thomas Jefferson's indelible mark is on this city: while he was American minister to France, the directors of public buildings requested that he assist them in developing a plan for a government building, the Virginia Capitol, and his noble design, based on the Roman temple at Nîmes in southern France known as the Maison Carrée, dominates the hill overlooking the James River.

I went to take my usual walk this morning, and found that the good citizens of Charleston were providing themselves with a most delightful promenade upon the river, a fine, broad, well-paved esplanade, of considerable length, open to the water on one side, and on the other over-looked by some very large and picturesque old houses, whose piazzas, arches, and sheltering evergreens reminded me of buildings in the vicinity of Naples. This delightful walk is not yet finished, and I fear, when it is, it will be little frequented; for the Southern women, by their own account, are miserable pedestrians. . . . I received a visit from a young lady residing in the same street where we lodged, who came in her carriage a distance of less than a quarter of a mile, to call upon me.

Frances Anne Kemble, *Journal of a Residence on a Georgia Plantation*, 1838–39

45 S. BARNARD *View along the East Battery, Charleston, South Carolina*, 1831. (Yale University Art Gallery, Mabel Brady Garvan Collection)

46 W. J. BENNETT after G. COOKE *Richmond from the Hill above the Waterworks*, 1834. (The I.N. Phelps Stokes Collection, The New York Public Library)

The different views of Richmond, with its immense Capitol, towering above the Town on a lofty eminence, with its antique appearance, arrested my attention. . . . The Town contains about 300 houses, some of them excellent brick and well built. It carries a great deal of business and will be a flourishing place when the navigation with the count[r]y is entirely opened, which will be in two or three years.

The Capitol, built on the model of the Temple of Nismes, is an immense pile of brick work. . . . Its uufinished state gives it a heavy, singular appearance, but when complete it will be a magnificent building. . . . The loftiness of this building, and its eminent situation render it a very striking object, and it is the first thing which strikes the traveler.

William Loughton Smith, *Journal*, 1791

We took for our model what is called the Maisonquarrèe of Nismes, one of the most beautiful, if not the most beautiful and precious morsel of architecture left us by antiquity. . . . It is very simple, but it is beyond expression, and would have done honour to our country as presenting to travellers a morsel of taste in our infancy promising much for our maturer age.

Thomas Jefferson to James Madison, September 20, 1785

Plantation economy

By 1860 the South had changed less than any other section of the country. Northern farmers, employing improved farming methods, had diversified their crops some time ago. Even the states of the upper South had turned increasingly to fruits, vegetables, corn, and livestock. But the states of the Deep South raised more cotton than ever. Between 1830 and 1860, helped by the development of Whitney's cotton gin (which separated fiber from seeds), production increased from some 700,000 to 3,800,000 bales. The number of slaves increased by a similar ratio. Cotton was still king, and slaves were his bondsmen.

Giroux's painting shows cotton fields, probably in Louisiana, with the gin houses in the distance. Persac's view of the Olivier Plantation – done with a mixture of paint and cut-out figures – records a house which reputedly burned in the Civil War, only a few years after the picture was painted.

September 1 Clear pleasant morning – Picked Last week 48 Bales Bothered two days for want of cotten & two days in Bad picking new ground grassy. over 125 Bales out last night. But for being Bothered about Gin house would have over 150 B. out, Courtneys *celebrated* overseer W. Bryant doubts my hands 69 Pickers picked over 16105 lb Saturday, & offers to Bet $700 they can't picke 16000 fair cotton, will take the Bet

*　　*　　*

January 1 Few clouds Early this morning, Warm spring day, Began work after the dullest Christmass I ever past, just now feel like having it. suffered Very much from Bad cold & sore throat, the Prospects of the cotten planter seems quite gloomy from the immense amt of cotten made, and still increasing – my own situation is better than for 10 years Back obtained a Loan of $24000 out of the Louisiana Bank on mortgage 8 pr ct interest I think will be able to get out of Debt without being cramped to Death, (BAD BEGINNING FOR NEW YEAR)

Bennet H. Barrow, *Plantation Diary*, 1844–45

47 C. GIROUX *Cotton Plantation*, c.1850–65 (Courtesy Museum of Fine Arts, Boston, M. and M. Karolik Collection)

48 MARIE ADRIEN PERSAC *The Olivier Plantation [near New Iberia], Louisiana,* 1861. (Courtesy Louisiana State Museum)

Upon the banks of the Mississippi . . . may be seen the appliances of plantation life in their perfection. The stately residence rises out from among grooves of lemon and orange-trees, of magnolia and live-oaks. . . . Grouped in the rear, in strange confusion, is a crowd of out-houses; useful as kitchens, store-rooms, baths, with a school-house, and perhaps a chapel. A little farther on is the neat stable of the saddle and carriage-horses, around all of which is drawn the protecting fence, that shuts up the "residence" from the plantation. Passing beyond this magic circle, you find yourself in the broad fields . . . and, in the distance, you see the village known as the "quarters."

Thomas Bangs Thorpe, "Sugar and the Sugar Region of Louisiana," 1853

After breakfast, the Governor drove out by the ever-silent levee for some miles, passing estate after estate, where grove nodded to grove. . . . The gangs of negroes at work were hidden in the deep corn, and their quarters were silent and deserted. We met but one planter. . . . His house was like a French chateau erected under tropical influences, and he led us through a handsome garden laid out with hothouses, conservatories, orange-trees, and date-palms, and ponds full of the magnificent Victoria Regia in flower.

William Howard Russell, *My Diary North and South,* 1861

Scenes exotic and sublime

Artists were not as eager to explore the Southern wilderness as were naturalists like Audubon, but with the encouragement of Jefferson, who frequently extolled the beauty of the Natural Bridge, and others, painters did venture into the countryside. The bridge became an icon visited almost as much as any other distinctive feature of the American landscape, except Niagara Falls.

The exotic tropical vegetation of the Deep South was also a source of curiosity, and the wonder and delight of the painter Harry Fenn, sent to Florida for that great celebration of the nation's landscape, Picturesque America, *are evident in his drawing of an old-established garden at St Augustine.*

The *Natural bridge*, the most sublime of Nature's works . . . is on the ascent of a hill, which seems to have been cloven through its length by some great convulsion. The fissure, just at the bridge, is, by some admeasurements, 270 feet deep, by others only 205. It is about 45 feet wide at the bottom. . . . It is impossible for the emotions, arising from the sublime, to be felt beyond what they are here; so beautiful an arch, so elevated, so light, and springing, as it were, up to heaven, the rapture of the Spectator is really indiscribable!

Thomas Jefferson, *Notes on the State of Virginia*, 1787 edition

49 After HARRY FENN *A Garden in Florida*, from *Picturesque America*, 1872–74

In ''A Garden in Florida'' we have, with surroundings of a more refined character, other specimens of Southern vegetation. The cactus on the right of the picture is an exceptional development of this singular plant, which is usually a humble occupier of the soil. Its habit is to push a few leaves upward, and then shed them one after another, something after the fashion crabs dispose of an offending claw. Each discarded leaf, however, sets up growing for itself, and thus the cactus, in a modest way, usurps large tracts of favorable soil, forming an undergrowth more impenetrable to man and beast than walls of wood or iron. But our cactus in the garden has been led by the skilful hand of the cultivator upward, and, by removing every exuberant bud, developed into proportions quite foreign to its customary experience. At the left of the picture we have, in the banana, another phase of tropical horticulture, with its broad leaves, that unfold in a single night from a long, slender stem, and its pendant clusters of fruit.

Such was the St. Augustine of a score of years back. Then the railroad came, and the magnate with his wand of gold built palaces, and St. Augustine, with its Ponce de Leon, its Alcazar, and its Cordova, became fashionable. With the change it has lost something of its quaintness, but there is left enough of the old Spanish flavor to still make the town a unique one.

Robert Carter in *Picturesque America*, 1872–74 and 1894. (The last paragraph was added in the later edition.)

50 DAVID JOHNSON *The Natural Bridge of Virginia*, 1860. (Collection of Jo Ann and Julian Ganz, Jr.)

A divided nation

As the Southern states expanded their slavery-based agricultural system westward, the ideological gap between them and the North, with its family farms and industry, widened. After Abraham Lincoln had been elected President, South Carolina seceded from the Union and attacked the U.S. garrison at Fort Sumter, located on a man-made island in Charleston harbor, on April 12, 1861, beginning the Civil War. Ten other states, convinced that the Republicans planned to abolish slavery, and with it their way of life, rapidly joined South Carolina in the Confederacy. The war initially favored the gallant and talented Southerners, who, in probes like Colonel Thomas J. "Stonewall" Jackson's at Harper's Ferry, West Virginia, in May, 1862, shocked the Union into the realization that the war would not be easily won. The North suffered monumental disasters before its unquestioned industrial edge, huge population advantage, and morally superior position ultimately enabled it to gain victory in a bitter and costly war.

Harper's Ferry is a stronghold of no little importance, most picturesquely situated on the Virginia side of the Potomac. . . . Here the United States Government had, many years before the war, established a very large arsenal and manufactory of small-arms. . . . Around the workshops of the arsenal . . . a little town had grown up, built partly upon a narrow tract of level ground . . . and partly upon a lofty hill looking down upon either stream. This eminence is itself commanded on the Maryland side by . . . the Maryland Heights, a position which had been strongly fortified, for the obvious reason that whoever became master of it might with little difficulty obtain possession of Harper's Ferry.

. . . About 10 o'clock the Federals commenced to move; their cavalry skirmishers advanced, and the lines of their infantry tirailleurs came in sight. The decisive moment had arrived, and every hand closed more firmly round its weapon. Already shots began to be exchanged, when suddenly a cry of joy, louder than the roar of cannon . . . brought delight to our hearts and carried despair to the foe, whose insolent advance it brought quickly to a halt – *"Harper's Ferry has surrendered to Jackson!"*

Heros von Borcke (a Prussian associate of Jeb Stuart), *Memoirs of the Confederate War For Independence*, 1866

The shore opposite Charleston is more than a mile distant, and is low and sandy. . . . From the mastheads of the few large vessels in harbour floated the Confederate flag. Looking to our right, the same standard was visible, waving on the low, white parapets of the earth-works which had been engaged in reducing Sumter.

That much-talked-of fortress lay . . . near the middle of the passage out to sea between James' Island and Sullivan's Island. . . . The land contracts on both sides opposite the fort, a projection of Morris' Island, called "Cumming's Point," running out on the left. There is a similar promontory from Sullivan's Island, on which is erected Fort Moultrie, on the right.

William Howard Russell, *My Diary North and South*, 1861

51 ALBERT BIERSTADT *The Bombardment of Fort Sumter*, 1862? (Courtesy a Massachusetts Collector)

52 WILLIAM MACLEOD *Maryland Heights: Siege of Harper's Ferry*, 1863. (In the Collection of the Corcoran Gallery of Art, Washington, D.C.)

The defeated South

Edward Lamson Henry, with General Ulysses S. Grant as he swept through the James River country of Virginia in October, 1864, observed Union troops as they bivouacked in front of William Byrd II's elegant eighteenth-century mansion, Westover, which they used as temporary headquarters. When he painted the scene, in 1869, the country had been at peace for four years.

The war did not end until Union troops had captured all the cities of significance, excepting the Confederate capital of Richmond. A period of Reconstruction followed, during which the chastened and politically disenfranchised Southerners were permitted to regain control of their states. The war was devastating, and Reconstruction was difficult, to be sure, but never before in such a bitter, internecine war had the victor been as kind to the vanquished.

A stately brick mansion, standing back from the highway, once the residence of a man of wealth and taste, with blinds, portico, and carriage-house, elaborate in design and finish, was in the last stages of ruin. The portico had settled away from the house. The roof was hollowed like a weak-backed horse, the chimneys were tumbling, blinds swinging by a hinge, windows smashed, outhouses tottering with age and neglect, all presenting a most repulsive appearance. How changed from former years, when the courteous, hospitable proprietor of the estate received his guests at the magnificent portico . . . !

Charles Carleton Coffin, *Four Years of Fighting*, 1866

My dear family,
    I am here at the old place amongst the ruins of the old homestead of one of the F.F.V.'s [First Families of Virginia]. Dreary and desolate it is. My headquarters is in a small outhouse — one used, I presume, for an office, perhaps to barter in human flesh. . . . But the desolating hand of war has laid all around me a heap of ruins. The handsome mansion, barn and outbuildings, fences, and all have shared alike the fate of the destroying hand.

General Robert McAllister, in a letter, 1862

53 EDWARD LAMSON HENRY *The Old Westover Mansion*, 1869. (In the Collection of the Corcoran Gallery of Art, Washington, D.C.)

The Crescent City

More than four hundred steamboats like the "Belle Creole" had helped New Orleans become the nation's leading cotton exporter before the Civil War, and with the establishment of peace it resumed its position as a port second only to New York. The cotton trade too resumed, bolstering the international ambiance of the city and profiting merchants such as Michel Musson, uncle of the French painter Edgar Degas, whose visit in 1872–73 resulted in this memorable record of Musson's cotton office. Musson himself is seated in the foreground, examining cotton; Degas' brothers are shown, one leaning against the window and the other studying a ledger at the right; and a cousin by marriage, William Bell, is displaying cotton at the table.

54 *The "Belle Creole" at New Orleans,* c.1845–49. (In the Collection of the Corcoran Gallery of Art, Washington, D.C.)

The town has much the appearance of a French ville de province, and is, in fact, an old French colony taken from Spain by France. The names of the streets are French, and the language about equally French and English. . . . We were much pleased by the chant with which the Negro boatmen regulate and beguile their labour on the river; it consists of but very few notes, but they are sweetly harmonious, and the Negro voice is almost always rich and powerful.

Mrs Trollope, *Domestic Manners of the Americans,* 1832

116

55 EDGAR DEGAS *The Cotton Office, New Orleans*, 1872–73. (Musée des Beaux-Arts, Pau)

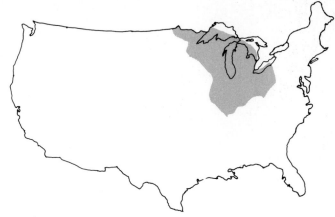

The Midwest

56 Peter Rindisbacher *Captain W. Andrew Bulger saying Farewell at Fort MacKay, Prairie du Chien, Wisconsin, on May 22, 1815,* c.1823. (Courtesy Amon Carter Museum, Fort Worth, Texas)

A frontier fort

The war that finally erupted between the United States and Great Britain in 1812 had been raging for several years on the frontier as various Indian allies of the British frustrated American attempts to establish a stronghold on the upper Mississippi. Finally in June, 1814, William Clark, governor of Missouri Territory and one of the leaders of the famous Lewis and Clark expedition, occupied the crossroads of Prairie du Chien in Wisconsin and built a fort there, christening it Fort Shelby. The British Indian allies promptly drove the Americans from the fort, and it was renamed Fort MacKay.

When the British had to turn the post back to the Americans at the end of the war, Captain Andrew Bulger oversaw the fort's destruction. The Americans built a new fort to serve in the chain of posts defending the frontier, and in the happier days of peace, Captain Bulger commissioned the young Swiss artist Peter Rindisbacher to depict his departure from Fort MacKay. Rindisbacher included a self-portrait, the top-hatted figure third from the right.

The next morning our fort was planned and marked out, the circumference measuring four hundred and fifty-five feet, which would require as many palisades to be made of trees, one with another, of a foot diameter each. . . . Each pine made three palisades of eighteen feet long, pointed at one end. While these were preparing, our other men dug a trench all round, of three feet deep, in which the palisades were to be planted. . . . When they were set up, our carpenters built a stage of boards all round within, about six feet high, for the men to stand on when to fire through the loopholes. We had one swivel gun, which we mounted on one of the angles . . . and thus our fort, if such a magnificent name may be given to so miserable a stockade, was finished in a week.

Benjamin Franklin, *Autobiography,* 1788

From fort to city

Many of the frontier forts developed into cities. Detroit was first a French, then a British fort. Cincinnati, founded by land speculators as Losantiville in 1788, developed around Fort Washington to become the hub of the old Northwest as farmers settled the fertile Ohio Valley. This view of Front Street and the public landing is one of the earliest close-up views of a Midwestern river town. The steamboat traffic and Conestoga wagons hint at the phenomenal growth of Cincinnati. "I don't believe there exists anywhere on earth a town which has had a growth so prodigious," wrote Gustave de Beaumont, who accompanied Alexis de Tocqueville to America in 1831. "Thirty years ago the banks of the Ohio were a wilderness. Now there are 30,000 inhabitants." By 1838 Cincinnati had ten newspapers, including the "Intelligencer," whose offices can be seen here on the quayside. (Foreign visitors were already astonished at the profusion — and bulk — of American newspapers.)

The city of Detroit is very beautifully situated. Its principal street and buildings are upon a bend of the river, of a mile or two in length, and they occupy the whole extent of it. The bend forms a semi-circle, and the banks of it are gently sloping. The houses and stores are near the summit of the bank, and the slopes form pleasant grounds for gardening. The streets intersect each other at right angles, and the situation is calculated for a large and elegant city. The Fort and Cantonment lie about forty rods west of the main street. From this street a spacious gate opens to them, and at a little distance from it, the road forks and leads to them respectively. The contrast between the numerous white buildings in both of these places, and the green grass contiguous to and around them is very pleasant. . . . The Government warehouse here is very large, and the Government wharf is long and commodious. There are several other wharves at Detroit, and the vessels lying at them make a pleasant appearance. From the lower part of the town the view, up the river, is remarkably fine. Here one may see, for the distance of four miles, a beautiful expanse of water, several islands almost lost to vision, and near them, on a point of land, several large windmills.

Estwick Evans, *A Pedestrious Tour of Four Thousand Miles Through the Western States and Territories,* 1819

57 UNKNOWN BRITISH OFFICER *View of Detroit,* 1794. (Courtesy of the Burton Historical Collection of the Detroit Public Library)

58 JOHN C. WILD *Cincinnati: the Public Landing*, 1835. (Courtesy of The Cincinnati Historical Society)

Dr. Drake took us a delightful drive, the pleasure of which was much enhanced by his very interesting conversation. . . . He had seen the foundations of the great city laid; he had watched its growth till he was now able to point out to the stranger, not only the apparatus for the exportation of 6,000,000 dollars' worth a year of produce and manufactures, but things which he values far more: the ten or twelve edifices erected for the use of the common schools, the new church of St. Paul, the two fine banking-houses, and the hundred and fifty handsome private dwellings, all the creations of the year 1835. He points to the periodicals, the respectable monthlies, and the four daily and six weekly papers of the city. He looks with a sort of paternal complacency on the 35,000 inhabitants, scarcely one of whom is without the comforts of life, the means of education, and a bright prospect for the future. Though a true Westerner, and devoutly believing the *buckeyes* (natives of Ohio) to be superior to all others of God's creatures, he hails every accession of intelligent members to his darling society.

Harriet Martineau, *Retrospect of Western Travel*, 1838

A pioneer settlement

Charles Alexandre Lesueur was a French artist-naturalist who set out on an exploration along the Mississippi and in the Great Lakes area, making sketches as he went. The settlement that he sketched on the Mississippi, consisting of little more than a log cabin, cleared field, and orchard, was optimistically named Commercetown — a characteristically American vote of confidence in the future.

Like the field around it, this rustic dwelling shows every sign of new and hurried work. It is seldom more than 30 feet long. It is 20 feet wide and 15 high. Both its walls and its roof are made of unsquared tree-trunks between which moss and earth have been rammed to keep the cold and rain out from the inside of the house. . . .

Such a cabin generally has but one window, at which perhaps a muslin curtain is hanging; for in these parts where necessities are not seldom lacking, superfluities often abound. A resinous fire crackles on the hearth of beaten earth, and, better than the daylight, lights up the inside of the place. Over this rustic fire one sees trophies of war or hunt: a long rifle, a deerskin, some eagle's feathers. To the right of the chimney a map of the United States is often stretched, and the draught that blows through the gaps in the wall keeps raising and fluttering it. By it on a single shelf of ill-squared planks are a few tattered books; there one finds a Bible with its cloth and boards already worn out by the piety of two generations, a prayerbook and, sometimes, a poem of Milton or a tragedy of Shakespeare.

Alexis de Tocqueville, *Journey to America*, 1831

59 CHARLES ALEXANDRE LESUEUR *Tyawapatia Bottom or Commercetown* [*on the Mississippi in Missouri*], April 13, 1826. (Collection C. A. Lesueur, Muséum d'Histoire Naturelle, Le Havre)

60 After CHARLES SULLIVAN *Great Mound at Marietta, Ohio,* from E. G. Squier and E. H. Davis, *Ancient Monuments of the Mississippi Valley,* 1848

Evidence of the Ancients

Lesueur as he travelled no doubt wondered about the mysterious earth mounds along the Ohio and Mississippi, but added nothing to the speculations that they might have been left by a prehistoric race, even unrecorded Danes who might later have amalgamated with the natives. In the 1780s the agent of the Ohio Company at Marietta, the Reverend Manasseh Cutler, had counted the rings of a tree felled on top of one of the mounds and concluded that the culture dated to before AD 1300, and Thomas Jefferson had excavated a mound on his property and proved to his satisfaction that it was of Indian origin. This picture of a mound at Marietta was published in an effort to prove the existence of a great race of mound-builders, but it was left to recent researchers to conclude that it was a burial ground for the Ohio Hopewell culture (c. 100 BC to c. 550 AD), so that its later use as a cemetery, with church nearby, was entirely appropriate.

As o'er the verdant waste I guide my steed,
Among the high rank grass that sweeps his sides,
The hollow beating of his footstep seems
A sacrilegious sound. I think of those
Upon whose rest he tramples: are they here,
The dead of other days? and did the dust
Of these fair solitudes once stir with life
And burn with passion? Let the mighty mounds
That overlook the rivers, or that rise
In the dim forest crowded with old oaks,
Answer. A race that long has passed away
Built them; . . . The red man came,
The roaming hunter tribes, warlike and fierce,
And the mound-builders vanished from the earth.

William Cullen Bryant, "The Prairies," 1832

123

St Louis, gateway to the West

Established in 1763 as a French fur-trading post, on the first high ground on the Mississippi below the mouths of the Missouri and Illinois rivers, St Louis languished under the succeeding Spanish rule, but after it became part of the United States in 1804 it served as an outfitting point for Western expeditions, and its success was assured. In 1831, shortly before the town was visited by George Catlin, its population was some 6,000, still concentrated in the old French quarter down by the river (see Pl. 73). By 1859, about the time of Edward Sachse's view, the population had leapt to 185,000 and the town was rapidly spreading inland on the typical American checkerboard plan. Sachse positioned himself in Lucas Place, where the grandest private houses stood. In the center is the new First Presbyterian Church, to the right the curiously turreted High School, and in the right center the dome of the Court House. East St Louis, in Illinois, lies across the steamboat-thronged river.

In point of heat, St. Louis certainly approaches the nearest to the Black Hole of Calcutta of any city that I have sojourned in. They have not the yellow-fever here; but during the autumn they have one which, under another name, is almost as fatal – the bilious congestive fever. I found sleep almost impossible from the sultriness of the air, and used to remain at the open window for the greater part of the night. I did not expect that the muddy Mississippi would be able to reflect the silver light of the moon; yet it did, and the effect was very beautiful. Truly it may be said of this river, as it is of many ladies, that it is a candlelight beauty.

Captain Frederick Marryat, *Diary in America*, 1839

St. Louis, on the Mississippi, is the great town of Missouri, and is considered by the Missourians to be the star of the West. It is not to be beaten in population, wealth, or natural advantages by any other city so far west. . . . The great glory of the town is . . . the long river beach up to which the steamers are brought with their bows to the shore. . . . They resemble huge wooden houses, apparently of frail architecture, floating upon the water.

Anthony Trollope, *North America*, 1862

124

61 EDWARD SACHSE *View of St Louis from Lucas Place* (detail), *c*.1860. (Courtesy Chicago Historical Society)

Along the rivers

As elsewhere in the new land, rivers were the major highways. Prosperous towns developed along the Ohio, Mississippi and Missouri, with warehouses on the shore, as here at Louisville, and at Cincinnati (Ill. 58). Also along the rivers there grew up one of the truly American characters – the riverman, immortalized in the literary portraits of Washington Irving and Mark Twain (whose "Huckleberry Finn" is set in the 1840s), and in the paintings of George Caleb Bingham, himself a Missouri man.

Louisville in Kentucky has always been a favourite place of mine. The beauty of its situation, on the banks of *La Belle Rivière*, just at the commencement of the famed rapids, commonly called the Falls of the Ohio, had attracted my notice, and when I removed to it . . . I found it more agreeable than ever. The prospect from the town is such that it would please even the eye of a Swiss. It extends along the river for seven or eight miles, and is bounded on the opposite side by a fine range of low mountains, known by the name of the Silver Hills. The rumbling sound of the waters, as they tumble over the rock-paved bed of the rapids, is at all times soothing to the ear. . . . But, above all, the generous hospitality of the inhabitants, and the urbanity of their manners, had induced me to fix upon it as a place of residence.

John James Audubon, *Delineations of American Scenery and Character*, 1834

Louisville is a considerable town of Kentucky, at the head of the Falls of the Ohio. Many boats unload here for the back country, others stop here to get a pilot to take them over the Falls, and sometimes at low water to get part of their lading carried by hand to below the Falls. It possesses some manufactories, and is a place of considerable trade, and with the exception of Cincinnatti, is by far the best town I have seen in the western country.

John Woods, *Two Years' Residence in the Settlement on the English Prairie, in the Illinois Country*, 1822

62 JOHN H. B. LATROBE *Louisville (Upper Landing)*, 1832. (Courtesy Amon Carter Museum, Fort Worth, Texas)

63 After GEORGE CALEB BINGHAM *The Jolly Flat Boat Men*, 1847. (Courtesy Amon Carter Museum, Fort Worth, Texas)

. . . a singular aquatic race . . . had grown up from the navigation of the rivers, the "boatmen of the Mississippi," who possessed habits, manners and almost a language, peculiarly their own and strongly technical. They at that time were extremely numerous, and conducted the chief navigation and commerce of the Ohio and the Mississippi, as the voyageurs did of the Canadian waters; but, like them, their consequence and characteristics are rapidly vanishing before the all pervading intrusion of steamboats.

Washington Irving, *Astoria*, 1836

There was thirteen men there [on the raft] – they was the watch on deck of course. And a mighty rough-looking lot, too. They had a jug, and tin cups, and they kept the jug moving. One man was singing – roaring, you may say; and it wasn't a nice song – for a parlor anyway. . . . Next they got out an old fiddle, . . . and the rest turned themselves loose on a regular old-fashioned keel-boat break-down. They couldn't keep that up very long without getting winded, so by and by they settled round the jug again.

They sung "jolly, jolly raftsman's the life for me," with a rousing chorus, and they got to talking about differences betwixt hogs, and their different kinds of habits; and next about women and their different ways.

Mark Twain, in the character of Huckleberry Finn, speaking *c.* 1840, in *Life on the Mississippi*, 1883

Across the country

Travel from the East Coast to St Louis was usually easier if one took a ship around Florida to New Orleans, then booked a steamboat for passage up the Mississippi to St Louis. Those who chose the more direct route had to contend with the haphazard conditions of rutted and at times impassably muddy tracks, and ford streams as bridges had not yet been built. The advent of the railroad, of course, revolutionized overland travel, but the artist Thomas Rossiter, who probably painted this canvas after a railroad-sponsored excursion, seemed to have considered the iron horse an assault on the wilderness.

By far the greatest portion of travellers one meets with, not to mention the ordinary stage-coach passengers, consists of teamsters and the emigrants. The former generally drive six horses before their enormous wagons – stout, heavy-looking beasts, descended, it is said, from the famous draught horses of Normandy. They go about twenty miles a day. The leading horses are often ornamented with a number of bells suspended from a square raised frame-work over their collars, originally adopted to warn these lumbering machines of each other's approach, and prevent their being brought up all standing in the narrow parts of the road.

Charles Fenno Hoffman, *A Winter in the West*, 1835

64 WILLIAM TYLEE RANNEY *Crossing the Ferry*, 1846. (The Thomas Gilcrease Institute of American History and Art, Tulsa, Oklahoma)

65 THOMAS PRICHARD ROSSITER *Opening of the Wilderness* (detail), c.1858. (Courtesy Museum of Fine Arts, Boston, M. and M. Karolik Collection)

There is a large variety in American roads. There are the excellent limestone roads which stretch out in three directions from Nashville, Tennessee, and some like them in Kentucky. . . . There is quite another sort of limestone road in Virginia, in traversing which the stage is dragged up from shelf to shelf, some of the shelves sloping so as to throw the passengers on one another, on either side alternatively. Then there are the rich mud roads of Ohio, through whose red sloughs the stage goes slowly sousing after rain, and gently upsetting when the rut on the one or the other side proves to be of a greater depth than was anticipated. . . . Lastly, there is the corduroy road, happily of rare occurrence, where, if the driver is merciful to his passengers, he drives them so as to give them the association of being on the way to a funeral, their involuntary sobs on each jolt helping the resemblance.

Harriet Martineau, *Retrospect of Western Travel*, 1838

The train calls at stations in the woods, where the wild impossibility of anybody having the smallest reason to get out, is only equalled by the apparently desperate hopelessness of there being anybody to get in. It rushes across the turnpike road, where there is no gate, no policeman, no signal: nothing but a rough wooden arch, on which is painted "WHEN THE BELL RINGS, LOOK OUT FOR THE LOCOMOTIVE." On it whirls headlong, dives through the woods again, emerges in the light . . . unaccustomed horses plunging and rearing, close to the very rails – there – on, on, on – tears the mad dragon of an engine with its train of cars; scattering in all directions a shower of burning sparks from its wood fire; screeching, hissing, yelling, panting; until at last the thirsty monster stops beneath a covered way to drink, the people cluster round, and you have time to breathe again.

Charles Dickens, *American Notes*, 1842

Farming on the prairie

By the turn of the nineteenth century the ideal American was more accurately the yeoman farmer than the noble savage. Statistics changed only slowly as the nation expanded into the Midwest, because the new land proved even more fertile and productive. Inventions also improved agriculture, as John Deere contrived a steel plow that would cut a deeper row and Cyrus McCormick and his son developed a reaper that revolutionized grain harvests. Karl Bodmer, traveling west with Prince Maximilian of Wied-Neuwied, appreciated the discipline that one family had brought to a large section of the Illinois prairie as he passed by in 1833, and an unknown artist depicted the prosperity of similar land forty years later.

66 KARL BODMER *View of a Farm on the Prairies of Illinois*, 1833. (The InterNorth Art Foundation, Joslyn Art Museum, Omaha, Nebraska)

67 *Farm Residence of H. B. Kay's, Magnolia Tp., Putnam Co., Ill., c.1875.* (Courtesy Amon Carter Museum, Fort Worth, Texas)

On the 13th of June [1834] we . . . left Vincennes [Indiana] by the stage. . . . We came to Washington and Mount Pleasant, where the farmers were cultivating their fields, in which isolated trees were frequently seen, but which afforded no shade from the sultry sun, for they were all destroyed by the fire. They are cut down, from time to time, when the people are in want of timber; and, as a sign that they are to be felled in the next winter, a circular ring is hewn into the bark. It is said to be very difficult to cultivate the land in Indiana, on account of the extremely vigorous vegetation. Except in the vicinity of the Wabash and the White River, it is, however, not so fertile as in Illinois, where, in the environs of Springfield, for instance, it is scarcely necessary to do more than hoe the ground, in order to obtain the finest crops. An acre of land there yields from sixty to eighty bushels of maize, and fifty bushels of wheat.

Maximilian of Wied-Neuwied, *Travels in . . . 1832, 1833, and 1834,* 1843

The State of Illinois [is] nearly the same length as England . . . On again reaching the black prairie, after having been for some time accustomed to the whitish grey soil of the southern prairie, it seemed to me that the land looked richer and the grass greener. But we were now traversing the richest part of Illinois, and for 100 miles north of Tacusah [now Assumption, Christian County; 100 miles takes one up to Putnam County] the whole country is very fine, much of it settled and enclosed, and dotted with houses, as far as the eye can see. The cultivation is on a larger and more regular scale, the Indian corn and wheat both showing evidence of more careful management. Hay and corn ricks are more numerous; woodland is to be seen in all directions. . . . At Bloomington, which is a very rising town, with 7000 people, 10,000 bushels of grain are sent off daily by railroad to Chicago in a good season. The country here is chiefly settled by farmers from the State of New York.

Sir James Caird, *Prairie Farming in America,* 1859

Chicago

One beneficiary of the fertility of the farm belt was Chicago, which began as a hamlet on the Chicago River at the tip of Lake Michigan in the 1830s and became, by 1871 when it was devastated by the great fire, a metropolis of more than 300,000 people. In the meantime, Chicago had become the railroad center for the Midwest and had developed the largest grain market, the largest livestock market, and the greatest meat packing center in the world. The fire, which almost entirely destroyed the city of largely wooden buildings, gave Chicago a rebirth as a city of brick and stone and significant architectural monuments.

At one o'clock we were wakened by shouts of people in the streets declaring the city was on fire – but then the fire was far away on the south side of the river. Mr. King [the writer's husband, a clothing merchant] went quite leisurely over town, but soon hurried back with the news that the courthouse, Sherman House, post office, Tremont House, and all the rest of the business portion of the city was in flames, and thought he would go back and keep an eye on his store. He had scarcely been gone fifteen minutes when I saw him rushing back with his porters, bringing the books and papers from the store, with news that everything was burning, that the bridges were on fire, and the North Side was in danger. From that moment the flames ran in our direction, coming faster than a man could run. The rapidity was almost incredible, the wind blew a hurricane, the air was full of burning boards and shingles flying in every direction, and falling everywhere around us. . . . The streets were full of wagons transporting household furniture, people carrying on their backs the little bundles they had saved. Now and then we would pass a friend seated on a truck or dray, huddling her children together and her two or three little treasures snatched from the burning.

Mrs Aurelia R. King, writing to friends, October 21, 1871

68 CURRIER & IVES *Chicago in Flames. Scene at Randolph Street Bridge*, 1871. (Library of Congress)

69 *The Great Union Stock Yards of Chicago*, 1878. (Library of Congress)

They say every Englishman goes to the Chicago stock-yards. You shall find them about six miles from the city; and once having seen them will never forget the sight. As far as the eye can reach stretches a township of cattle-pens, cunningly divided into blocks so that the animals of any pen can be speedily driven out close to an inclined timber path which leads to an elevated covered way straddling high above the pens. These viaducts are two-storied. On the upper story tramp the doomed cattle, stolidly for the most part. On the lower, with a scuffling of sharp hooves and multitudinous yells, run the pigs. The same end is appointed for each.

Rudyard Kipling, *American Notes*, 1891

The extensive enclosure is entered through a modest gray sandstone, turreted gateway, surmounted by a carved bull's head, and the cattle pens stretch far away on either hand. This stock yard is a town of itself, with its own banks and hotel, "Board of Trade," post-office, town-hall, and special fire department, the latter being a necessity, as it occasionally has very destructive fires. About £400,000 has been invested in this undertaking, which covers nearly a square mile.

Anonymous, "A Visit to the States," 1887

Midwestern metropolises

Cleveland and Cincinnati were founded within a few years of each other just before the turn of the eighteenth century, Cleveland on a plateau overlooking Lake Erie and Cincinnati on the north bank of the Ohio River in the opposite corner of Ohio. Both prospered with canal, river, and, finally, rail transportation. Cincinnati became a great stockyards center, Cleveland one of the world's greatest ore markets. By 1876 both had become thriving cities of substantial homes.

It is a beautiful town . . . with several good public buildings, with trees in the streets, and a busy gay look about it – the "Queen City of the West." In one thing it resembles an English City – there is *smoke to be seen*, for west of the Alleghanies lie the bituminous coalfields, and Cincinnati having certain factories about it, is really not so new and American-looking as the Eastern cities. . . .

The suburbs of Cincinnati are extremely pretty (really very pretty) with good houses and good gardens. We went to see some of them – a young Mr. Longworth's place and a Mr. Wheeler's. At the former we saw the lady of the house. . . . She is an agreeable person and gave us some very fair Catawba and a button-hole bouquet.

Henry Arthur Bright, *Travel Diary*, 1852

70 *Edmund Dexter's Residence,
N.E. Corner of Fourth St. &
Broadway, Cincinnati, c.1861–69.*
(Courtesy Cincinnati Art Museum,
Gift of Mrs William M. Chatfield)

71 After J. Douglas Woodward
*Superior Street, Cleveland, from
Presbyterian Church,* from
Picturesque America, 1872–74. We
are looking across the Public
Square down toward the "Flat."

Above the lake on either side of the river stretch
the long avenues, with miles of pleasant residences,
gardens, velvet lawns, vines, and flowers. Each
house is isolated in green, and one of the avenues is
lined with rows of country-seats, with extensive
grounds, such as are seldom seen within the limits
of a city. But Cleveland on the hill is not like a
city; it is like a suburban village multiplied by ten,
and miraculously endowed with gas and pavements.
Even in its central square, with its post-office,
court-house, business-blocks, and street-cars, it has
an air of leisure; and the statue of Commodore
Perry, the flag-staff, and the little seats scattered
over the grass, seem quite appropriate to its elegant
ease. But step to the verge of the hill, and
everything is different. Down on the Flat [by the
river] we see Cleveland at work, Cleveland grimy,
Cleveland toiling in the sweat of her brow. . . .

As Buffalo has its elevators, so Cleveland has its
oil-refineries, which line the river-valley for miles.
Hither, from the petroleum district, comes that fiery
fluid which, hidden through all these centuries, has
crowned the nineteenth with its luminous splendor.
Here it is purified and sent forth into the wide
world to fulfil its mission.

Constance F. Woolson in *Picturesque America,* 1872–74

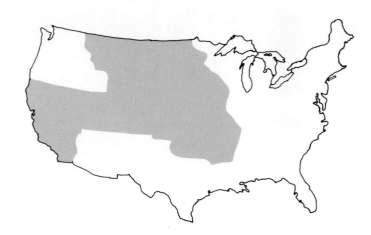

The West

72 SAMUEL SEYMOUR *Cliffs of Red Sandstone Near the Rocky Mts., c.1820.* (Courtesy Beinecke Rare Book and Manuscript Library, Yale University)

American ventures

Spanish, British and French explorers predated Americans west of the Mississippi, but it was the Lewis and Clark expedition of 1804–06 that opened the Great West to settlement and established American claims to territory beyond the Rocky Mountains, and it was another American expedition, led by Major Stephen H. Long in 1819–20, that brought back the first pictures of the Rocky Mountains. They were drawn by Samuel Seymour, an English-born engraver and lithographer from Philadelphia.

The woodless plain is terminated by a range of naked and almost perpendicular rocks, visible at a distance of several miles, and resembling a vast wall, parallel to the base of the mountain. These rocks are sandstone similar in composition and character to that on the Cannon-ball creek. . . .

It is difficult, when contemplating the present appearance and situation of these rocks, to prevent the imagination from wandering back to that remote period, when the billows of an ocean lashed the base of the Andes, depositing, during a succession of ages, that vast accumulation of . . . rocks, which now extends without interruption from the base of this range to the summits of the Alleghany mountains.

Edwin James, *Account of an Expedition from Pittsburgh to the Rocky Mountains . . . under . . . Maj. S. H. Long*, 1821–23

Rivers of the West

Vast interconnecting rivers led explorers and travelers deep into the West. From St Louis, where it spills into the Mississippi, the Missouri stretches back to its source in Montana. The painter George Catlin in 1832, and, a year later, Prince Maximilian of Wied-Neuwied and the artist Karl Bodmer, left St Louis aboard the steamboat "Yellowstone", bound for the upper reaches of the Missouri. Catlin stopped at Fort Union in North Dakota, but Maximilian and Bodmer carried on up into Montana, where they saw the extraordinary rock formations known as the Stone Walls.

Also from St Louis, the Oregon Trail followed the Kansas River to its junction with the "thousand miles long and six inches deep" Platte River. The Trail clung to the Platte's North Fork, past Fort Laramie to the Rockies; the painter Worthington Whittredge, with General John Pope's troops in 1866, rode up its South Fork to Denver, and was so captivated he returned in 1870.

73 GEORGE CATLIN *St Louis from the River below* (detail), 1832–33. (Courtesy National Museum of American Art (formerly National Collection of Fine Arts), Smithsonian Institution, Washington, D.C., Gift of Mrs Sarah Harrison)

As it was my intention to travel through the interior of the western part of North America, and, if possible, the Rocky Mountains, St. Louis was unquestionably the most proper basis for such an enterprise. The question was, whether it was more advisable to go by the caravans by land to Santa Fé, or to proceed by water up the Missouri? . . . the plan of following the course of the Missouri seemed to be the most suitable for my purposes; for, first, I should not be able to observe any Indians on the land journey; for if you happen to meet with them, you must fight them, and therefore, cannot become well acquainted with them; and, secondly, it is extremely difficult, nay impossible, to make considerable collections of natural history on such a journey. These reasons were decisive: I hoped, therefore, to obtain from the gentlemen of the American Fur Company, a passage up the Missouri in their steam-boat, the Yellow Stone . . .

Maximilian of Wied-Neuwied, *Travels in . . . 1832, 1833, and 1834*, 1843

74 KARL BODMER *View of the Stone Walls. On the upper Missouri* (detail), 1840. (Courtesy Amon Carter Museum, Fort Worth, Texas)

The part of the country called The Stone Walls, which now opened before us, has nothing like it on the whole course of the Missouri; and we did not leave the deck for a single moment the whole forenoon. . . . Here, on both sides of the river, the most strange forms are seen, and you may fancy that you see colonnades, small round pillars with large globes or a flat slab at the top, little towers, pulpits, organs with their pipes, old ruins, fortresses, castles, churches, with pointed towers, &c., &c., almost every mountain bearing on its summit some similar structure.

. . . All these eminences are inhabited by numerous troops of the wild mountain sheep.

Maximilian of Wied-Neuwied, *Travels in . . . 1832, 1833, and 1834*, 1843

I had never seen the plains or anything like them. . . . Whoever crossed the plains at that period, notwithstanding its herds of buffalo and flocks of antelope, its wild horses, deer and fleet rabbits, could hardly fail to be impressed with its vastness and silence and the appearance everywhere of an innocent primitive existence. . . . We usually made a march of thirty-three miles a day, which was performed between daybreak and one o'clock in the afternoon. On arriving in camp I gave my horse to an orderly and went at once to the wagon for my sketch box which was usually covered deep with camp furniture, but I always got it out, and while the officers were lounging in their tents and awaiting their dinners, I went to make a sketch seldom returning before sundown. Then I had to partake of a cold dinner, if there was anything left for me at all.

Worthington Whittredge, *Autobiography*

75 WORTHINGTON WHITTREDGE *Indian Encampment on the Platte River* (detail), 1870–72. (Collection of Jo Ann and Julian Ganz, Jr.)

76 GEORGE CATLIN *White Cloud, Chief of the Tribe* [*Iowa*], 1844. (National Gallery of Art, Washington, D.C., Paul Mellon Collection)

The native sons

77 GEORGE CATLIN *The Bull Dance, Mandan O-kee-pa Ceremony* (detail), *c.*1832. (The Anschutz Collection)

Compelled by a desire to document the Indians of the West before they had been "contaminated" by civilization or became extinct, various artists compiled a splendid record of these native American sons before the mid-century. One of the first was George Catlin, a self-trained artist in his mid-thirties who in 1830 forsook a legal career and travelled up the Missouri to become the historian of the Western tribes.

This young man, only 32 years of age, has, by several humane and noble acts since he inherited the office [of chief], proved himself well worthy of it, and has thereby gained the love of all his tribe, and also the admiration of the President of the United States, who has granted him the unusual permission to make the journey to Europe, and to select such a party as he chose to bring with him; and he . . . has brought the aristocracy of the tribe.

George Catlin, *Fourteen Ioway Indians*, 1844

This very curious and exceedingly grotesque part of their performance, which they denominated *Bellohck nah-pick* (the bull-dance) . . . I have selected for my second picture, and the principal actors in it were eight men, with the entire skins of buffaloes thrown over their backs, with the horns and hoofs and tails remaining on; their bodies in a horizontal position, enabling them to imitate the actions of the buffalo, whilst they were looking out of its eyes as through a mask. . . .

This most remarkable scene, then, which is witnessed more or less often on each day, takes place in presence of the whole nation, who are generally gathered around, on the tops of the wigwams or otherwise, as spectators. . . .

George Catlin, *Letters and Notes on the . . . North American Indians*, 1866

Hunting the bison

The entirety of the Plains Indian culture rested on the noble shoulders of the bison. From him the Indians obtained food, tools, shelter, and sport. He was the physical manifestation of their gods' approval, and, when the white man entered the West, he was numberless. Immense herds roamed the Plains, perhaps thirty million in all. The bison was an apparently eternal source of life for the Indians, who devised ingenious ways of worshipping – and killing – him. The vast herds began to dwindle rapidly once the white man began to hunt, and once he had provided the Indian with the long rifle, a much more effective weapon of death. With the coming of the railways the slaughter became indiscriminate, and by 1888 a researcher could not find a single herd anywhere in the West.

78 After JOHN MIX STANLEY *Herd of Bison, near Lake Jessie* [*North Dakota*], 1855, from the Pacific Railroad Survey *Reports*. (Courtesy Amon Carter Museum, Fort Worth, Texas)

The face of the country was dotted far and wide with countless hundreds of buffalo. They trooped along in files and columns, bulls, cows, and calves, on the green faces of the declivities in front. They scrambled away over the hills to the right and left; and far off, the pale blue swells in the extreme distance were dotted with innumerable specks. . . . The prairie teemed with life. Again and again I looked toward the crowded hillsides, and was sure I saw horsemen; and riding near . . . I found them transformed into a group of buffalo. There was nothing in human shape amid all this vast congregation of brute forms.

Francis Parkman, *The Oregon Trail*, 1849

79 ALFRED JACOB MILLER *Indians tantalizing a wounded Buffalo*, 1837. (Courtesy Amon Carter Museum, Fort Worth, Texas)

80 CURRIER & IVES after ARTHUR F. TAIT *Life on the Prairie. The "Buffalo Hunt,"* 1862. (Courtesy Amon Carter Museum, Fort Worth, Texas)

81 KARL BODMER *Bellevue Agency –
Post of Major Dougherty*, 1833.
(The InterNorth Art Foundation,
Joslyn Art Museum, Omaha,
Nebraska)

82 KARL BODMER *Mahchsi Karehde,
Mandan Indian*, 1833–34. (The
InterNorth Art Foundation, Joslyn
Art Museum, Omaha, Nebraska)

Noble Savages

*When the scholarly German Prince Maximilian of
Wied-Neuwied and the Swiss artist Karl Bodmer
traveled up the Missouri into Montana in 1833–34
they were helped by government Indian agents, like
Major Dougherty of Bellevue (near present-day
Omaha, Nebraska), and fur dealers, who knew the
Indians and could speak their language. Through them
the travellers came to know individual Indians, so
that their record is one of the most complete and
understanding ever made. They were particularly
impressed with the appearance of the young warrior
Mahchsi Karehde, who was over six feet tall: Bodmer
painted him dressed in his beaded buffalo robe,
leggings and moccasins, with his prestigious bear-claw
necklace (compare Pl. 76) and eagle-wing fan. The
wolves' tails trailing from his heels indicate that he
had killed two enemies in battle. (For a complete
description of his costume see the note to Pl. 82.)*

*Only three years later, the Mandans were virtually
exterminated by an epidemic of smallpox.*

Below, on the bank, there are some huts, and on
the top the buildings of the agents, where a sub-
agent, Major Beauchamp, a blacksmith, and some
servants of the company, all lived with their
families, who attend to the plantations and affairs
of the company. These men were mostly married to
women of the tribes of the Otos and Omahas; all, on
our landing, immediately came on board. Their
dress was of red or blue cloth, with a white border,
and cut in the Indian fashion. . . . Their children
had dark brown hair, and agreeable features.
[Later, the travellers heard that cholera had broken
out in St Louis, and been carried upriver by the
steamboats – as the smallpox would be:] at
Bellevue, Major Dougherty's post, seven of the ten
white inhabitants had died in a few days. The
major himself had been very ill, but had happily
recovered.

        *   *   *

The tallest man now living was Mahchsi-Karehde
(the flying war eagle) . . . Even in the midst of
winter, the Mandans wear nothing on the upper
part of the body, under their buffalo robe. . . . The
face is, for the most part, painted all over with
vermilion, or yellow, in which latter case the
circumference of the eyes and the chin are red. . . .

Maximilian of Wied-Neuwied, *Travels in . . . 1832, 1833, and
1834*, 1843

83 After FREDERICK PIERCY *Council Bluffs Ferry and group of Cotton-wood Trees*, from Piercy's *Route from Liverpool to Great Salt Lake Valley*, 1855. (Courtesy Amon Carter Museum, Fort Worth, Texas)

The Mormon emigrants usually start from Council Bluffs [in Iowa], on the left bank of the Missouri River . . . According to the "Overland Guide," Council Bluffs is the natural crossing of the Missouri River, on the route destined by nature for the great thoroughfare to the Pacific. This was the road selected by "nature's civil engineers," the buffalo and the elk, for their western travel. The Indians followed them in the same trail; then the travellers; next the settlers came.

Sir Richard F. Burton, *The City of the Saints*, 1861

The Mormon migrations

One of the most remarkable of the Western migrations was that of the Mormon pioneers under Brigham Young. Founded in 1830 in New York by Joseph Smith, Jr, the Church of Jesus Christ of the Latter-Day Saints (Mormons) eventually moved to Nauvoo, Illinois. There they encountered the hostility of their neighbors, and Smith was murdered by a lynch mob in 1844. Taking command of the demoralized group, Young led it westward. Some 1,600 Mormons made their way across the frozen Mississippi River to the Missouri and up the Platte and along its North Fork. Following the soon-to-be-famous Oregon Trail through South Pass, they defied contrary advice and crossed over the Uinta and Wasatch ranges. When Young saw the Great Salt Lake, he announced that the journey was at an end.

Salt Lake City grew rapidly as Mormon converts poured into the new Zion. The Tabernacle, completed in 1867, was visible proof of Mormon prosperity and ingenuity.

I found Kanesville to be a very dirty, unhealthy place, and withal a very dear place to make an outfit for the Plains, notwithstanding the assertions of holders of property and merchants settled there to the contrary. . . . Sometimes emigrants to California get sick of the journey by the time they

have arrived at Kanesville, and sell out by auction in the street. The ringing of a large bell announces the sale, and it seldom fails to collect a crowd. . . . Gambling houses and lawyers abound also. Where there are so many wolves there must consequently be a number of victims.

Frederick Piercy, *Route from Liverpool to Great Salt Lake Valley,* 1855

SALT LAKE CITY wears a pleasant aspect to the emigrant or traveler. . . . The houses – generally small and of one story – are all built of adobe (sun-hardened brick), and have a neat and quiet look; while the uniform breadth of the streets (eight rods) and the ''magnificent distances'' usually preserved by the buildings (each block containing ten acres, divided into eight lots, giving a quarter of an acre for buildings and an acre for garden, fruit, etc., to each householder), make up an *ensemble* seldom equaled. Then the rills of bright . . . water which . . . flow through each street and are conducted at will into every garden, diffuse an air of freshness and coolness which none can fail to enjoy, but which only a traveler in summer across the Plains can fully appreciate.

Horace Greeley, *An Overland Journey from New York to San Francisco,* 1860

84 After FREDERICK PIERCY *Entrance to Kanesville [Iowa]* (detail), from Piercy's *Route from Liverpool to Great Salt Lake Valley,* 1855. (Courtesy Amon Carter Museum, Fort Worth, Texas)

85 After CHRISTIAN INGER *View of Great Salt Lake City* (detail), 1867. (Courtesy Amon Carter Museum, Fort Worth, Texas)

Miller and the route West

Alfred Jacob Miller made his colorful and romantic record of the Oregon Trail in 1837 when he accompanied Captain William Drummond Stewart to the Wind River Mountains in the Rockies. He was the only artist to see the original Fort Laramie, which lay on the North Fork of the Platte in Wyoming; beyond it they entered the mountains, and the tenderfoot

Miller frequently mentions the difficult weather they had to endure. His painting of their goal, the site of the trappers' rendezvous, shows the various amusements the Indians engaged in while at the rendezvous; but Miller shows no trappers or traders — probably to make the scene more exotic for Easterners, impressed by wild Indians in their mountain habitat.

This post . . . built by the American Fur Co. situated about 800 miles West of St. Louis, is of a quadrangular form, with bastions at the diagonal corners to sweep the fronts in case of attack; over the ground entrance is a large block house, or tower, in which is placed a cannon. . . . Tribes of Indians encamp here 3 or 4 times a year, bringing with them peltries to be traded or exchanged for dry-goods, tobacco, vermillion, brass, and diluted alcohol.

Alfred Jacob Miller, manuscript caption, c. 1850

. . . a furious blast of sleet and hail drove full in our faces, icy cold, and urged with such demoniac vehemence that it felt like a storm of needles. It was curious to see the horses; they faced about in extreme displeasure, holding their tails like whipped dogs, and shivering as the angry gusts, howling louder than a concert of wolves, swept over us. Wright's long train of mules came sweeping round before the storm, like a flight of snowbirds driven by a winter tempest.

Francis Parkman, *The Oregon Trail*, 1849

86 ALFRED JACOB MILLER *Fort Laramie* (detail), 1851. (The Thomas Gilcrease Institute of American History and Art, Tulsa, Oklahoma)

87 ALFRED JACOB MILLER *Storm: Waiting for the Caravan*, 1858–60. (Courtesy the Walters Art Gallery, Baltimore)

88 ALFRED JACOB MILLER *Indian Village*, in the Wind River Mountains, Wyoming, *c.*1850. (Courtesy Amon Carter Museum, Fort Worth, Texas)

The Gold Rush

In 1848 James W. Marshall found some bright metal beneath the mill he was building near present-day Sacramento, and John Augustus Sutter, the German Swiss colonizer of the Sacramento Valley, pronounced it to be gold. The word soon leaked out, and Sutter's peaceful community was overrun by probably the greatest gold rush of the nineteenth century.

89 *The Independent Gold Hunter on his Way to California,* c.1850. (Courtesy Amon Carter Museum, Fort Worth, Texas)

All sorts of people, from the polished Broadway dandy, who never handled an instrument heavier than a whalebone walking-stick, to the sturdy labourer who had spent his life in wielding the pickaxe and the shovel, had come to California, and all for one common object – to dig gold.

E. Gould Buffum, *Six Months in the Gold Mines,* 1850

90 CHARLES C. KUCHEL AND EMIL DRESEL *Scotts Bar and French Bar, On Scotts River, Siskiyou County, California,* 1856. (Courtesy Amon Carter Museum, Fort Worth, Texas)
91 After S. F. MARRYAT *San Francisco* (detail), 1851. (Courtesy Amon Carter Museum, Fort Worth, Texas)

Over a quarter of a million immigrants poured into California during the next five years, including thousands of Chinese who were drawn by jobs in the mines. The Mexican colonizers of California were completely swept up in the boom economy that erupted virtually overnight, with San Francisco as the entrepôt.

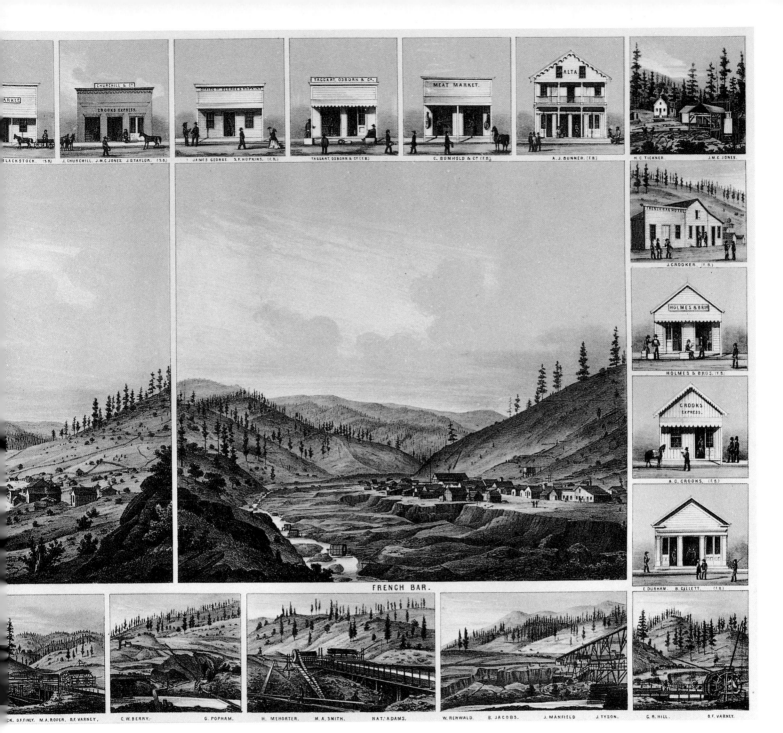

BLACKSTOCK. (S.B.) J. CHURCHILL. J.M.C.JONES. J.O.TAYLOR. (S.B.) JAMES GEORGE. S.F.HOPKINS. (F.B.) TAGGART, OSBORN & C? (F.B.) C. BOMHOLD & C? (F.B.) A.J.BUNNER. (F.B.) H.C.TICKNER. J.M.C.JONES.

J.CROOKER. (F.B.)

HOLMES & BROS. (F.B.)

A.C.CROOKS. (F.B.)

E.DURHAM. B.CALLETT. (F.B.)

FRENCH BAR.

CK. O.F.FINLY. M.A.ROPER. B.F.VARNEY. C.W.BERRY. G. POPHAM. H. MEHORTER. M.A.SMITH. NAT. ADAMS. W. RENWALD. B.JACOBS. J.MANFIELD. J.TYSON. G.R.HILL. B.F.VARNEY.

Ditches and banks of gravel, denuded hillsides, stumps, and decayed trunks of trees, took the place of woodland and ravine, and indicated his approach to civilization. Then a church steeple came in sight, and he knew that he had reached home. In a few moments he was clattering down the single narrow street that lost itself in a chaotic ruin of races, ditches, and tailings at the foot of the hill, and dismounted before the gilded windows of the Magnolia saloon.

Bret Harte, "Brown of Calaveras," 1870

151

The Overland Trail

Following in the trail of fur trappers and early explorers such as the inveterate map-maker John Charles Frémont, pioneers travelled overland to settle in the West. Soon the 2,000-mile Oregon Trail, from Independence, Missouri, to the Pacific coast was rutted and clearly marked – often by animal carcasses and new graves – and the Catholic and pastoral character of California was completely changed.

The German-American painter Albert Bierstadt made his second trip West in 1863. As he and his friend, Fitz Hugh Ludlow, neared Fort Kearney in Nebraska, they passed a wagon train of Germans en route to Oregon, who presented a very different picture from the poor, strained, and often ill-fated emigrants that Francis Parkman had encountered.

They had a large herd of cattle and fifty wagons, mostly drawn by oxen, though some of the more prosperous "outfits" were attached to horses or mules. The people themselves represented the better class of Prussian or North German peasantry. A number of strapping teamsters, in gay costumes, appeared like Westphalians. Some of them wore canary shirts and blue pantaloons; with these were intermingled blouses of claret, rich warm brown, and most vivid red. All the women and children had some positive color about them, if it only amounted to a knot of ribbons, or the glimpse of a petticoat. I never saw so many bright and comely faces in an emigrant train. . . . Every wagon was a gem of an interior such as no Fleming ever put on canvas, and every group a *genre* piece. . . .

Fitz Hugh Ludlow, *The Heart of the Continent*, 1870

They were ill-looking fellows, thin and swarthy, with care-worn anxious faces, and lips rigidly compressed. . . . Since leaving the settlements they had met with nothing but misfortune. Some of their party had died; one man had been killed by the Pawnees; and about a week before they had been plundered by the Dahcotahs of all their best horses . . .

Francis Parkman, *The Oregon Trail*, 1849

The station-keeper up-ended a disk of last week's bread, of the shape and size of an old-time cheese, and carved some slabs from it which were as good as Nicholson pavement, and tenderer.
    He sliced off a piece of bacon for each man, but only the experienced old hands made out to eat it, for it was condemned army bacon which the United States would not feed to its soldiers in the forts, and the stage company had bought it cheap. . . .
    Then he poured for us a beverage which he called "*Slumgullion*," and it is hard to think he was not inspired when he named it. It really pretended to be tea, but there was too much dish-rag, and sand, and old bacon-rind in it to deceive the intelligent traveler. . . .
    Our breakfast was before us, but our teeth were idle.

Mark Twain, *Roughing It*, 1872

92 ALBERT BIERSTADT *Emigrants crossing the Plains* (detail), 1867. (Courtesy The National Cowboy Hall of Fame and Western Heritage Center, Oklahoma City)

93 CARL WILLIAM HAHN *California Stage Coach Halt* (detail), 1875. (The Anschutz Collection)

The urban West

The hope for quick riches transformed Western towns overnight from peaceful villages with only a few hundred residents to boomtowns. Sacramento was little more than the site of Sutter's trading post before gold was discovered. Los Angeles was a sleepy Spanish pueblo *almost seventy years old when the Forty-Niners began to arrive, and Denver in Colorado was founded upon the remains of a rather modest discovery of gold in 1858, which was widely promoted as another bonanza. The cities continued to grow as the Homestead Act encouraged immigration and the railroad provided easier and faster transportation westward.*

One never sees summer clothing or mosquitoes in San Francisco – but they can be found in Sacramento. Not always and unvaryingly, but about one hundred and forty-three months out of twelve years, perhaps. Flowers bloom there, always, the reader can easily believe – people suffer and sweat, morning, noon and night, and wear out their staunchest energies fanning themselves. . . . In Sacramento it is fiery summer always, and you can gather roses, and eat strawberries and ice-cream, and wear white linen clothes, and pant and perspire, at eight or nine o'clock in the morning, and then take the cars, and at noon put on your furs and your skates, and go skimming over frozen Donner Lake, seven thousand feet above the valley.

Mark Twain, *Roughing It*, 1872

94 After GEORGE V. COOPER *Sacramento City Ca. From the Foot of J. Street, Showing I. J. & K. Sts. With the Sierra Nevada in the Distance, December 20, 1849* (detail), 1850. (Courtesy Amon Carter Museum, Fort Worth, Texas)

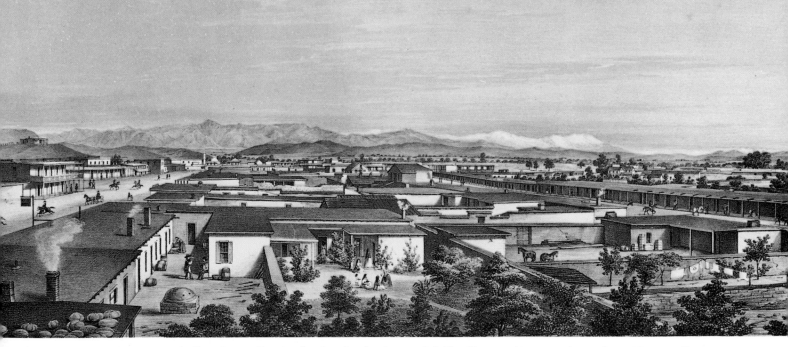

95 CHARLES C. KUCHEL AND EMIL DRESEL *Los Angeles, Los Angeles County, Cal.* (detail), 1857. (Courtesy Amon Carter Museum, Fort Worth, Texas)

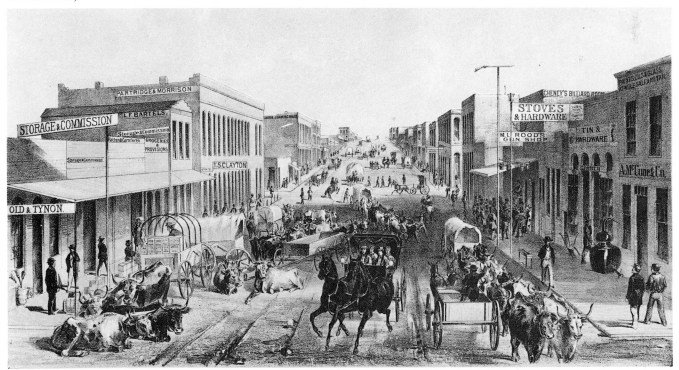

96 After ALFRED E. MATTHEWS *F Street, Denver*, 1866. (Courtesy Amon Carter Museum, Fort Worth, Texas)

Denver is no longer the Denver of Hepworth Dixon. A shooting affray in the street is as rare as in Liverpool, and one no longer sees men dangling to the lamp-posts when one looks out in the morning! It is a busy place, the *entrepôt* and distributing point for an immense district, with good shops, some factories, fair hotels, and the usual deformities and refinements of civilization. Peltry shops abound, and sportsman, hunter, miner, teamster, emigrant, can be completely rigged out at fifty different stores. At Denver, people who come from the East to try the "camp cure" now so fashionable, get their outfit of wagon, driver, horses, tent, bedding, and stove, and start for the mountains.

Isabella L. Bird, in a letter of October 23, 1873

155

Yosemite

The trapper and explorer Joseph R. Walker was probably the first American to see the Yosemite Valley, in the fall of 1833, but it remained in the hands of Indians until they were driven out in 1851. Within four years the first party of tourists had been brought into the valley to see Half Dome, the giant sequoia trees, and the countless streams and waterfalls. Most of the painters who visited California, including Albert Bierstadt and Carl William Hahn (see Pl. 130), succumbed to its pristine beauty. It became a state park in 1864 and later a national park. Bierstadt first visited it in 1863, with Fitz Hugh Ludlow and other friends and artists.

I know of no single wonder of nature on earth which can claim a superiority over the Yosemite. Just dream yourself for one hour in a chasm nearly ten miles long, with egress save for birds and water, but at three points, up the face of precipices from three thousand to four thousand feet high, the chasm scarcely more than a mile wide at any point, and tapering to a mere gorge, or cañon, at either end, with walls of mainly naked and perpendicular white granite . . . so that looking up to the sky from it, is like looking out of an unfathomable profound – and you will have some conception of the Yosemite.

Horace Greeley, *An Overland Journey from New York to San Francisco*, 1860

The artists with their camp-stools and color-boxes, the sages with their goggles, nets, botany-boxes, and bug-holders, the gentlemen of elegant leisure with their naked eyes and a fish-rod or a gun, all rode away whither they listed. . . . Sitting in their divine workshop, by a little after sunrise our artists began labor in that only method which can ever make a true painter or a living landscape, color-studies on the spot; and though I am not here to speak of their results, I will assert that during their seven weeks' camp in the Valley they learned more and gained greater material for future triumphs than they had gotten in all their lives before. . . . At evening, when the artists returned, half an hour was passed in a "private view" of their day's studies; then came another dinner, called a supper; then the tea-kettle was emptied into a pan, and brush-washing with talk and pipes led the rest of the genial way to bed-time.

Fitz Hugh Ludlow, *The Heart of the Continent*, 1870

97 ALBERT BIERSTADT *Sunrise, Yosemite Valley*. (Courtesy Amon Carter Museum, Fort Worth, Texas)

The transcontinental railroad is complete

The need for a transcontinental railroad was clearly established and the routes surveyed before the Civil War. With the surrender of the Confederacy, the Union Pacific and the Central Pacific railroads resumed construction, using thousands of Chinese workers imported for that purpose. But the hostile terrain was not the only problem the engineers had to overcome, as heavy snows, prairie fires, and, sometimes, buffalo herds on the move postponed the joining of the rails, at Promontory Point, Utah, until May, 1869. The hazards remained, and were catered for: snow fences and snow sheds were erected, to protect the line from drifting, and American trains long retained their characteristic "cow-catchers."

We had no means of fighting the snows in the Laramie Plains except by fences and sheds, and none were put up until the year 1870, so that when the heavy snows fell in the winter of 1869–70, it caught six of our trains west of Laramie that were snowed in there some weeks. . . . These six trains . . . were supplied with sledges and snow-shoes from Laramie. They had with them, in charge of the six trains, Mr. H. M. Hoxie, the Assistant Superintendent, who managed to get the trains together, but the blizzards were so many and so fierce that it was impossible for men to work out in the open. . . . Mr. Hoxie handled his forces with great ability and fed and entertained his passengers in good shape. In one train was an opera company bound for California, that Mr. Hoxie used to entertain the passengers with, so that when the trains reached Salt Lake City, the passengers held a meeting and passed resolutions complimentary to Mr. Hoxie and the Union Pacific in bringing them safely through.

Major General Grenville M. Dodge, *How We Built the Union Pacific Railway*, 1911

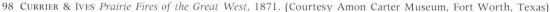

98 CURRIER & IVES *Prairie Fires of the Great West*, 1871. (Courtesy Amon Carter Museum, Fort Worth, Texas)

99 JOSEPH BECKER *Snow Sheds on the Central Pacific Railroad in the Sierra Nevada Mountains, May 1869.* (The Thomas Gilcrease Institute of American History and Art, Tulsa, Oklahoma)

At Colfax [California], a station at a height of 2,400 feet, I got out and walked the length of the train. First came two great gaudy engines, the Grizzly Bear and the White Fox, with their respective tenders loaded with logs of wood, the engines with great, solitary, reflecting lamps in front above the cow guards, a quantity of polished brass-work, comfortable glass houses, and well-stuffed seats for the engine-drivers. The engines and tenders were succeeded by a baggage car, the latter loaded with bullion and valuable parcels, and in charge of two "express agents." Each of these cars is forty-five feet long. Then came two cars loaded with peaches and grapes; then two "silver palace" cars, each sixty feet long; then a smoking car, at that time occupied mainly by Chinamen; and then five ordinary passenger cars, with platforms like all the others, making altogether a train about 700 feet in length. . . .

Shivering in the keen, frosty air near the summit pass of the Sierras, we entered the "snow-sheds," wooden galleries, which for about fifty miles shut out all the splendid views of the region, as given in dioramas, not even allowing a glimpse of "the Gem of the Sierras," the lovely Donner Lake. One of these sheds is twenty-seven miles long.

Isabella L. Bird, in a letter of September 2, 1873

Thomas Moran's West

One of the first artists to take advantage of the newly-completed transcontinental railroad to head west was the English-born painter Thomas Moran, who accompanied Dr Ferdinand V. Hayden's U.S. Geological Survey expedition into the Yellowstone in 1871. Moran took the train as far as the Green River, in southwestern Wyoming, then headed up the river to meet Hayden's party. Passing the stunning cliffs, he sketched for the first time a scene that proved to be a lasting image for him.

"The place where Hell bubbled up" had been known by the Indians for hundreds of years before the first white man, John Colter, who had left the Lewis and Clark expedition on its return trip, saw it in 1807. Mountain men followed Colter into the Yellowstone region, but no one believed the stories of geysers, hot springs, and mirror-smooth lakes. Proof came as the documents from Hayden's expedition — Moran's paintings, and photographs by William H. Jackson — were disseminated among the members of Congress. Impressed by the evidence, Congress in 1872 declared Yellowstone the first national park.

100 THOMAS MORAN *Cliffs of the Green River*, 1874. (Courtesy Amon Carter Museum, Fort Worth, Texas)

Our way for nearly fifty miles was through the Green River Bad Lands, a region of desolation. The rocks are sandstones and shales, gray and buff, red and brown, blue and black strata in many alternations, lying nearly horizontal, and almost without soil or vegetation; but they are all very soft and friable, and are strangely carved by the rains and streams. The fantastic rain-sculpture imitates architectural forms, and suggests rude and weird statuary. . . .

John Wesley Powell, "The Cañons of the Colorado," 1875

We encamped on the evening of August 5th in the middle of the Upper Geyser Basin. . . . Soon after reaching camp a tremendous rumbling was heard, shaking the ground in every direction, and soon a column of steam burst forth from a crater near the east side of the river. Following the steam by a succession of impulses, a column of water, apparently 6 ft. in diameter, rose to the height of 200 ft., while the steam ascended 1,000 ft. or more.

F. V. Hayden on the Grand Geyser, in *The Englishman's Illustrated Guide Book to the United States and Canada*, 1879

160

101 THOMAS MORAN *Old Faithful*, 1873. (Private collection)

The cowboy conquers the Plains

The institution by which the Great American Desert was finally conquered was the ranch. The vast grasslands, which even the earliest explorers had noted, and the thousands of immigrants thronging the Overland Trail, provided sustenance and a market for the herds of wild Longhorn cattle that had existed in Texas for decades. The post-Civil War trail drives, carried out with methods the Texans had inherited from both Spanish and English forebears, got the cattle from the South Texas plains to ranches in the West and to railheads in Kansas, for shipment to the Chicago stockyards and points east.

The small engraving from "A Visit to Texas" (1834), probably one of the earliest sporting scenes of the West, demonstrates that it was in Texas that the cattle- and horse-handling techniques of the Spaniard combined with those of the Anglo-Saxon South to mold the American cowboy. The famous chroniclers of the cow puncher, Charles M. Russell and Frederic Remington, arrived late, and before 1880 it was the illustrated magazines, such as "Harper's Weekly," that fed public curiosity about his distinctive way of life.

The small horses of the country, called *mustangs*, introduced by the Spaniards, and now numerous in the more northern prairies, run wild in droves over these parts of Texas, and are easily taken and rendered serviceable by the inhabitants. . . . These horses are very useful in the country, and may perhaps become at some future time a valuable article of export, as they are innumerable, and cost only the trouble of catching. This is done with a strong noosed cord, made of twisted strips of raw hide, and called a *lazo*, which is the Spanish word for a band or bond. It has been often described, as well as the manner of throwing it, as it is in common use for catching animals, and sometimes for choking men, in different parts of America. . . . A man on horseback, with a rope of this kind coiled in his left hand, and one end of it fastened to the horse, whirls the noosed end in the air over his head as he approaches the animal he intends to seize: and, on finding an opportunity, throws it over its head or horns, and checks his horse. The noose is instantly drawn tight, and the poor creature is thrown violently down . . .

A Visit to Texas, 1834

102 J. T. HAMMOND *Lazooing a Horse on the Prairie*, from *A Visit to Texas*, 1834. (Courtesy Amon Carter Museum, Fort Worth, Texas)

103 After W. J. PALMER *Driving Cattle into a Corral in the Far West* (detail), from *Harper's Weekly*, September 11, 1875. (Courtesy Amon Carter Museum, Fort Worth, Texas)

. . . beyond the railroad tracks are nothing but the brown plains, with their lonely sights — now a solitary horseman at a traveling amble, then a party of Indians in paint and feathers, . . . then a drove of ridgy-spined, long-horned cattle, which have been several months eating their way from Texas, with their escort of four or five much-spurred horsemen, in peaked hats, blue-hooded coats, and high boots, heavily armed with revolvers and repeating rifles, and riding small wiry horses.

Isabella L. Bird, in a letter from Cheyenne, Wyoming, September 8, 1873

Everybody knows that a large proportion of the beef that finds its way to our tables comes from Texan cattle. These are driven in large numbers from the Far Southwest up to Kansas, where they are transferred to the cars, and sent eastward by railroad. The droves vary from 500 to 8,000, and are guarded by well-mounted and well-armed herdsmen, who are inured to fatigue and to fighting hostile Indians. The cattle feed during the long march on the luxurious grazing grounds of the Indian Territory. The entire journey, from Texas to Kansas occupies from four to five months, as the herds must move very slowly, and what with stoppages to feed, water, and rest, only a few miles are made in a day. At various points along the route are great yards, called corrals, inclosed by tall, strong fences. These corrals are secure resting-places into which the cattle are driven temporarily. In our double-page illustration the herdsmen are seen in the act of driving a large number of cattle into one of these enclosures. One of the beasts, less manageable than the rest, has broken loose, and threatens to give the herdsmen plenty of hard work before they capture him.

Harper's Weekly, September 11, 1875

The bountiful land

Many of the Forty-Niners who went broke in the gold fields in the 1850s and '60s turned to farming to earn their living in the 1870s, and found that comparatively little effort usually produced a bountiful crop. As one San Francisco clergyman explained it, California was "the beloved Benjamin of American States, whose autumn sack is filled with grain, while the mouth of it contains a cup of gold."

The vast size of many of the holdings, combined with the need to harvest quickly in the dry California air, led to the rapid mechanization of farming. The farm depicted by Hahn was perhaps already a little old-fashioned: the thresher in the field is powered not by steam but by a team of vigorous horses and mules.

From off the boundless harvest fields the grain was carried in June, and it is now stacked in sacks along the track, awaiting freightage. California is a "land flowing with milk and honey." The barns are bursting with fullness. In the dusty orchards the apple and pear branches are supported, that they may not break down under the weight of fruit; melons, tomatoes, and squashes of gigantic size lie almost unheeded on the ground; fat cattle, gorged almost to repletion, shade themselves under the oaks; superb "red" horses shine, not with grooming, but with condition; and thriving farms everywhere show on what a solid basis the prosperity of the "Golden State" is founded.

Isabella L. Bird, in a letter of September 2, 1873

104 CARL WILLIAM HAHN *Harvest Time* (detail), 1875. (The Fine Arts Museums of San Francisco, Gift of Mrs Harold R. McKinnon and Mrs Harry L. Brown)

In the grain harvest (which begins in the second week of June) the "wholesale" mode of procedure is equally prevalent. The scythe is used only to cut the way, and that on small farms; then follows the reaper, hired if not owned by the farmer himself. But the binding and shocking process that is to succeed is far too slow for the large grain-grower, who has his hundreds, and sometimes thousands of acres to reap. . . . His implement is the giant header, pushed into the golden fields by from four to eight horses. Its vibrating cutters clip off the heads with only a few inches of straw attached . . . [so that] within half an hour, the grain that was waving in the morning breeze may be sacked ready for shipment to Liverpool. . . . Where farming is

not done on quite so energetic a plan, the reaped and bound grain being at that season perfectly safe from rain, is left either in shocks or stacks until the threshing party comes around, mostly with a portable engine often fed with straw alone, to drive the huge "separator," whose combined din and puffing will sometimes startle late sleepers, as it suddenly starts up in the morning from most unexpected places. Two wagons . . . feed the devouring monster. In an incredibly short time the shocks or stacks are cleared away and in their stead appear square piles of turgid grain-sacks and broad, low hillocks of straw.

E. W. Hilgard, "The Agriculture and Soils of California," 1878

165

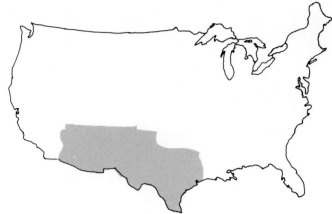

The Southwest

Church at El Paso del Norte

105 JOHN RUSSELL BARTLETT? *Church at El Paso del Norte, Chihuahua, c.*1851. (Courtesy The John Carter Brown Library, Providence, Rhode Island)

The Mexican Southwest

Spaniards were the first Europeans to explore the Southwest. Santa Fe was founded in 1610 as part of a series of frontier outposts in what later became the states of Texas, New Mexico, Arizona, and California; and Spanish missions, established among the sedentary Indians in the hope of converting them to Christianity and stabilizing the frontier, led to settlements at El Paso, San Antonio and Nacogdoches.

When Mexico won its independence from Spain in 1821 it welcomed American settlers, a disastrous policy that resulted in Texas becoming independent in its turn in 1836. Mexico ultimately lost more than half of its territory in the war with the United States in 1846–48, but Hispanic culture had indelibly marked the American Southwest.

There is a venerable looking church here, constructed of adobe, which the cura [priest] . . . informed me had been built more than 200 years [ago] . . . The other three sides [of the plaza] present externally an unbroken and prison-like appearance.

There are a few respectable old Spanish families at El Paso, who possess much intelligence, as well as that elegance and dignity of manner which characterized their ancestors. Among these may be found many names which are illustrious in Spanish history and literature, but there is no great middle class, as in the United States and England. A vast gulf intervenes between these Castillians and the masses.

John Russell Bartlett, *Personal Narrative of Explorations and Incidents*, 1854

167

Texas and the war with Mexico

When Texas joined the Union in 1846, war was inevitable. Radical politicians in Mexico demanded that the loss of Texas be avenged, while many in Washington coveted additional Mexican territory. The conflict began when an American advance guard encountered Mexican scouts north of the Rio Grande. As General Zachary Taylor advanced into Mexico, General John E. Wool marched from San Antonio, Texas, with 3,400 men, intent on the conquest of Chihuahua. This picture of Wool's march through the Military Plaza en route to Mexico was painted from memory by one of the participants. Another, Edward Everett, a British artist attached to Wool's command, paused to document the old Spanish missions near the city, including the handsomest, San José, which had been completed in 1778.

106 SAMUEL CHAMBERLAIN *General Wool crossing the Military Plaza, San Antonio, c.1856.* (Courtesy San Jacinto Museum of History, Houston)

General Wool's Division left San Antonio for Mexico on September 25 [1846]. The command made quite an imposing appearance as they marched through the Grand Plaza of San Antonio, which was crowded with a motley assembly of wild looking Texans, Mexicans in their everlasting blankets, Negro Slaves, a sprinkling of Lipan Indians in full dress of paint and feathers, white women, squaws and senoritas.

Samuel E. Chamberlain, *My Confession*, 1844–49

107 EDWARD EVERETT *Mission of San José near San Antonio de Bexar*, 1846. (Courtesy Amon Carter Museum, Fort Worth, Texas)

The Mission of San José is about a mile and a half down the river. . . . The church stands apart from the other buildings, in the square, but not in the centre; the west door is surrounded with most elaborate stone carving of flowers, angels, and apostles. The interior is plain. To the right is a handsome belfry tower, and above the altar a large stone cupola. Behind the church, and in connexion with it, is a long range of rooms for the missionaries, opening upon a covered gallery or *portales* of nine arches. Though the Texan troops were long quartered here, the stone carvings have not been injured. The church has been repaired, and Divine service is performed in it.

George W. Kendall, *Across the Great Southwestern Prairies*, 1844

169

Trade and exploration

108 *March of the Caravan*, from Josiah Gregg, *Commerce on the Prairies*, 1844. (Courtesy Amon Carter Museum, Fort Worth, Texas)

A lucrative trade had developed between the New Mexican capital of Santa Fe and Independence, Missouri, via the famed Santa Fe Trail, and attracted so many Anglos that by 1846 it seemed natural for that area as well as Texas to be added to the United States. The wagons did not stop rolling until the railroad reached Santa Fe in 1880.

As the caravan was passing under the northern base of the Round Mound, it presented a very fine and imposing spectacle to those who were upon its summit. The wagons marched slowly in four parallel columns, but in broken lines, often at intervals of many rods between. The unceasing ''crack, crack,'' of the wagoners' whips, resembling the frequent reports of distant guns, almost made one believe that a skirmish was actually taking place between two hostile parties. . . . As our camp was pitched but a mile west of the Round Mound, those who lingered upon its summit could have an interesting view of the evolutions of ''forming'' the wagons, in which the drivers by this time had become very expert. When marching four abreast, the two exterior lines spread out and then meet at the front angle; while the two inner lines keep close together until they reach the point of the rear angle, when they wheel suddenly out and close with the hinder ends of the other two; thus systematically concluding a right-lined quadrangle, with a gap left at the rear corner for the introduction of the animals.

Josiah Gregg, *Commerce on the Prairies*, 1844

170

109 After JOHN MIX STANLEY *Mouth of Night Creek*, from W. H. Emory, *Notes of a Military Reconnoissance*, 1848. (Courtesy Amon Carter Museum, Fort Worth, Texas)

110 After JAMES W. ABERT *Pueblo de Santo Domingo*, from Abert's *Report of . . . New Mexico*, 1848. (Courtesy Amon Carter Museum, Fort Worth, Texas)

After the war with Mexico had started, Colonel Stephen W. Kearny and his "Army of the West" were dispatched to capture New Mexico and then California. They were joined at Fort Leavenworth, Kansas, by a scientific expedition led by Lieutenant W. H. Emory, of the Topographical Engineers. John Mix Stanley, a seasoned artist, was in the party which reconnoitred along the Arkansas, Gila, and Maricopa rivers to San Diego in 1846–47. Lieutenant James W. Abert, just four years out of West Point, was due to join Kearny and Emory: kept by illness from accompanying them to California, he was instead charged with mapping New Mexico. The exploration results were published in 1848.

We wended our way through the narrow valley of Night creek.

On each side were huge stone buttes shooting up into the skies.

At one place we were compelled to mount one of these spurs almost perpendicular. This gave us an opportunity of seeing what a mule could do. My conclusion was, from what I saw, that they could climb nearly as steep a wall as a cat. A pack slipped from a mule, and, though not shaped favorably for the purpose, rolled entirely to the base of the hill, over which the mules had climbed.

W. H. Emory, *Notes of a Military Reconnoissance*, 1848

We passed through unfenced fields of melons and corn. Here [we] saw many clumps of leafless trees covered with melons drying in the sun. At St. D. we noticed that the houses were built in a few blocks so that 60 or 70 families lived in one house. The walls were covered over with red peppers and long spiral curls of the dried melons. One ascends to the second story of their houses in order to enter.

J. W. Abert, *Report of . . . New Mexico*, 1848

Santo Domingo . . . is a pueblo or Indian town, containing about eight hundred inhabitants. It is laid out in streets running perpendicularly to the Rio Grande. The houses are constructed of *adobes*; are two stories in height, the upper one set retreatingly on the lower, so as to make the superior covering or ceiling of the lower answer for a terrace or platform for the upper; and have roofs which are nearly flat. . . . The height of the stories is about eight or nine feet. The lower stories have very small windows, and no doors; the lights of the windows, wherever there were any, being made of selenite – the crystallized foliated form of gypsum. The mode of access to the building is by exterior ladders, which may be seen leaning against every house.

James H. Simpson, *Navaho Expedition*, 1849

171

Richard Kern in New Mexico

Richard Kern, one of three brothers from Philadelphia who had an active role in the exploration and documentation of the Southwest, was among the first artists to visit northern New Mexico after the Americans took possession. A member of Frémont's ill-fated fourth expedition that set out in the fall of 1848 only to be stranded in Rocky Mountains snowstorms, Kern made his way to New Mexico, where he painted this series of watercolor sketches, and joined Lieutenant James H. Simpson's punitive expedition against the Navahos in 1849. He later accompanied Captain John W. Gunnison's Pacific Railroad Survey team and was killed, along with the Captain, by Ute Indians in October, 1853.

Kern's painting labeled "Robidoux's Pass" probably shows Hardscrabble Canyon, in the Sangre de Cristo Mountains of Northern New Mexico. The Parroquia of Santa Fe, with the priest's colonnaded house beside it, was torn down a quarter of a century later and replaced by the existing Gothic cathedral.

111 RICHARD H. KERN *"Robidoux's Pass, White Mountains, New Mexico,"* 1848. (Courtesy Amon Carter Museum, Fort Worth, Texas)

112 RICHARD H. KERN *La Parroquia, Santa Fe, New Mexico,* 1849. (Courtesy Amon Carter Museum, Fort Worth, Texas)

113 RICHARD H. KERN *Valley of Taos, looking South, New Mexico*, 1849. (Courtesy Amon Carter Museum, Fort Worth, Texas)

We were early awakened with the ringing of the campanetas, summoning the good citizens of Santa Fe to morning mass at the parroquia, or parish church. . . .

The body of the building is very long [and] narrow and the roof lofty, the ground plan resembling a cross. Midway on each side were wax figures the size of life [that] represented hooded friars with shaven heads except a crown of hair that encircled the head like a wreath. These figures were draped, one in white, the other in blue, their garments long and flowing, with long girdles around the waist. . . . In the evening I made a sketch of the Parroquia. Though mud walls are not generally remarkable for effect, still the great size of the building compared with those around produces an imposing effect.

J. W. Abert, in *Report of . . . New Mexico*, 1848, and in his diary

El Valle de Taos is situated eighty miles to the northward of Santa Fe, on the eastern side of the Del Norte. . . . The soil is exceedingly fertile, and produces excellent wheat and other grain. The climate being rigorous, and the summers short, fruit does not ripen to perfection, but vegetables of all kinds are good and abundant, onions in particular growing to great size.

George Frederick Ruxton, *Wild Life in the Rocky Mountains*, 1846

114 JOHN RUSSELL BARTLETT *Ascent to the Quicksilver Mines, New Almaden, California, c.1851.* (Courtesy The John Carter Brown Library, Providence, Rhode Island)

The Southwestern surveys

Once the area was firmly under control, the United States government undertook to survey the new territory, both to establish an accurate boundary with Mexico and to locate the best route for a transcontinental railroad. Teams set out from San Diego in June, 1849, to mark the border between the two countries. After a trip to San Francisco to clear government drafts so he could pay his men, who were threatening to leave for the goldfields, the Boundary Survey Commissioner, John Russell Bartlett, returned south via the quicksilver mines of New Almaden. The manager gave the visitors a tour, showing them the cinnabar as it was heated and distilled and permitting them to test their weight against that of mercury. Bartlett made a series of sketches of the mines, leaving one unfinished when the wind changed and he was almost overcome by poisonous fumes. The

boundary survey was essentially completed by September, 1853; and the United States then purchased additional land from Mexico to secure a much-needed railroad route across the southern part of the country.

Early morning at New Almaden is worth getting up betimes to see. Sometimes the valley is like a great lake filled with billows of fog – pearly white billows, tumbling and surging with noiseless motion. . . . On windy mornings, the fog rolls grandly out to sea along the defiles of the triple chain of hills; when there is no wind, it rises and drifts in masses over the mountains, making the clear sunlight hazy for a moment before dissolving into it. . . .

Mary Hallock Foote, "A California Mining Camp," 1878

174

The houses at El Paso are all of one story, and built of *adobe*, i.e. the mud of the valley formed into bricks from twelve to eighteen inches long, and four inches thick, and baked in the sun. This material, with slight repairs, will endure for centuries. Sometimes chopped straw and gravel are mixed with it, which greatly improves its quality. The houses of the better classes are large, and built in the form of a hollow square. The walls are from two to three feet in thickness, and have but few openings. When plastered and whitewashed they look very neat, and make comfortable dwellings. All the floors are laid with mud, concrete, or brick. Such a thing as a wooden floor is unknown in the country.

John Russell Bartlett, *Personal Narrative of Explorations and Incidents*, 1854

Meanwhile, Congress authorized extensive exploration of all the possible transcontinental railroad routes. Artists accompanying the expeditions created an unparalleled visual record of the western half of the country.

115 JOHN RUSSELL BARTLETT *El Paso, Texas*, 1852. (Courtesy The John Carter Brown Library, Providence, Rhode Island)

116 *Mission Church of San Xavier del Bac* (detail), 1854, from the Pacific Railroad Survey *Report* on the 32nd parallel, 1855–60. (Courtesy Amon Carter Museum, Fort Worth, Texas)

117 Worthington Whittredge *Santa Fe*, July 20, 1866. (Yale University Art Gallery, Gift from the estate of William W. Farnam)

Santa Fe

Long the object of American commerce, Santa Fe was the largest and oldest European settlement in New Mexico Territory. Despite being occupied by the American army in 1846, the city retained much of its Spanish character, with its distinctive low adobe houses and public buildings fronted by timber colonnades.

Reaching Santa Fe with General John Pope's expedition in July, 1866, Worthington Whittredge walked around the village, then settled down to paint a vista with the "low adobe huts in the foreground and looking off over their flat grassgrown roofs to the great valley of the Rio Grande with the beautiful San Dia mountains in the distance." He soon met another resident. "An exceedingly rough-looking fellow with a broken nose and hair matted like the hair of a buffalo stepped up behind me and, with a loud voice,

demanded to know what I asked for the picture." Whittredge explained that the sketch was to be used as a guide to make the finished work and was not for sale. The aesthetically-inclined ruffian persisted: "'You think probably that I haven't any money to buy your picture.'" He pulled out his pistol and continued: "'I have got money enough to buy all the pictures you could paint in a hundred years and I made it all in sight of this ramshackle town, and I want that picture . . . and I'm going to have it.'" Whittredge admitted that things were getting "pretty serious," and he agreed to sell the man the painting after he returned to New York. "'Money,' he ejaculated, 'what will the big picture cost?' I told him about $10,000 without the frame. The frame would cost him about $2,000 more. . . . I handed him my studio address." Whittredge heard no more of him.

176

The houses are of mud bricks, in the Spanish style, generally of one story, and built on a square. The interior of the square is an open court, and the principal rooms open into it. They are forbidding in appearance from the outside, but nothing can exceed the comfort and convenience of the interior. The thick walls make them cool in summer and warm in winter.

W. H. Emory, *Notes of a Military Reconnoissance*, 1848

Santa Fe, the capital of the province of Nuevo Mejico, contains about three thousand inhabitants, and . . . is a wretched collection of mud-houses, without a single building of stone, although it boasts a *palacio* – as the adobe residence of the Governor is called – a long low building, taking up the greater part of one side of the plaza or public square. . . . The appearance of the town defies description, and I can compare it to nothing but a dilapidated brick-kiln or a prairie-dog town.

George Frederick Ruxton, *Wild Life in the Rocky Mountains*, 1846

The Colorado River of the West

The Spaniards had discovered the Grand Canyon during Coronado's march into the Southwestern desert, but few Americans had laid eyes on it when Lieutenant James Christmas Ives pushed up the Colorado River, through the Mojave Canyon, and into the Grand Canyon in 1857 and 1858. His party, including the artist H. B. Möllhausen, went in a shallow-draft steamboat, the U.S.S. "Explorer," which Ives had ordered constructed in Philadelphia the previous summer and had dismantled and reassembled once he reached the mouth of the Colorado. Clusters of Indians lined the riverbank, laughing as the red steamer lurched from sand bar to sand bar, but they soon proved to be a navigational aid to the pilot, who learned to watch for trouble when he saw a crowd of natives.

Lieutenant Ives was probably the first American to walk on the floor of the Grand Canyon, but his report, as complete as it was, paled by comparison to Thomas Moran's paintings of the canyon, especially one that recorded a sudden apocalyptic storm. As Major John Wesley Powell, head of the 1873 expedition that Moran accompanied, explained, "The landscape is too vast, too complex, too grand for verbal description."

The walls, now, are more than a mile in height – a vertical distance difficult to appreciate. . . . A thousand feet of this is up through granite crags, then steep slopes and perpendicular cliffs rise, one above another, to the summit. The gorge is black and narrow below, red and gray and flaring above, with crags and angular projections on the walls, which, cut in many places by side cañons, seem to be a vast wilderness of rocks. . . . Ever, as we go, there is some new pinnacle or tower, some crag or peak, some distant view of the upper plateau, some strange-shaped rock, or some deep, narrow side cañon.

John Wesley Powell, *Exploration of the Colorado River of the West and its Tributaries*, 1875

118 After H. B. MÖLLHAUSEN *Chimney Peak* (detail), from J. C. Ives, *Report Upon the Colorado River of the West*, 1861. (Courtesy Amon Carter Museum, Fort Worth, Texas)

119 After H. B. MÖLLHAUSEN *Mohave Cañon* (detail), 1861, from Ives's *Report Upon the Colorado*. (Courtesy Amon Carter Museum, Fort Worth, Texas)

120 *Overleaf* THOMAS MORAN *Chasm of the Colorado*, 1873–74. (U.S. Department of the Interior)

The Northwest

121 JOSÉ CARDERO *Funeral Pyre and Tombs of the Family of the present An-kay, Port Mulgrave*, 1792. (Museo Naval, Madrid)

Spanish explorers in Alaska

The Pacific Northwest was far away and virtually unknown as the Spanish pushed up the west coast. They soon confronted Russian traders, moving southward from Alaska. England joined the contest when Captain James Cook explored the region in 1778, and President Thomas Jefferson was to involve the United States when he dispatched the Lewis and Clark expedition to the Pacific in 1803.

The Spanish scientific and geographical exploring voyage of Alejandro Malaspina landed on the Northwest coast in 1791 and spent several months searching for a Northwest Passage as well as measuring, recording, drawing, and collecting specimens. José Cardero, a cabin boy turned artist, drew this scene as the Indians of Yakutat Bay, Alaska (which the fur traders called Port Mulgrave), befriended the Spaniards and showed them their burial ground, with its ornate structures.

The bodies here are burned, and the ashes, together with the bones that remain unconsumed, deposited in wooden boxes, which are placed on pillars, that have different figures painted and carved on them, according to the wealth of the deceased. . . . On the death of a toyon, or other distinguished person, one of his slaves is deprived of life, and burned with him. . . . The bodies of those who lose their lives in war are also burned, except the head, which is preserved in a separate wooden box from that in which the ashes and bones are placed. This mode of destroying dead bodies originated, I was informed, in the ridiculous idea, that a piece of the flesh gave to the person who possessed it, the power of doing what mischief he pleased.

Urey Lisiansky, *A Voyage Round the World in the Years 1803, 4, 5, & 6 . . . in the Ship Neva*, 1814

The Colville Indians

Spain and Russia soon relinquished their claims in favour of the Americans, leaving them to squabble with the British over the ultimate fate of the Northwest. The two antagonists agreed to a truce, each hoping that it could bring more settlers into the Oregon Country and successfully press its claim. When a treaty was finally signed in June, 1846, the United States had completed its march to the Pacific.

The Canadian artist Paul Kane, who traveled overland in 1846–48 to document the Indians of the Pacific Northwest, found the Colville Indians living an idyllic existence along the Columbia River. In a climate kept mild by Pacific currents, they were able to catch enough salmon during the spawning season to last them the rest of the year. Early travelers, smelling the rotting salmon, found the habits of the Colvilles repulsive, but a taste of the salmon proved to even the most skeptical that the Indians enjoyed one of nature's greatest blessings.

122 PAUL KANE *Drying Salmon near Colville on the Columbia River* (detail), c.1846. (Courtesy Stark Museum of Art, Orange, Texas)

Salmon is almost the only food used by the Indians on the Lower Columbia River, the two months' fishing affording a sufficient supply to last them the whole year round. The mode in which they cure them is by splitting them down the back, after which each half is again split, making them sufficiently thin to dry with facility, a process occupying in general from four to five days. The salmon are afterwards sewed up in rush mats, containing about ninety or one hundred pounds, and put up on scallfolds to keep the dogs from them.

Paul Kane, *Wanderings of an Artist Among the Indians of North America*, 1859

The Indian village is situated about two miles below the fort, on a rocky eminence overlooking the Kettle Falls. These are the highest in the Columbia River. They are about one thousand yards across, and eighteen feet high. The immense body of water tumbling amongst the broken rocks renders them exceedingly picturesque and grand.

Paul Kane, *Wanderings of an Artist Among the Indians of North America*, 1859

123 PAUL KANE *Falls at Colville* (detail), *c.*1848. (Courtesy Royal Ontario Museum, Toronto)

Indians linger on the Columbia as long as a salmon can be caught. Unconscious of the approaching winter, they do not lay in sufficient stock of provisions, and till late in the fall they may be seen picking up the dead and dying fishes which float in great numbers on the surface. In the immediate neighborhood of a camp the air is infected with the scent of salmon in a state of putrefaction; they are suspended on trees, or on scaffolds, and to this unwholesome and detestable food has the improvident Indian recourse, when the days of his long lent commence.

Father P. J. DeSmet, S. J., *Oregon Missions and Travels Over the Rocky Mountains*, 1847

Disputed territory: Washington State

Vigorous American efforts in 1844 to seize the Oregon Territory motivated the British government to send Lieutenant Henry J. Warre on a military reconnaissance of the country. With secret instructions, Warre and his aide-de-camp and nephew, Lieutenant Vavasour, set out from Montreal on May 5, 1845, as if they were two young gentlemen off on a sporting expedition. They arrived at Fort Vancouver, the principal Hudson's Bay Company post in the region (across the Columbia from Portland, Oregon), at the end of the summer and spent the winter nearby. "We were most cordially welcomed to the wooden walls of Fort Vancouver, when obliged to seek shelter from the perpetual rain, which commenced in November and continued with little intermission til the following march," Warre wrote in his report. By the time he returned to Canada to present that report, Britain and the United States had agreed on the 49th parallel as the boundary, and Washington State, with its rich land and spectacular scenery, was no longer in dispute.

The fort stands at some distance beyond the village, and to the eye appears like an upright wall of pickets, twenty-five feet high: this encloses the houses, shops, and magazines of the Company. . . . At one end is Dr. M'Laughlin's house. . . . Between the steps are two old cannons on sea-carriages, with a few shot, to speak defiance to the natives, who no doubt look upon them as very formidable weapons of destruction. I mention these, as they are the only warlike instruments to my knowledge that are within the pickets of Vancouver.

Charles Wilkes, *Narrative of the United States Exploring Expedition*, 1845

124 After HENRY JAMES WARRE *Fort Vancouver*, from Warre's *Sketches in North America and the Oregon Territory*, 1848. (Courtesy Amon Carter Museum, Fort Worth, Texas)

125 After HENRY JAMES WARRE *Fall of the Peloos River*, from Warre's *Sketches*. (Courtesy Amon Carter Museum, Fort Worth, Texas)

The Chief of this place . . . told me that there was a fall up the Pelouse that no white man had ever seen, and that he would conduct me up the bed of the river, as it was sufficiently shallow for our horses. I accepted his proposal, and rode eight or ten miles through a wild and savage gorge. . . . The chief came up to us and guided us to the falls through one of the boldest and most sublime passes the eye ever beheld. . . . The water falls in one perpendicular sheet of about 600 feet in height, from between rocks of greyish-yellow colour, which rise to about 400 feet above the summit of the fall. The water tumbles into a rocky basin below, with a continuous hollow echoing roar, and courses with great velocity along its bed.

Paul Kane, *Wanderings of an Artist Among the Indians of North America*, 1859

Explorer artists

In the course of his two years' stay in the Northwest, Paul Kane stopped on March 26, 1847, at the mouth of the Kattlepoutal River, twenty-six miles from Fort Vancouver, to draw Mount St Helen's: "This mountain has never been visited by either Whites or Indians. . . . I offered a considerable bribe to any Indian who would accompany me in its exploration, but could not find one hardy enough to venture."

John Mix Stanley was in the region on two different occasions: first, in July and August of 1847, after he had left Colonel Kearny's expedition in California; and second, in the fall of 1853, as artist attached to Stevens's northern railroad survey. His "Scene on the Columbia River" was probably the result of his first trip, when he was more interested in painting the Indians of the Northwest for his proposed Indian Gallery.

126 JOHN MIX STANLEY *Scene on the Columbia River* (detail), c.1852. (Courtesy Amon Carter Museum, Fort Worth, Texas)

St Helen's with smoke from
hovering in a peculiar form
top of the mountain

127 PAUL KANE *Mount St Helen's with smoke from the crater hovering in a peculiar form over the top of the mountain*, 1847. (Courtesy Stark Museum of Art, Orange, Texas)

I stopped to make a sketch of the volcano, Mount St. Helen's, distant, I suppose, about thirty or forty miles. . . . It is of very great height, and being eternally covered with snow, is seen at a great distance. There was not a cloud visible in the sky at the time I commenced my sketch, and not a breath of air was perceptible: suddenly a stream of white smoke shot up from the crater of the mountain, and hovered a short time over its summit; it then settled down like a cap. . . .

About three years before this mountain was in a violent state of irruption for three or four days, and threw up burning stones and lava to an immense height, which ran in burning torrents down its snow-clad sides.

Paul Kane, *Wanderings of an Artist Among the Indians of North America*, 1859

Towns of the Willamette Valley

Immigrants poured into the small towns as traffic along the Oregon Trail increased. The 1847 massacre at the Whitman Mission at the Dalles, on the Columbia, by the Cayuse Indians slowed the migration, then thousands of Forty-Niners, inspired by the discovery of gold in California and the rumours of paradise in Oregon, began to arrive. New houses were put up daily in the flourishing villages along the Willamette Valley as the Oregon Country more than fulfilled the dreams of the hopeful settlers.

Portland was founded in 1845 by two Easterners, who named it after the older town in Maine. By the end of 1851 there were more than 2,000 residents, enough for Portland to eclipse Oregon City as the major settlement on the Willamette. Making good use of its superior port facilities and nearby farmlands, Portland became a supply center for the Northwest and for a burgeoning trade with China. The number of brick structures visible in this view of the west bank and vignettes of individual buildings indicates the town's prosperity.

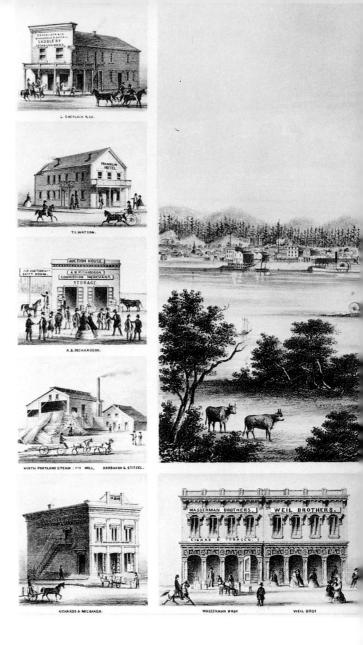

129 *Right* After GRAFTON T. BROWN *City of Portland, Oregon* (detail), *c.*1861. (Courtesy Amon Carter Museum, Fort Worth, Texas)

128 *Below* JOHN MIX STANLEY *Oregon City on the Willamette River* (detail), *c.*1848. (Courtesy Amon Carter Museum, Fort Worth, Texas)

Passing through the timber that lies to the east of the city, we beheld Oregon [City] and the Falls of the Willamette at the same moment. We were so filled with gratitude that we had reached the settlements of the white man, and with admiration at the appearance of the large sheet of water rolling over the Falls, that we stopped, and in this moment of happiness recounted our toils. . . . Among the public buildings, the most conspicuous were the neat Methodist church, which is located near the upper part of the town, and a splendid Catholic chapel, which stands near the river and the bluff bank at the lower part of the town site. . . . The population is computed at about six hundred white inhabitants, exclusive of a few lodges of Indians.

Joel Palmer, *Journal of Travels over the Rocky Mountains to the Mouth of the Columbia River*, 1847

The entire population of Oregon, may now be estimated at about twenty-four thousand, including both whites and Indians, and the white population, including Canadians and half-breeds, now amounts to about four thousand. . . . The American population, and the Canadians and half-breeds . . . are, as before remarked, chiefly settled at the falls of the Wallammette, the Fualitine plain, and the Wallammette valley. They are industrious, orderly, and good citizens; devoting their entire time and attention to the improvement of their farms, the growing of grain, and rearing of herds; they all appear to be intent, only upon the advancement of the general good.

Lansford W. Hastings, *The Emigrants' Guide*, 1845

130 CARL WILLIAM HAHN *Looking down at Yosemite Valley from Glacier Point*, 1874. (Collection of the California Historical Society, San Francisco/San Marino)

By 1876 tourists were close on the heels of the explorers. The Grand Canyon and Yellowstone might still be the domain of Powell and Hayden, but the Yosemite was already in the hands of the tour guides and the travelers.

Inevitably, civilization changed the face of America. But almost at the same time as the discoveries came the conviction that part at least of this untouched land must be kept intact for future generations. It was the origin of the idea of the state park and the national park, both American inventions. Yosemite was among the first. It was a tourist attraction almost from the day the Indians relinquished it; but as it looked then, so it looks today – a corner of America exempt from change.

The Yosemite! . . . The overpowering sense of the sublime, of awful desolation, of transcending marvelousness and unexpectedness, that swept over us, as we reined our horses sharply out of green forests and stood upon a high jutting rock that overlooked this rolling, upheaving sea of granite mountains . . . comes at rare intervals in any life. It was the confrontal of God face to face, as in great danger, in solemn, sudden death. . . . Under sunshine and shadow; by rich, mellow moonlight; by stars opening double wide their eager eyes; through a peculiar August haze, delicate, glowing, creamy, yet hardly perceptible as a distinct element . . . have we seen these, the great natural wonders and beauties of this western world.

Samuel Bowles, *Across the Continent: A Summer's Journey*, 1865

Bibliography

As the original editions of many of these works are scarce, republications that may be more accessible have frequently been cited.

ABERT, J.W. *Report of Lieutenant J.W. Abert, of His Examination of New Mexico, in the Years 1846–47.* House Executive Document No. 41, 30th Congress, 1st Session, 1848. Sometimes bound with Emory, q.v.

The American War of Independence, 1775–83. London: British Museum, 1975

ANGLE, P.M., ed. *Prairie State: Impressions of Illinois, 1673–1967, By Travelers and Other Observers.* Chicago: Univ. of Chicago Press, 1968

ARKELIAN, M.D. *William Hahn, Genre Painter, 1829–1887.* Oakland, Cal.: Oakland Museum, 1976

AUDUBON, J.J. *Audubon and His Journals* (1897). Ed. E. Coues. Freeport, New York: Books for Libraries Press, 1972

AUDUBON, J.J. *Delineations of American Scenery and Character* (1834). London: Simpkin, Marshall, Hamilton, Kent, 1926

AUDUBON, J.J. *Ornithological Biography.* Edinburgh: A. & C. Black, 1831–39

BADGER, D.D. *Illustrations of Iron Architecture, Made by the Architectural Iron Works of the City of New York* (1865). In *The Origins of Cast Iron Architecture in America.* Ed. W.K. Sturges. New York: Da Capo, 1970

BARROW, B.H. *Plantation Diary* (1844–45). See Davis

BARTLETT, J.R. *Personal Narrative of Explorations and Incidents in Texas, New Mexico, California, Sonora, and Chihuahua* (1854). Chicago: Rio Grande Press, 1965

BIEBER, R.H., and HAFEN, L.R., eds. *Southwest Historical Series.* Glendale, Cal.: Arthur H. Clark Co., 1931–43. 12 vols.

BIRD (later Bishop), I.L. *The Englishwoman in America.* London: John Murray, 1856. (This work, published anonymously, is the source of the quote on p.91. The quotes from letters are taken from the following work.)

BIRD (later Bishop), I.L. *A Lady's Life in the Rocky Mountains* (1879). Norman: Univ. of Oklahoma Press, 1960

BOMFORD, G. (1824). Quoted in Mirsky, q.v.

BOONE, D. Quoted in Slotkin, q.v.

von BORCKE, H. *Memoirs of the Confederate War for Independence.* Edinburgh: William Blackwood, 1866

BOWLES, S. *Across the Continent: A Summer's Journey.* Springfield, Mo.: Samuel Bowles & Co., 1865

BRADFORD, W. Quoted in Nash, q.v.

BRIGHT, H.A. *Happy Country This America.* Ed. Anne Henry Ehrenpreis. Columbus: Ohio State Univ. Press, 1978

BRISSOT de WARVILLE, J.P. *New Travels in the United States of America, 1788.* Trans. M.S. Vamos and D. Echeverria. Cambridge, Mass.: Belknap Press of Harvard Univ. Press, 1964

BRYANT, W.C. *The Poetical Works of William Cullen Bryant.* Ed. P. Godwin. New York: D. Appleton, 1883

— See *Picturesque America*

BUFFUM, E.G. *Six Months in the Gold Mines* (1850). Ann Arbor, Mich.: University Microfilms, Inc., 1966

BURTON, R.F. *The City of the Saints and Across the Rocky Mountains to California.* Ed. Fawn M. Brodie. New York: Alfred A. Knopf, 1963

CAIRD, J. In Angle, q.v.

CARVER, J. *Travels Through the Interior Parts of North America in the Years 1766, 1767, and 1768.* London: the author, 1778

CASTAÑEDA DE NAXERA, P. de *Narrative.* In Hammond, q.v.

CATESBY, M. *The Natural History of Carolina, Florida and the Bahama Islands.* London: the author, 1731 (Vol.I), 1743 (Vol.II), [1748] (Appendix). Rev. by G. Edwards. London: C. Marsh, T. Wilcox, B. Stichall, 1754

CATLIN, G. *Fourteen Ioway Indians.* London: W.S. Johnson, 1844

CATLIN, G. *Illustrations of the Manners, Customs, and Condition of the North American Indians, with Letters and Notes* (1841). 10th edn. London: Henry G. Bohn, 1866

CHAMBERLAIN, S.E. *My Confession* (1844–49). Introduction and postscript by R. Butterfield. New York: Harper & Bros., 1956

CHATEAUBRIAND, F.R. de *Travels in America* (1791). Trans. R. Switzer. Lexington: Univ. of Kentucky Press, 1969

CLAPPER, J.C. *Notebook* (1828). In Sibley, q.v.

CLARK, C. *Thomas Moran: Watercolors of the American West.* Austin: Univ. of Texas Press, 1980

CLARK, W., and LEWIS, M. *The Journals of Lewis and Clark.* Ed. B. DeVoto. Boston: Houghton, Mifflin, 1953

COFFIN, C.C. *Four Years of Fighting* (1866). New York: Arno Press, 1970

COLE, T. "Essay on American Scenery." In McCoubrey, q.v.

The Journal of Christopher Columbus. Trans. C. Jane. New York: Bramhall House, 1960

CORONADO, F.V. de Quoted in Hammond, q.v.

CREVECOEUR, J.H. ST J. de *Journey into Northern Pennsylvania and the State of New York* (1801). Trans. C. Spencer Battelmann. Ann Arbor: Univ. of Michigan Press, 1964

CRÈVECOEUR, M.G.J. de *Letters From an American Farmer* (1782). New York: E.P. Dutton & Co., 1957

Daily National Intelligencer on Seymour. Nov.23, 1820

DAVIS, E.A. *Plantation Life in the Florida Parishes of Louisiana, 1836–1846.* New York: Columbia Univ. Press, 1943

DESMET, P.J. *Oregon Missions and Travels Over the Rocky Mountains* (1847). In *Early Western Travels* (see Thwaites) Vol. 29

DICKENS, C. *American Notes* [1842] *and Pictures From Italy.* London: Oxford Univ. Press, 1957

DODGE, G.M. *How We Built the Union Pacific Railway* (1911). Denver: Sage Books, 1965

DUNLAP, W. *A History of the Rise and Progress of the Arts of Design in the United States.* New edn. New York: Dover, 1969

DUNTON, J. *Letters Written From New-England* (1686). American Classics in History and Social Science, no. 2. New York: Burt Franklin, n. d.

EMERSON, R. W. *The Selected Writings of Ralph Waldo Emerson.* Ed. B. Atkinson. New York: Modern Library, 1950

EMORY, W.H. *Notes of a Military Reconnoissance, from Fort Leavenworth, in Missouri, to San Diego, in California, including Part of the Arkansas, Del Norte, and Gila Rivers.* Washington, D.C.: Wendell & Van Bouthuysen, 1848. For further details see the note to Pl. 10g.

EVANS, E. *A Pedestrious Tour of Four Thousand Miles Through the Western States and Territories* (1819). In *Early Western Travels* (see Thwaites), Vol. 8

FLEXNER, J.T. *That Wilder Image: The Painting of America's National School from Thomas Cole to Winslow Homer.* Boston: Little, Brown, 1962

FLINT, T. *A Condensed Geography and History of the Western States* (1828). In McDermott, q.v.

FOOTE, M.H. "A California Mining Camp," *Scribner's Monthly,* 15 (Feb., 1878)

FRANKLIN, B. *The Autobiography of Benjamin Franklin* (1788). Ed. D. Wecter. New York: Holt, Rinehart & Winston, 1948

FRENEAU, P. Quoted in Nash, q.v.

GOETZMANN, W.H. *Exploration and Empire: The Explorer and the Scientist in the Winning of the American West.* New York: Alfred A. Knopf, 1967

GORDON, P. *The Journal of Peter Gordon, 1732–1735.* Ed. E.M. Coulter. Athens: Univ. of Georgia Press, 1963

GREELEY, H. *An Overland Journey from New York to San Francisco* (1860). Ann Arbor, Mich.: University Microfilms Inc., 1966

GREGG, J. *Commerce on the Prairies, or the Journal of a Santa Fe Trader, during Eight Expeditions across the Great Western Prairies, and a Residence of nearly Nine Years in Northern Mexico.* New York: G. Langley, 1844. Ed. M.L. Moorhead. Norman: Univ. of Oklahoma Press, 1954

HAHN, C.W. See Arkelian

HAMMOND, G., and REY, A., eds. *Narratives of the Coronado Expedition, 1540–1542.* Albuquerque: Univ. of New Mexico Press, 1949

HARTE, B. "Brown of Calaveras" (1870), in *The Outcasts of Poker Flat and Other Tales.* New York: New American Library, 1961

HASTINGS, L.W. *The Emigrants' Guide.* Cincinnati: George Conclin, 1845

HAYDEN, F.V. In *The Englishman's Illustrated Guide Book to the United States and Canada.* London: Longmans, Green, Reader, and Dyer, 1879

HAYDEN, F.V. *Preliminary Report of the United States Geological Survey.* House Executive Document No. 325. 42nd Congress, 2nd Session, 1872

HAYDEN, F.V. *Preliminary Report of the United States Geological Survey of Montana and Portions of Adjacent Territories (5th Annual Report).* Washington, D.C.: U.S. Government Printing Office, 1872

HAYDEN, F.V. "The Wonders of the West — II: More About the Yellowstone," *Scribner's Monthly,* 3 (Feb., 1872)

HILGARD, E.W. "The Agriculture and Soils of California" (1878). In *Agriculture in the United States: A Documentary History.* Ed. W.D. Rasmussen. New York: Random House, 1975

HOFFMAN, C.F. *A Winter in the West* (1835). Ann Arbor, Mich.: University Microfilms Inc., 1966

HOLLIDAY, J.S. *The World Rushed In: The California Gold Rush Experience*. New York: Simon & Schuster, 1981

HONOUR, H. *The European Vision of America*. Cleveland: Cleveland Museum of Art, 1975

HONOUR, H. *The New Golden Land: European Images of America from the Discoveries to the Present Time*. New York: Pantheon Books, 1975

HULTON, P., and QUINN, D.B. *The American Drawings of John White, 1577–1590, with Drawings of European and Oriental Subjects*. London: British Museum, 1964

IRVING, W. *Astoria* (1836). Ed. R.D. Rust. Boston: Twayne, 1976

IRVING, W. *A History of New York, by Diedrich Knickerbocker* (1809), in *Selected Writings of Washington Irving*. New York: Modern Library, 1945

IVES, J.C. *Report Upon the Colorado River of the West, Explored in 1857 and 1858*. House Executive Document No. 90. 36th Congress, 1st Session, 1861

JACKSON, W.H. *Time Exposure: The Autobiography of William Henry Jackson*. New York: G.P. Putnam's Sons, 1940

JAMES, E. *Account of an Expedition from Pittsburgh to the Rocky Mountains . . . under . . . Maj. S.H. Long* (Philadelphia: Carey and Lea, 1821–23). Reprinted in *Early Western Travels* (see Thwaites), Vols. 14–16

JARVES, J.J. Quoted in Wilmerding, q.v.

JEFFERSON, T. Letter to Madison quoted in Reps, q.v.

JEFFERSON, T. *Notes on the State of Virginia* (1785, 1787) Ed. W. Peden. Chapel Hill: Univ. of North Carolina Press, 1955

JOSEPHY, A., Jr. *The Artist Was a Young Man: The Life Story of Peter Rindisbacher*. Fort Worth, Tex.: Amon Carter Museum of Western Art, 1970

KANE, P. *Wanderings of an Artist Among the Indians of North America* (1859). In *Paul Kane's Frontier*. Ed. J.R. Harper. Austin: Univ. of Texas Press, 1971

KEMBLE, F.A. *Journal of a Residence on a Georgia Plantation* (1838–39). Ed. J.A. Scott. New York: Alfred A. Knopf, 1961

KENDALL, G.W. *Across the Great Southwestern Prairies* (1844). Ann Arbor, Mich.: University Microfilms, Inc., 1966

KING, Mrs A. In Angle, q.v.

KIPLING, R. *American Notes* (1891). Freeport, N.Y.: Books for Libraries Press, 1972

LEVINGE, R.G.A. *Echoes from the Backwoods; or Sketches of Transatlantic Life*. London: Henry Colburn, 1846

LISIANSKY, U. *A Voyage Round the World in the Years 1803, 4, 5, & 6 . . . in the Ship Neva* (1814). New York: DaCapo, 1968

The Lowell Offering (1844). In *American Issues: The Social Record*. 4th edn. Ed. M. Curti, W. Thorp, and C. Baker. Philadelphia: J.B. Lippincott, 1960

LORANT, S., ed. *The New World: The First Pictures of America*. Rev. ed. New York: Duell, Sloan and Pearce, 1964

LUDLOW, F.H. *The Heart of the Continent*. London: Sampson Low, 1870

MARRYAT, F. *Diary in America* (1839). Ed. J. Zanger. Bloomington: Indiana Univ. Press, 1960

MARTINEAU, H. *Retrospect of Western Travel*. London: Saunders & Otley, 1838

MARX, L. *The Machine in the Garden: Technology and the Pastoral Ideal in America*. New York: Oxford Univ. Press, 1964

MARZIO, P.C. *The Democratic Art: Chromolithography, 1840–1900; Pictures for a 19th-Century America*. Boston: David R. Godine, 1979

MATHER, C. Quoted in Nash q.v.

MCALLISTER, R. *The Civil War Letters of General Robert McAllister*. Ed. J.I. Robertson, Jr. New Brunswick, N.J.: Rutgers Univ. Press, 1965

MCCOUBREY, J., ed. *American Art, 1700–1960: Sources and Documents in the History of Art Series*. Englewood Cliffs, N.J.: Prentice-Hall, 1965

MCDERMOTT, J.F., ed. *Before Mark Twain*. Carbondale: Southern Illinois Univ. Press, 1968

MELVILLE, H. "The Tartarus of Maids" (1855), in *Selected Tales and Poems of Herman Melville*. Ed. R. Chase. New York: Holt, Rinehart & Winston, 1950

MIRSKY, J., and NEVINS, A. *The World of Eli Whitney*. New York: Macmillan, 1952

Monthly Review on Seymour. 102 (Sept., 1823)

MORAN, T. See Clark, C.; *Nation*; *Times*; and Wilkins

"Thomas Moran's Water-Color Drawings," *Scribner's Monthly*, 5 (Jan., 1873)

MOURE, N. "Five Eastern Artists Out West," *American Art Journal*, 5 (Nov., 1973)

NASH, R. *Wilderness and the American Mind*. Rev. edn. New Haven, Conn.: Yale Univ. Press, 1973

Nation on Moran. Sept. 5, 1872

• *New Englands First Fruits* (1643). In *The Founding of Harvard College*, by S.E. Morison. Cambridge, Mass.: Harvard Univ. Press, 1935

Niles Weekly Register on Seymour. 23 (Feb.8, 1823)

North American Review on the Pacific Railroad Surveys. 82 (1856)

NOVAK, B. *American Painting of the Nineteenth Century*. New York: Praeger 1969

NOVAK, B. *Nature and Culture: American Landscape and Painting, 1825–1875*. London: Thames and Hudson; New York: Oxford Univ. Press, 1980

PARKMAN, F. *The Oregon Trial* (1849). Boston: Little, Brown, 1925

PENN, T. Quoted in Snyder, q.v.

Picturesque America; or, the Land we live in. Ed. W.C. Bryant. New York: D. Appleton, 1872–74; rev. edn. 1894

PIERCY, F. *Route From Liverpool to Great Salt Lake Valley* (1853). Ed. J. Linforth. London: Latter-Day Saints' Book Depot; Liverpool: Franklin Richards, 1855

POWELL, J.W. "The Cañons of the Colorado," *Scribner's Monthly*, 9 (Jan., Feb., 1875)

POWELL, J.W. *Canyons of the Colorado* (1895). New York: Dover, 1961

POWELL, J.W. *Exploration of the Colorado River of the West and its Tributaries* (1875). In *Grand Canyon: An Anthology*. Ed. B. Babbitt. Flagstaff, Ariz.: Northland Press, 1978

PREUSS, C. *Exploring With Frémont*. Trans. and ed. by E.G. and E.K. Gudde. Norman: Univ. of Oklahoma Press, 1958

Reports of Explorations and Surveys, to Ascertain the Most Practicable and Economic Route for a Railroad from the Mississippi River to the Pacific Ocean. Washington, D.C., 1855–60. 12 vols.

REPS, J.W. *Tidewater Towns: City Planning in Colonial Virginia and Maryland*. Williamsburg, Va.: Colonial Williamsburg, Inc., 1972

RINDISBACHER, P. See Josephy

RUSH, B. Quoted in Nash, q.v.

RUSSELL, W.H. *My Diary North and South* (1861). Ed. F. Pratt. New York: Harper & Bros., 1954

RUXTON, G.F. *Wild Life in the Rocky Mountains* (1846). New York: Macmillan, 1916

SCHWAAB, E.L. and BULL, J., eds. *Travels in the Old South: Selected from Periodicals of the Times*. Lexington: Univ. of Kentucky Press, 1973

SHUMWAY, G. and FREY, H.C., eds. *Conestoga Wagon 1750–1850*. 3rd edn. York, Pa.: George Shumway 1968

SIBLEY, M.McA. *Travelers in Texas, 1761–1860*. Austin: Univ. of Texas Press, 1967

SIMPSON, J.H. *Navaho Exhibition: Journal of a Military Reconnaissance from Santa Fe, New Mexico to the Navaho Country, 1849*. Ed. F. McNitt. Norman: Univ. of Oklahoma Press, 1964

SLOTKIN, R. *Regeneration through Violence: The Mythology of the American Frontier, 1600–1860*. Middletown, Conn.: Wesleyan Univ. Press, 1973

SMITH, W.L. *Journal of William Loughton Smith, 1790–1791*. In Reps, q.v.

SNYDER, M.P. *City of Independence: Views of Philadelphia before 1800*. New York: Praeger 1975

STEGNER, W. *The Gathering of Zion: The Story of the Mormon Trail*. New York: McGraw-Hill, 1964

TAFT, R. *Artists and Illustrators of the Old West, 1850–1900*. New York: Charles Scribner's Sons, 1953

TAYLOR, J.C. *The Fine Arts in America*. Chicago: Univ. of Chicago Press, 1979

THOREAU, H.D. *Walden and Other Writings*. Ed. B. Atkinson. New York: Modern Library, 1950

THORPE, T.B. "Sugar and the Sugar Region of Louisiana" (1853). In Schwaab, q.v.

THWAITES, REUBEN GOLD, ed. *Early Western Travels, 1748–1846*. Cleveland: Arthur H. Clark, 1904–07. 32 vols.

Times on Moran. In Marzio, q.v.

TOCQUEVILLE, A. de *Journey to America* (1831). Trans. G. Lawrence. Ed. J.P. Mayer. New Haven, Conn.: Yale Univ. Press, 1959

TROLLOPE, A. *North America* (1862). Ed. D. Smalley and B.A. Booth. New York: Alfred A. Knopf, 1951

TROLLOPE, Mrs F. *Domestic Manners of the Americans*. London: Whittaker, Treacher, 1832

TRUETTNER, W.H. *National Parks and the American Government*. Washington, D.C.: Smithsonian Institution Press, 1972

TUCKERMAN, H.T. *Book of the Artists*. New York, 1867

TURNER, F.J. "The Significance of the Frontier in American History," in American Historical Association *Annual Report, 1893*. Washington, D.C., 1893

TWAIN, M. *Life on the Mississippi* (1883). New York: New American Library, 1961

TWAIN, M. *Roughing It* (1872). Ed. Franklin R. Rogers and Paul Baender. Berkeley: Univ. of California Press, 1972

"A Visit to the States" (1887). In *As Others See Chicago*. Ed. B.L. Pierce. Chicago: Univ. of Chicago Press, 1933

A Visit to Texas: Being the Journal of a Traveler through those Parts most interesting to American Settlers (attrib. Asahel Langworthy). New York: Goodrich & Wiley, 1834

WHITE, JOHN. See Hulton

WHITING, W.H.C. *Journal* (1849). In Southwest Historical Series (see Bieber), Vol. 7

WHITMAN, W. *Complete Poetry and Selected Prose of Walt Whitman*. Ed. J.E. Miller, Jr. Boston: Houghton, Mifflin, 1959

WHITMAN, W. *Specimen Days in America* (1882). In *The Best of Whitman*. Ed. H.W. Blodgett. New York: Ronald Press, 1953

WHITTREDGE, W. *Autobiography* (c. 1905). Ed. J.I.H. Baur. *Brooklyn Museum Journal*, 1942

WIED-NEUWIED, M. of *Travels in the Interior of North America* (1843). In *Early Western Travels* (see Thwaites), Vols. 22–24

WIED-NEUWIED, M. of *People of the First Man*. Ed. D. Thomas and K. Ronnefeldt. New York: E.P. Dutton, 1977

WILKES, C. *Narrative of the United States Exploring Expedition*. Philadelphia: Lea & Blanchard, 1845

WILKINS, T. *Thomas Moran, Artist of the Mountains*. Norman: Univ. of Oklahoma Press, 1966

WILLARD, M.W., ed. *Letters on the American Revolution, 1774–1776*. Boston: Houghton, Mifflin, 1925

WILMERDING, J. *American Light: The Luminist Movement, 1850–1875; Paintings, Drawings, Photographs*. Washington, D.C.: National Gallery of Art, 1980

WOODS, J. *Two Years' Residence in the Settlement on the English Prairie, in the Illinois Country, United States* (1822). Ed. P.M. Angle. Chicago: R.R. Donnelley & Sons, 1968

Annotated catalogue of the illustrations

Measurements, which are in centimeters, relate to the image only; height precedes width. Printed books that appear in the Bibliography (pp.193–94) are given in abridged form here. Square brackets are used to indicate authors and titles that have been assigned.

p.2 Jasper F. Cropsey, *Niagara Falls*, 1860
Oil on canvas, 91.4 × 64.5
Collection of Jo Ann and Julian Ganz, Jr.
Cropsey (1823–1900) was one of the most popular painters in America at mid-century. Born in Rossville, New York, he spent a considerable time in Europe, and this picture was painted during an extended stay in 1856–63 in England, where a swell of interest in Hudson River pictures led him to paint several typical views. *Niagara Falls*, which shows figures on Goat Island with Horseshoe Falls and the Canadian side of the Falls in the background, arrived in the United States in 1861. The *New York Tribune* reviewed it as a "novel view of that very hackneyed subject." Perhaps Cropsey painted it as a reaction to Church's definitive image of the Falls from the usual point of view (Pl.21).

p.10 Unknown artist, *Insula Hyspana*. From Christopher Columbus, "Letter to Gabriel Sánchez" (Basel, 1493)
Woodcut, max. 11.3 × 7.5
The New York Public Library, Astor, Lenox and Tilden Foundations
The Basel printer seems to have modified a design previously used to illustrate Mediterranean voyages, labeling it "Insula Hyspana" – "the Spanish island." The oar-powered galley is a Mediterranean, not ocean-going, vessel.

p.11 Unknown artist, [The King of Spain directs Columbus's landing in the Indies]. From Giuliano Dati, *La lettera dellisole che ha trouato nuouamente il Re dispagna* (Florence, 1493)
Woodcut, 11.7 × 11.3
British Library, London
Published on the cover of a 68-stanza Italian verse translation of Columbus's letter, this woodcut appears to be the first image specially designed to depict America. The king is presumably Ferdinand, in whose service Columbus sailed.

pp.12–13
Jan Mostaert, " *An Episode in the Conquest of America*," or "*West Indian Landscape*," c. 1542
Oil on oak panel, 86.5 × 152.5
State-Owned Art Collections Department, The Hague (Dienst Verspreide Rijkskollekties te den Haag)
This picture has perplexed scholars ever since its discovery in 1909. It is probably the one described by Carel van Mander in his *Het Schilder-boeck* (Alkmaar, 1604) as "a West Indian Landscape." In 1931 Edouard Michel correctly noted that West Indies to Mostaert could have been anywhere in the New World and surmised that it might have depicted a scene from Cortez's conquest of Mexico. Not until 1948 did R. van Luttervelt suggest that it might be, instead, taken from Coronado's march into the American Southwest.
Mostaert (c. 1475–1555/56) was born in Haarlem. He probably traveled around Europe for several years before settling down to become court painter to the Regent Margaret.

p.14 Theodor de Bry after Jacques Le Moyne de Morgues, [Map-view of part of Florida, showing "Cedar Island"]. From de Bry, *Indorum Floridam provinciam inhabitantium eicones* (Frankfurt, 1591)
Engraving, 15.9 × 20.6
British Library, London

p.15 Jacques Le Moyne de Morgues, *René de Laudonnière and Chief Athore*, 1564
Gouache, 17.8 × 26
The New York Public Library, Astor, Lenox and Tilden Foundations
This image was known from Theodor de Bry's engraving (*Indorum Floridam . . . eicones*, pl.VIII), but the original painting was lost until 1901, when it was identified in a private collection in Paris.
The engraving is titled "The natives of Florida worship the column erected by the commander on his first voyage." Le Moyne noted that the chief was "very handsome, prudent, honorable, and of very great stature, being more than half a foot taller than the tallest of our men."

p.17 John White, *Indians fishing*, c. 1585
Watercolor heightened with white over black lead outlines, 35.3 × 23.5
British Museum, London

p.18 Theodor de Bry after Jacques Le Moyne de Morgues, [A council of state between the chiefs and principal councillors]. From de Bry, *Indorum Floridam provinciam inhabitantium eicones* (Frankfurt, 1591)
Engraving, 15 × 20.4
British Library, London
The chief consulted with the principal men of the tribe to discuss important affairs. As he called on the men to respond to his questions, the women served *casina*, a drink boiled from a root that was so potent that it immediately induced a sweat, and men who could not keep it down were considered unreliable for a difficult mission or military responsibility.

p.21 After Father Louis Hennepin, [Niagara Falls]. From Hennepin, *Voyage curieux . . . qui contient une nouvelle découverte . . . dans l'Amérique* (The Hague, 1704)
Engraving, 14.3 × 16.9
British Library, London
Hennepin wrote of Niagara Falls in his first book, *Description de la Louisiane* (Paris, 1683), describing the turbulence of the water and its thundering roar, and giving the Falls' height as over 500 feet (it is actually 193 feet). In his second book, *Nouvelle découverte d'un très grand pays situé dans l'Amérique* (Utrecht, 1697), he made the description more dramatic, increasing the height to over 600 feet, and included this illustration. The pages of the *Nouvelle découverte* were bound up again, with additional matter, in 1704, under the title *Voyage curieux*. In his 1697 book Hennepin, making use of various sources, recounted a journey he claimed to have made the full length of the Mississippi two years before La Salle. As a result his reputation as an explorer is severely tarnished.

p.22 Thomas Jefferys after George Heap, *An East Prospect of the City of Philadelphia; taken by George Heap from the Jersey Shore, under the Direction of Nicholas Scull, Surveyor General of the Province of Pennsylvania*, 1756
Engraving, 49.2 × 91.1
The Library Company of Philadelphia
The original, large, version of the "Scull and Heap" view was produced in 1754. Heap had made a drawing of the city and was taking it to London to have it engraved when he suddenly died. Scull, who had collaborated with him on a map of the city, purchased the drawing from

Heap's widow, and Thomas Penn had it engraved in four sections which, combined, are over 2 m. long.

Penn did not like the huge size of that view, nor did it clearly show that Philadelphia is a river port; so he employed Jefferys, a London engraver, to make this reduction, which is slightly less than half-size. The view was republished in several different versions over the years.

p.23 Michael Angelo Rooker, probably after Jonathan Carver, "The falls of St. Anthony in the River Mississippi, near 2400 miles from its entrance into the Gulf of Mexico." From Carver, *Travels Through the Interior Parts of North America* (1778)
Engraving, 10.1 × 17.5
Amon Carter Museum, Fort Worth, Texas
Returning to England in 1769 to get his journal published, Carver failed to get government support, and finally published it himself.

p.24 Paul Revere, *The Bloody Massacre perpetrated in King Street, Boston on March 5th 1770*
Engraving (hand colored), 19.7 × 22.1
The Metropolitan Museum of Art, New York, Gift of Mrs Russell Sage, 1910
Three weeks after the incident Paul Revere produced 200 copies of this print for Edes and Gill of Boston at a cost of £5. The coloring was probably done by Christian Remick, a mariner and artist, who was born in Eastham, Massachusetts, in 1726. It is Revere's best known print, even though he was accused of plagiarism at the time by Henry Pelham, the Boston painter and engraver, who placed an almost identical print on sale the following week.

pp.26–27 Pierre L'Enfant, [Panorama of West Point, New York] (detail), 1778?
Watercolor, 26 × 41
Library of Congress, Washington, D.C.
L'Enfant's four-part panoramic view was probably made in the late summer of 1778, while he was attached to General Baron von Steuben's staff. It shows the American troop encampments near the Hudson River.

Louis Nicolas van Blarenberghe, *The Siege of Yorktown in Virginia, October 18, 1781* (detail), 1784
Gouache, 58.8 × 94
Musée National du Château de Versailles
Van Blarenberghe (1716/19–94) depicts the scene leading up to Lord Cornwallis's surrender on the following day. Maneuvers can be seen in the left foreground as French troops march toward the front in trenches, which protect them from cannon shot. In the center of the group, with the Cross of St Louis pinned to his coat, is the Comte de Rochambeau. The man with the map, in the center of the group behind Rochambeau, is probably Duportail, the chief engineer in the Continental Army, who played an important role in the Yorktown campaign. Smoke rises from the redoubts in the distance, signifying that the battle is under way.

Van Blarenberghe based the painting on eyewitness sketches made by Louis-Alexandre Berthier, a French engineer and illustrator who was a member of Rochambeau's army. He presented another version of the painting to Rochambeau.

p.28 James Otto Lewis after Chester Harding, *Col. Daniel Boon* [sic], 1820
Stipple engraving, 29.9 × 20.5

St Louis Art Museum
Little is known of James Otto Lewis (1799–1858), who was born in Philadelphia and died in obscurity in New York City. He was producing engravings in Philadelphia by 1815, and his major work is the *Aboriginal Port-Folio: A Collection of Portraits of the Most Celebrated Chiefs of the North American Indians* (Philadelphia, 1835–36). This portrait of Daniel Boone was copied after an oil painting by Chester Harding (1792–1866), a soldier, sign painter, tavern keeper, and portrait painter who had settled around 1818 in Paris, Kentucky, where he no doubt heard much of the Boone legend.

p.30 Charles Willson Peale, *Meriwether Lewis* (detail), 1807
Oil on wood panel, 58.4 × 47.6
Independence National Historical Park Collection, Philadelphia
In 1782, as he was developing what became the first public museum in America, Peale built a long gallery onto his house, which would serve as an exhibition area for his portraits of "distinguished characters." Among the statesmen, military heroes, writers, artists, and scientists who made up this gallery four years later were the young explorers who were helping gather knowledge about the continent, including Lewis. Peale's portraits were done in a simple and unadorned style, suggesting that the virtues of the sitters were apparent without enhancement.

p.31 Charles Willson Peale, *Stephen H. Long* (detail), 1819
Oil on canvas, 61.6 × 51.4
Independence National Historical Park, Philadelphia
Peale was almost eighty when Long began to plan his expedition into the West in 1818. When Peale was in Washington that year he took time to paint portraits of Long and the scientist members of his expedition, in a successful effort to secure a place in the party for his son, Titian.

Samuel Seymour, *Pawnee Council*, 1819
Watercolor, 20.5 × 15
Beinecke Rare Book and Manuscript Library, Yale University
Made in October when Long's party were settled at "Engineer Cantonment" (see the following note), this painting shows the conference that Long and Benjamin O'Fallon arranged with three Pawnee tribes, to make them give back property that they had taken from Thomas Say, the expedition naturalist, and members of his party a few weeks before. The Indians sit facing the army officers and a small military band. The American flag flies by the tents, and soldiers in dress uniforms patrol the camp.

p.32 Titian Ramsay Peale, *Engineer Cantonment, Feb. 1820*
Watercolor, 12.1 × 19
American Philosophical Society Library, Philadelphia
"Engineer Cantonment," the expedition's winter base, was on the west side of the Missouri, 8 km. from the "Council Bluff" of Lewis and Clark (opposite the present Council Bluffs, Iowa). This is one of Peale's rare surviving landscapes. Most of his known sketches are of wildlife.

p.33 F. Kearney after Samuel Seymour, *View of the*

Rocky Mountains on the Platte 50 Miles from Their Base. From Edwin James, *Account of an Expedition . . . under . . . Maj. S.H. Long* (atlas, 1822)
Engraving, 13.5 × 21.1
Amon Carter Museum, Fort Worth, Texas
The original drawing was made in early July, 1820, as the Long expedition caught its first glimpse of the Rockies.

Peter Rindisbacher, *Assiniboin hunting on Snowshoes* (detail), 1833
Watercolor, 24.6 × 41.5
Amon Carter Museum, Fort Worth, Texas

p.34 George Catlin, *William Clark* (detail), 1830
Oil on canvas, 72.4 × 59.7
National Portrait Gallery, Smithsonian Institution, Washington, D.C.
Catlin painted this portrait of General Clark (1770–1838) in the summer of 1830.

p.35 George Catlin, *Catlin painting the Portrait of Mah-to-toh-pa – Mandan* (detail), 1857–69
Oil on cardboard, 39 × 60.6
National Gallery of Art, Washington, D.C.

George Catlin, *Little Bear, A Hunkpapa Brave*, 1832
Oil on canvas, 76.6 × 61
National Museum of American Art (formerly National Collection of Fine Arts), Smithsonian Institution, Washington, D.C., Gift of Mrs Joseph Harrison

p.36 George Catlin, *The Cutting Scene*, 1832
Oil on canvas, 60 × 70.8
Harmsen Collection, Denver
In the climax of the O-kee-pa ceremony, inside the Mandan lodge, the initiates, with wood spikes through their back and pectoral muscles, are quickly hoisted in the air. Those who had survived the ceremony previously lined the lodge to watch.

p.37 A. Manceau after Karl Bodmer, *The Travellers meeting with Minatarre Indians. Near Fort Clark* (detail), 1840. From Maximilian of Wied-Neuwied, *Voyage dans l'interieur de l'Amérique du Nord . . .* (Paris: Arthus Bertrand, 1840–43)
Aquatint and etching with stipple, 19.7 × 29.8
Amon Carter Museum, Fort Worth, Texas
Prince Maximilian, David Dreidoppel, and Karl Bodmer (a native of Zurich and student of Ingres) landed in Boston in the summer of 1832 and traveled westward va New York and Pennsylvania to Harmony, Indiana, where they spent the winter in the company of the entomologist Thomas Say (who had been on Major Long's expedition) and the French naturalist C.A. Lesueur (see Pl.59). Continuing to St Louis, they set out up the Missouri in April, 1833, reaching their farthest point, Fort McKenzie in Montana, in the summer. They turned back in September, and overwintered at Fort Clark, in Mandan and Minnetaree (Hidatsa) country. Passing again through St Louis and Harmony, they returned via Lake Erie and Niagara Falls to New York, where they embarked for Europe in July, 1834.

There, Maximilian settled down to edit his hundreds of pages of notes, and Bodmer went to Paris, to begin work on the 81 plates based on his field watercolors that would appear, in a separate atlas volume, with the Prince's text. Many of the prints were virtual copies of the sketches, but others were combinations of individual portraits. The Prince's book was first published in German in 1839–41 (*Reise in* das Innere Nord-America in den Jahren 1832 bis 1834) at Coblenz, then in French in 1840–43, and finally in English in 1843. The plates remained the same, having been prepared with trilingual captions. The most expensive sets were fully hand-colored, but partially colored and uncolored sets were available. Bodmer spent four years supervising their production.

Our illustrations are taken from a copy of the French edition, our text quotations from the English translation. The plates themselves are undated, and the date I have ascribed to them, 1840, can only be approximate.

A. Manceau and J. Hürlimann after Karl Bodmer, *Fort Mackenzie [sic], August 28th, 1833*, 1840. From Maximilian of Wied-Neuwied, *Voyage* (see the preceding note)
Engraving, 30.4 × 44
Amon Carter Museum, Fort Worth, Texas
The watercolor or sketch from which this unusual print was made is not known to exist, and the print is only infrequently colored.

p.38 J. Hürlimann after Karl Bodmer, *Mato-Topé. A Mandan Chief*, 1840. From Maximilian of Wied-Neuwied, *Voyage* (see the note to the first illustration on p.37)
Engraving, 41.5 × 32
Maximilian wrote of Mato-Topé: "He has been so often mentioned in my narrative that I must here subjoin a few words respecting this eminent man, for he was fully entitled to this appellation, being not only a distinguished warrior, but possessing many fine and noble traits of character.

Mato-Topé after repeated solicitations, prevailed on Mr. Bodmer to paint for him a white-headed eagle, holding in his claws a bloody scalp, to which he, doubtless, attached some superstitious notion, but I could not see exactly what it might be. Mato-Topé gave me very accurate information respecting his own language, and that of the neighboring Indian nations, and took great pleasure in communicating to me the words of the Mandan and Arikkara languages, the latter of which he spoke fluently."

p.39 Alfred Jacob Miller, *Self-Portrait*, c. 1837
Pencil, 18.6 × 22.8
The InterNorth Art Foundation, Joslyn Art Museum, Omaha
Miller sketched this on the back of a watercolor of fur trappers and voyageurs probably soon after he had started on his Western adventure.

Alfred Jacob Miller, *Indian Encampment near the Wind River Mountains*, c. 1837
Pencil with black and gray washes, 16.2 × 24.1
Whitney Gallery of Western Art, Buffalo Bill Historical Center, Cody, Wyoming, Gift of the Joseph M. Roebling Estate
After Miller returned to New Orleans and began in the fall of 1837 to work his sketches into finished paintings for Captain Stewart, he also produced a set of wash drawings that illustrate the entire expedition, which Stewart, upon his return to Murthly Castle, kept in a "richly bound portfolio" in the drawing room. They contain more frequent portraits of the captain than Miller's other work. This drawing comes from that set.

p.40 Alfred Jacob Miller, *The Trapper's Bride (Bartering for a Bride)*, 1845
Oil on canvas, 91.4 × 71.1
Courtesy Harrison Eiteljorg, Indianapolis, Indiana

This painting is based on an incident that Miller observed at the rendezvous. A half-breed trapper named François purchased an Indian woman for his wife, paying the bride's father the equivalent of $600 in guns, horse blankets, red flannels, alcohol, and sugar, tobacco, beads, and other trade goods. After Miller arrived at Murthly Castle to continue painting for Stewart, he began work on a canvas of this scene over 3 meters high, one of his largest paintings and proudest accomplishments. It was auctioned in Edinburgh in 1871 and has not been located since.

Alfred Jacob Miller, *Trapping Beaver* (detail), 1858–60
Watercolor, 22.5 × 32.4
Walters Art Gallery, Baltimore
Having searched the area for "sign" of beaver, such as footprints in the muddy or sandy bank, these trappers are now in the process of setting their traps in the beds that they have dug with their knives. Each trap will be firmly tied to a tree or a stick driven into the mud.

p.41 Charles Preuss (?), *The Pyramid Lake*. From John C. Frémont, *Report of the Exploring Expedition to the Rocky Mountains in the Year 1842, and to OregoN and North California in the Years 1843–44* (Washington, 1845)
Lithograph, 10.3 × 18.3
Amon Carter Museum, Fort Worth, Texas
"In short daily journeys we came to a deep lake . . . [that] has no outlet," wrote Preuss of Pyramid Lake, which is now within the boundaries of the Pyramid Lake Indian Reservation. "It teems with the most magnificent salmon trout . . . Strange volcanic rocks."

Bass Otis, *John Charles Frémont* (detail), 1856
Oil on canvas, 122.5 × 108
The University of Michigan Museum of Art, Ann Arbor, Bequest of Henry C. Lewis
Bass Otis (1784–1858), a New York City and Philadelphia portrait painter whose chief claim to fame was that he made the first lithograph in America, painted this campaign portrait of Frémont in the year when the "great pathfinder" won nomination as the first Republican candidate for president. (He was defeated by Buchanan.)

p.43 John Russell Bartlett, *Crossing the Pecos*, c. 1851
Pencil and sepia wash, 22.8 × 30.5
John Carter Brown Library, Providence, R.I.
En route from San Antonio to El Paso to take command of the boundary survey, Bartlett had to cross the Pecos River, which at this time of year was on the rampage. Several of the wagons of the caravan got stuck in the mud and almost overturned in the current. Bartlett abandoned his heavily armed and weighted carriage and rode to shore on the back of one of his men. The illustration is included in his *Personal Narrative*, Vol. II, p.98.

John Russell Bartlett, *Guadalupe Mountain, Texas*, c. 1852
Pencil and sepia wash, 24.1 × 33
John Carter Brown Library, Providence, R.I.
After crossing the Pecos, Bartlett encountered the "bare rocky shelf" of Guadalupe Pass and the 2,667-meters-high Guadalupe Peak, now a part of the Guadalupe Mountains National Park. He paused to produce one of the most striking drawings of his entire trip West. It is reproduced in his *Personal Narrative*, Vol. I, p.118.

p.44–45 John Mix Stanley after Gustavus Sohon, *Main chain of the Rocky Mountains, as seen from the east – extending from a point north of the Marias Pass to near the Little Blackfoot Pass*. From *Reports of Explorations and Surveys . . . for a Railroad . . . to the Pacific Ocean* (1855–60), Vol. XII
Colored lithograph, 32.6 × 60
Amon Carter Museum, Fort Worth, Texas
Gustavus Sohon (1825–1903) came to the United States in 1842. Ten years later he volunteered for the army and found himself a member of Isaac Stevens's survey from the Mississippi River to Puget Sound. In the summer of 1855, after his party had crossed the Rockies, Sohon produced this panorama, extending southward from Chief Mountain near the Canadian border.

p.47 Thomas Cole, *Landscape with Tree Trunks*, 1825
Oil on canvas, 67.3 × 82
Museum of Art, Rhode Island School of Design, Providence, Walter H. Kimball Fund
"All nature here is new to art, no Tivolis, Ternis, Mount Blancs, Plinlimmons, hackneyed and worn by the daily pencils of hundreds," wrote Cole, "but primeval forests, virgin lakes and waterfalls."

p.49 Thomas Cole, *The Oxbow (The Connecticut River near Northampton)*, 1836
Oil on canvas, 130.8 × 193
The Metropolitan Museum of Art, New York, Gift of Mrs Russell Sage, 1908
Oxbow, something of a change of pace for Cole, who was working hard on his series entitled *The Course of Empire*, was painted for the 1836 National Academy of Design exhibition.

p.50 Asher B. Durand, *Study from Nature – Rocks and Trees*, c. 1855
Oil on canvas, 43.1 × 54.6
The New-York Historical Society, New York City, Gift of Mrs Lucy M. Durand Woodman, 1907

p.51 Asher B. Durand, *The American Wilderness*, 1864
Oil on canvas, 64.1 × 101.6
Cincinnati Art Museum, The Edwin & Virginia Irwin Memorial

p.52 Fitz Hugh Lane, *Brace's Rock, Eastern Point, Gloucester*, 1863
Oil on canvas, 25.4 × 38.1
Private collection
Lane was a careful draughtsman, being trained as a printmaker and employing some of the tricks of that trade throughout his career to obtain the clarity and exactness of line that characterize his paintings.

p.53 John Frederick Kensett, *Upper Mississippi*, 1855
Oil on canvas, 47 × 77.5
St Louis Art Museum, Eliza McMillan Fund
Of this painting a reporter for *The Crayon*, a New York journal devoted to the arts, wrote: "Mr. Kensett has just completed a medium sized picture of a view on the Mississippi River, embracing a range of 'bluffs' on the banks of that stream. The eye takes in a series of bluffs on the left, running off into perspective; the remaining portion of the picture being the surface of the river. The latter is enlivened by a couple of birds just rising from the water, in the foreground. The time is toward sunset, indicated by the sunlight striking on the top of

the rocks projecting above the foliage. This picture is an interesting representation of one phase of our peculiar scenery."

p.55 Sanford R. Gifford, *Valley of the Chug Water, Wyoming Ter., Aug. 9th 1870*
Oil on canvas, 21 × 33.8
Amon Carter Museum, Fort Worth, Texas
Gifford and the photographer William Henry Jackson became good friends during Gifford's first trip West, in 1870, and traveled together on several occasions. To this friendship we owe one of the most unusual documents of painters in the West. Jackson wrote in his autobiography that "Gifford . . . and I would go off to record our respective impressions of a striking landmark": while Gifford, sitting on a rocky hillside, sketched this small oil, Jackson set up his bulky camera and photographed the artist, picture on his knee. The photograph is in the collection of the U.S. Geological Survey Library, Denver, Colorado.

p.56 William H. Holmes, *William H. Holmes and George B. Chittenden measuring a High Mountain Station, 1874*
Black and white wash, 23 × 16.4
National Museum of American Art (formerly National Collection of Fine Arts), Smithsonian Institution, Washington, D.C.
Holmes (1846–1933) worked at the Smithsonian Institution as a scientific illustrator, then joined the 1872 Hayden expedition into the Yellowstone. He followed Hayden into Colorado, where this dramatic wash drawing was made, perhaps after a Jackson photograph (U.S. Geological Survey collection). His major works are the illustrations for Major Clarence Dutton's *The Tertiary History of the Grand Canyon District* (1882).

p.57 Thomas Moran, *The Grand Canyon of the Yellowstone*, 1872
Oil on canvas, 219 × 358
U.S. Department of the Interior, on loan to the National Museum of American Art (formerly National Collection of Fine Arts), Smithsonian Institution, Washington, D.C.

p.59 After Thomas Almond Ayres, *General View of the Great Yo-semite Valley, Mariposa County, California*, 1859
Toned lithograph (hand colored), 45.7 × 60.9
Amon Carter Museum, Fort Worth, Texas
Ayres (c. 1818–58) arrived in San Francisco during the height of the Gold Rush. He evidently spent some time in the mines, but by 1850 he had begun to move throughout the north-central part of the state sketching and selling pictures. In 1855 Ayres was employed by James Mason Hutchings to accompany him to Yosemite to make pictures for his proposed *California Illustrated Magazine*, and made a second trip to Yosemite the following year. In 1857 he took some thirteen views of the valley to New York and exhibited them at the Art Union. Impressed by his ability, Harper Brothers sent him back to California to do a series of sketches for their magazine. After he had spent some time in Southern California, he boarded the *Laura Bevan* bound for San Francisco. It sank in a storm off Point Dume, and all aboard perished. Ayres's prints of Yosemite were issued the following year.

p.60 Thomas Eakins, *Pushing for Rail*, 1874
Oil on canvas, 30.5 × 76.2
The Metropolitan Museum of Art, New York, Arthur H. Hearn Fund, 1916

pp.62–63
Sketch map of the United States. (The relationship between boundaries and rivers is shown in purely schematic form.) Drawn by Hanni Bailey

1 Asher B. Durand, *Kindred Spirits*, 1849
Oil on canvas, 116.8 × 94
Art and Architecture Division, The New York Public Library, Astor, Lenox and Tilden Foundations
Bryant (1794–1878) and Cole (1801–48) – the leading nature poet and painter of the time, and old friends – stand on a mountain ledge that is a bit larger in relation to the composition than most landscape painters would permit, but it is a balanced work that contains the intense detail that Durand had learned as an engraver, although he had, by this time, begun painting bold plein-air compositions.
Kindred Spirits was painted at the suggestion of Jonathan Sturges, the patron of Cole and Durand. He had lent Durand money for a European trip, and gave him $300 credit for the picture, which he presented to Bryant as a memorial, in acknowledgement of his funeral oration for Cole, who had died the previous year.

2 Jan Vinckeboons, *Nieuw-Amsterdam ofte nue Nieuw Iorx opt Eijlant Man* (New Amsterdam or now New York on the Island of Man[hattan]) (detail), c. 1650–64
Watercolor, 41.9 × 61.3
Algemeen Rijksarchief, The Hague
Vinckeboons, an engraver and cartographer born in Amsterdam, probably drew this view from a sketch made on the spot.

3 John Harris after William Burgis, *A South East View of the Great Town of Boston in New England in America* (detail), 1725, 1736
Engraving, 60.2 × 131
British Library, London
This, Burgis's second view of Boston, is taken from the southeast, with the Long Wharf appearing near the center of the picture. The Town House (later the State House) can be seen near the land end of the wharf, with other clearly recognizable buildings on either side.
This version of the print contains "pasters," engraved additions that have been cut out and pasted onto the print, to update it to 1736. (The Hollis Street Meeting House (1731) has been added on the Neck, in the far left of the print, and the spires of Trinity Church (1734) and Lynds Street Meeting House (1736) have been added, with supplementary identifications pasted onto the legend.)

4 Lieutenant William Pierie, [Map and views of Boston and the surrounding area], 1773
Watercolor, 56 × 87
British Library, London
By the time Britain was finally at war with the colonies, the military had excellent documentation of the principal colonial seaports and coastline because of their previous reconnaissance. This view, by Lieutenant Pierie (fl. 1759–77), was made after the Boston "Massacre" but before the "Tea Party."

5 Dominic Serres, *Capt. Hyde Parker in the Phoenix going up the North River, New York*, 1776
Watercolor, 29 × 48
British Museum, London
Serres (dates unknown), the son of Dominique Serres (1722–93), is best known as a landscapist

and teacher of drawing. A version of this picture was included in Joseph Frederick Wallet Des Barres, *The Atlantic Neptune, published for the use of the Royal Navy of Great Britain* (London, 1774–81), Vol. II, No. 24.

6 J. Tingle after W.H. Bartlett, *Branch Bank of the United States, Philadelphia*. From Nathaniel P. Willis, *American Scenery; or, Land, Lake, and River: Illustrations of Transatlantic Nature* (London: George Virtue, 1840), Vol. II
Engraving, 12 × 18.9
The Historical Society of Pennsylvania, Philadelphia
Willis and Bartlett traveled in America in 1837–38 to gather material for their book, which included more than 100 engravings after Bartlett's fine sketches. By the time they saw the once-proud Branch Bank of the United States building, it was occupied by the Second Bank of the United States, operating under a state charter and on the verge of collapse. Bankruptcy occurred the following year, and the building became the U.S. Customs House in 1844. Since 1956 it has been part of Independence National Historic Park.

7 William Birch, *High Street, from Ninth Street, Philadelphia* (detail), 1799. From Birch and Son, *The City of Philadelphia, in the State of Pennsylvania North America; as it Appeared in the Year 1800* . . . (Philadelphia: R. Campbell & Co., 1800)
Engraving (hand colored), 21.6 × 28.6
The New York State Historical Association, Cooperstown
By 1798, William Birch (1755–1834) and his son, Thomas (1779–1851), had set out to depict the whole of Philadelphia, which was then the American capital. It was a huge and painstaking endeavor, for Birch was a perfectionist who required that the copper engraving plates be remade if they did not meet his expectations. Samuel Seymour, who later accompanied Major Stephen H. Long on his western expedition (see pp.31–33), assisted with the engraving.

8 John Rubens Smith (attrib.), *Nos. 168–172 Fulton Street, New York, showing the Shop and Warehouse of Duncan Phyfe*, 1816–17
Watercolor, pen, and brown ink, 40 × 48
The Metropolitan Museum of Art, New York, Rogers Fund, 1922
Duncan Phyfe arrived in America from his native Scotland shortly after the Revolution. He first settled in Albany, then moved to New York City, where he established a shop and warehouse on Fulton Street. He was an immensely talented and prosperous furniture maker. This watercolor has recently been attributed to John Rubens Smith (1775–1849), the English-born son of the engraver John Raphael Smith.

9 James B. Marston, *State Street, Boston* (detail), 1801
Oil on wood, 100 × 135
The Massachusetts Historical Society, Boston
Marston is recorded as a Boston portrait painter about 1807.

10 George Tattersall, *Highways and Byways of the Forest, a Scene on "the Road"* (No. 11 in the Album: American, Western Sketches), 1838
Brown and white wash on gray paper, 21 × 29.9
Museum of Fine Arts, Boston, M. and M. Karolik Collection

An Englishman trained as an architect, Tattersall (1817–49) visited America in 1836 and recorded his memories in a bound volume, which he presented to his wife in 1839.

11 J.H. Bufford after W. Wilson, *View of the Upper Village of Lockport, N.Y.* (detail), 1836
Lithograph, 34.9 × 49.5
The New-York Historical Society, New York City
Lockport, with its five ascending and five descending locks, was "the most stupendous work on the whole route" of the Erie Canal. It grew from just two houses in 1821 to quite a city by the time this print was made.

12 John Hill after William Guy Wall, *Palisades* (detail), *c.* 1820. From *The Hudson River Portfolio* (New York: Henry J. Megarey, 1824), No. 19
Aquatint and etching (hand colored), 35.5 × 54
Amon Carter Museum, Fort Worth, Texas
The *Hudson River Portfolio* has been called "the finest collection of New York State views ever published." The set was issued by Wall (1792–after 1864) in parts, each consisting of four views. The aquatints were made by John Hill (1770–1850), who came to America from England in 1815. The New-York Historical Society owns the watercolor after which this print was made.
The steamboat in the foreground is identified as the *Clermont*, which was the name of Robert Fulton's boat, but there is no record of a vessel by that name operating on the Hudson after 1813.

13 John Hill after T. Hornor, *Broadway, New-York. Shewing each Building from the Hygeian Depot corner of Canal Street to beyond Niblo's Garden* (detail), 1836
Aquatint (hand colored), 27.4 × 17.12
The New York Public Library
This superb view gives a good idea of the many horse-drawn vehicles in use in New York, as well as the street vendors and shops. Tattersall's, located in the building with the gable roof on the right hand side of Broadway, was the largest horse market in the United States by 1846.
Thomas Hornor, born in 1785, was a surveyor and artist from Hull, England, who moved to London and specialized in bird's-eye-views. He made the drawings for a giant 360° panorama of that city, to be shown in a vast purpose-built structure, the Colosseum. When that venture failed in 1829 he fled to America.

14 Benjamin Henry Latrobe, *Elevation of the South front of the President's house, copied from the design as proposed to be altered in 1807*, 1817
Watercolor, pen, and ink, 40 × 53.5
Library of Congress, Washington, D.C.
The Irish architect James Hoban designed the original President's Palace in 1792. Thomas Jefferson, while he was president, consulted an architect more to his liking, Benjamin Latrobe, who added the colonnades that can be seen to the left and right in this drawing, and designed the semicircular south portico. After the fire in 1814, Hoban was called back to supervise reconstruction of the mansion, which President James Madison occupied in 1817, the year in which Latrobe, who had been placed in charge of the reconstruction of the Capitol, painted this watercolour. The south front as restored seems to have combined Hoban's original scheme with Latrobe's proposal.

15 Edward Sachse, *View of Washington*, 1852
Lithograph (hand colored), 27.4 × 17.15
Library of Congress, Washington, D.C.
The artist felt compelled to add features that did not yet exist, probably in the hope that his view would not be so quickly outdated. In the left background stands the Washington Monument – as designed, with a circular portico, which was never built.
Little is known of Edward Sachse & Company, except that Sachse (1804–73) worked out of three different locations in Baltimore – 3 North Liberty Street, Sun Iron Building, and 104 South Charles Street – and did a number of views, primarily of the South. He was a native of Gorlitz, Germany, who came to America in the late 1840s. He established the lithographic firm in Baltimore with his brother and family.

16 Alburtius del Orient Browere, *Catskill*, 1849
Oil on canvas, 86.4 × 111.7
The Brooklyn Museum, Dick S. Ramsay Fund
Browere (1814–87) was born in Tarrytown, New York, the eldest son of H.I. Browere, who became fairly well known by making life masks of prominent Americans. He spent most of his life in New York, with the exception of two trips to California in quest of gold, in 1852–56 and 1858–61. This careful painting of a summer day along the Hudson, looking across to the village of Catskill, is typical of his sensitive work, distinguishing among the species of trees, grass, and weeds.

17 Thomas Cole, *Genesee Scenery (Mountain Landscape with Waterfall)*, 1847
Oil on canvas, 129.5 × 103
Museum of Art, Rhode Island School of Design, Jesse Metcalf Fund (38.054)
Painted from sketches made earlier in his career, Cole's *Genesee Scenery* is apparently intended as a generalized scene despite its specific locale, a cascade on the upper Genesee River. The picture has often been confused with another Cole painting, entitled *Falls of Nunda, near Portage on the Genesee River* (usually referred to as the *Falls of Munda* because of a typographical error in a catalogue published by the Wadsworth Atheneum, Hartford, in 1948). The whereabouts of that painting are unknown.

18 Francis Alexander, *Ralph Wheelock's Farm, c.* 1822
Oil on canvas, 63.9 × 122.3
National Gallery of Art, Washington, D.C., Gift of Edgar William and Bernice Chrysler Garbisch 1965
Alexander (1800–1880) was a portrait, genre, and still-life painter and a lithographer in Killingly, Connecticut, and Providence, Rhode Island, in the 1820s. He later settled in Boston and was a successful portraitist. In 1853 he moved to Europe and settled in Florence, returning to the United States only once, in 1868–69.

19 Thomas Cole, *Home in the Woods, c.* 1846
Oil on canvas, 111.7 × 167.6
Reynolda House Museum of American Art, Winston-Salem, N.C.
For this picture in Cole's *oeuvre* see above, p. 46.

20 Edward Hicks, *An Indian Summer View of the Farm & Stock of James C. Cornell of Northampton, Bucks county, Pennsylvania. That took the Premium in the Agricultural Society, October the 12, 1848*

Oil on canvas, 93.3 × 124.4
National Gallery of Art, Washington, D.C., Gift of Edgar William and Bernice Chrysler Garbisch
A coach and sign painter by trade, Hicks (1780–1849) was born in Langhorne, Pennsylvania. He is best known for his series of paintings entitled *Peaceable Kingdom*.

21 Frederic Edwin Church, *Niagara Falls*, 1857
Oil on canvas, 107.3 × 229.8
The Corcoran Gallery of Art, Washington, D.C.
Unlike most other American artists who searched for primeval nature, Church did not go to the West. He painted this magnificent picture just after reading Ruskin's discussions of Turner's technique, in which the critic had pointed out that trying to paint water was "like trying to paint a soul." This view, actually a composite of several of Church's sketches, was long considered the "finest picture ever painted on this side of the Atlantic" and was the primary American entry at the Paris International Exposition in 1867. A chromolithograph of it was issued in London in 1857.

22 Currier & Ives after Frances F. Palmer, *The "Lightning Express" Trains. "Leaving the Junction"*, 1863
Lithograph (hand colored), 44.5 × 70.5
Amon Carter Museum, Fort Worth, Texas
Currier & Ives were talented in selecting subjects that captured the imagination of the American people. First was their dramatic series on Mississippi riverboats. Then, as the railroad began to supplant the boat as the major form of transportation, they produced a series of railroad prints that are still valued for their accurate technical drawing as well as their composition and colorfulness. The artist who composed most of these scenes was English-born Fanny Palmer (1812–76), who apparently was a well educated lady who had come to America after her family had fallen on hard times. One of the other artists who worked for Currier & Ives recalled that Palmer had been with the company for some time when he joined in 1852, and she worked for them until her death.

23 George Inness, *The Lackawanna Valley, or The First Roundhouse of the Delaware, Lackawanna and Western Railroad at Scranton, Pennsylvania*, 1855
Oil on canvas, 86 × 127.5
National Gallery of Art, Washington, D.C., Gift of Mrs Huttleston Rogers, 1945
Inness (1825–94) was commissioned to paint this scene by the president of the railroad, who apparently did not like it, for the artist later found it in a Mexican curiosity shop and saved it. "I had to show the double tracks and the roundhouse," Inness wrote, "whether they were in perspective or not. But . . . the distance is excellent." Perhaps more than any other painting, this picture has stimulated the controversy over machine and nature.

24 Samuel Colman, *Storm King on the Hudson* (detail), 1866
Oil on canvas, 80.6 × 150.5
National Museum of American Art (formerly National Collection of Fine Arts), Smithsonian Institution, Washington, D.C., Gift of John Gellatly
This is one of Colman's finest works, reminiscent in the handling of paint of his watercolors, a medium that he favored much

later, during the last years of his life. In 1879 the art historian S.G.W. Benjamin wrote of Colman: "he has painted some very strong effects of light and shade, and his coloring has a brilliance that is so harmonious as to influence one like a strain of music."

25 Martin Johnson Heade, *Thunderstorm Over Narragansett Bay*, 1868
Oil on canvas, 81.6 × 138.4
Amon Carter Museum, Fort Worth, Texas
Here Heade has captured that moment just before a howling and furious thunderstorm strikes the becalmed Narragansett Bay. Lightning flashes silently in the background as the fishermen hurry across the glassy water toward the shore. One boat has already landed. Another is hastily lowering its sail, on the left, as the pilot anticipates the coming winds. On the right, a fisherman pulls on the oars to hurry his boat to safety.

The painting is now recognized as a masterpiece of American landscape, but it was not received as well at its debut. One critic commented that it "shows a painful amount of labor with a corresponding feeling of hardness in color and execution." There is no other such work in Heade's *oeuvre* – perhaps because he was discouraged by this critics, perhaps because he felt he could not surpass this statement.

26 Crow, Thomas & Co., *Grover & Baker Sewing Machine Co., 495 Broadway, New York*, c. 1860
Chromolithograph, 45.3 × 61
Library of Congress, Washington, D.C.

27 The Hatch Co., *Western Union Telegraph Company, Broadway, New York*, c. 1875
Chromolithograph, 53.7 × 36.5
Museum of the City of New York, Gift of Grace M. Mayer
Probably done upon the completion of the building.

28 Max Rosenthal, *Interior view of L.J. Levy & Co's Dry Goods Store, Chestnut St. Phila.*, c. 1857
Chromolithograph, 50.2 × 67.3
The Free Library of Philadelphia
Probably issued in celebration of the opening of the store on December 31, 1857. John Fraser was the architect of the building, which stood at 809–811 Chestnut Street and was known as the "palace of trade."

Rosenthal, born in Germany in 1833, studied in Berlin and Paris before settling in Philadelphia, where he became known as a painter of portraits and history subjects and a printmaker.

29 William Giles Munson, *The Eli Whitney Gun Factory, Connecticut* (detail), 1826–28
Oil of canvas, 61.6 × 75
Yale University Art Gallery, The Mabel Brady Garvan Collection
Munson (1801–78) was a New Haven dentist who made a hobby of painting local scenes. The Whitney factory was located near East Rock, close to the New Haven of Munson and Whitney.

30 Winslow Homer, *The Morning Bell*, c. 1866/70
Oil on canvas, 61 × 96.5
Yale University Art Gallery, Bequest of Stephen Carlton Clark, B.A. 1903
An engraving after this picture appeared in *Harper's Weekly* for December 13, 1873, raising the possibility that it might have been painted later.

31 William Burgis, *A Prospect of the Colledges in Cambridge in New England*, 1726
Engraving, 23.15 × 18.10
Massachusetts Historical Society, Boston
This is the earliest known view of Harvard College. Harvard (1672–82), Stoughton (1698–1700), and Massachusetts (1718–20) Halls are shown around the Harvard Yard. The only known copy of the first state of this view is illustrated here; a second state was issued in 1739 or 1740.

32 John Hill after George Catlin, *West Point Military Academy*, 1828
Aquatint, 29.8 × 46.3
Courtesy Kenneth M. Newman, The Old Print Shop, New York City
By 1821 Catlin had begun to exhibit his pictures in the annual shows of the Pennsylvania Academy of the Fine Arts. He later moved to New York City and accepted commissions, including one to paint landscapes of West Point that could be copied as prints.

33 Enrico Meneghelli, *The Lawrence Room, Museum of Fine Arts, Boston*, 1879
Oil on canvas, 40.6 × 50.8
Museum of Fine Arts, Boston, Gift of M. Knoedler and Co.
Enrico Meneghelli (1853–?) arrived in Boston from Italy soon after 1869, when Colonel T.B. Lawrence left his collection of arms and armor to the Boston Athenaeum, together with $25,000 toward the construction of the new Museum of Fine Arts. The armor was destroyed in a fire in 1872, but Mrs Lawrence used the insurance money to furnish a gallery in the museum with rare English paneling to house the collection of carvings and embroideries shown in the painting.

34 Sanford R. Gifford, *The Artist sketching at Mount Desert, Maine*, 1864–65
Oil on canvas, 27.9 × 48.3
Collection of Jo Ann and Julian Ganz, Jr.
In his *Autobiography*, Worthington Whittredge recorded that Gifford, following Asher B. Durand in going "out-of-doors to paint directly from nature," "procured a sketch box at an early day and had it so arranged that he could button it to a strap over his shoulder and detach it at short notice." Gifford's delicate and shimmering landscapes are unequalled among his contemporaries.

35 Jasper F. Cropsey, *The Narrows from Staten Island*, 1868
Oil on canvas, 106.9 × 183.2
Amon Carter Museum, Fort Worth, Texas
Cropsey began work on this giant canvas shortly after his return in 1863 from a seven-year stay abroad. At the height of his powers and with commissions from such wealthy patrons as the Vanderbilts, he painted several Staten Island pictures. This, the largest of all, was not reviewed well when it appeared in an 1870 exhibition, despite the fact that it represents Cropsey at his best, because tastes in landscapes had begun to change.

36 John White, *The Village of Secoton*, c. 1585–87
Watercolor and pencil, 32.4 × 19.9
British Museum, London
For a discussion of this picture see above, p.16.

37 Jean-Baptiste Michel Le Bouteaux, *View of the Camp of John Law's Concession at New Biloxi, Louisiana* (detail), December, 1720
Pen, ink, and wash, 49.5 × 89.8

Edward E. Ayer Collection, The Newberry Library, Chicago

38 Mark Catesby, *Bison by Acacia Tree*. From Catesby, *The Natural History of Carolina, Florida, and the Bahama Islands . . .* (1754)
Engraving (hand colored), 34.2 × 26.6
Amon Carter Museum, Fort Worth, Texas
For Catesby see above, pp.22–23.
In his image of a bison Catesby was proud to have given "a perfect likeness of this awful Creature." The animal stands under a *Robinia hispida*, with "faint purple or rose"-colored flowers. "I never saw any of these trees but at one place near the *Apalatchian* mountains, where Bufellos had left their dung; and some of the trees had their branches pulled down, from which I conjecture they had been browsing on the leaves."

The engraving appeared originally as pl.20 of the Appendix (1748). The version reproduced is from the first posthumous edition, in which the printing plates used were the same, but the hand coloring occasionally differs slightly – sometimes, though not in this case, being brighter.

39 Robert Havell, Jr., after John James Audubon, *Long-Billed Curlew (City of Charleston)*, 1834. From Audubon, *The Birds of America* (London, 1827–38), no. 231
Aquatint (hand colored), 67.3 × 100.3
Amon Carter Museum, Fort Worth, Texas
Audubon, born in Haiti in 1785, came to American in 1803 and eventually settled in Louisville, Kentucky. He sailed for England in 1826 to supervise the engraving of his *Birds of America*, which were published in 87 parts each consisting of 5 hand colored prints, making total of 435. The subscription price was $1,000. All but four of the original watercolors are in the New-York Historical Society, which raised $4,000 by public subscription to purchase them in 1863, twelve years after Audubon's death in that city.

Audubon gathered the skins which he worked up into this composition during a return visit to America in 1831. Before he could finish, however, he needed more from Bachman: "*Long billed Curlew*, . . . send me several skins. I must ask you in the most earnest manner to assist all you can and merely enable me to publish *no trash*."

40 Pierre Fourdrinier after Peter Gordon, *A View of Savannah as it stood the 29th of March, 1734*, 1734
Engraving, 40 × 55
Amon Carter Museum, Fort Worth, Texas
In his journal, Baron von Reck, leader of the Salzburgers who settled at Ebenezer, wrote of Savannah: "The Town is regularly laid out, divided into four Wards, in each of which is left a spacious Square for holding of Markets and other publick Uses. The Streets are all straight, and the Houses are all of the same Model and Dimensions, and well contrived for Conveniency."

41 John L. Boqueta de Woiseri, *A View of New Orleans taken from the Plantation of Marigny*, November, 1803
Aquatint and engraving, 28.6 × 55.2
The Historic New Orleans Collection
Little is known about Boqueta de Woiseri, who described himself as a "designer, drawer, geographer, and engineer." He may have been one of the first in the United States to employ the aquatint process, demonstrated in this

print. He arrived in the Crescent City probably in the spring of 1803 and advertised his services as a portrait painter in the newspapers in May. By 1804 he was in Philadelphia. He is listed in New York City directories from 1807 to 1811, but his whereabouts after that are unknown.

The original painting, perhaps a patriotic gesture in honor of the Louisiana Purchase, hangs in the Chicago Historical Society. A smaller version is in the Mariners' Museum, Newport News, Virginia. The aquatint was first offered to the public in an advertisement in the *Philadelphia General Advertisor* on February 21, 1804. For $10 the purchaser could get both it and "A Plan of New Orleans."

42 Firmin Cerveau, *View of Savannah, looking inland from Bay Street* (detail), 1837
Gouache and tempera, 69.8 × 125.7
The Georgia Historical Society, Savannah
In the center is Johnson Square, with a monument to the Revolutionary General Nathanael Greene and, on the left, the Episcopal Church. The spire in the distance marks Trinity Methodist Church.

43 Captain (later Sir) Richard George Augustus Levinge, *The Paddle Steamer "Ouishita" on the Red River, Louisiana Territory*, c. 1836
Watercolor on paper, 21.2 × 31.6
Amon Carter Museum, Fort Worth, Texas
Levinge (1811–89), with the Monmouthshire Light Infantry, landed in Quebec in 1836 and traveled extensively in Canada and America, going down the Ohio and Mississippi rivers to the Red River, a major tributary of the Mississippi. He wrote *Echoes from the Backwoods* (1846), a guidebook for sportsmen. He boarded the *Ouishita* at the junction of the Mississippi and Red rivers, and sailed up the latter as far as Alexandria, Louisiana. There the British officers came upon "the ruffians who composed the invading army to Texas," were suspected of being spies, and turned back eastward.

44 Marie Adrien Persac, *Interior of the Steamboat "Princess,"* 1861
Watercolor and collage, 43.1 × 56.6
Anglo-American Art Museum, Louisiana State University, Baton Rouge, Gift of Mrs Mamie Persac Lusk
Persac (?–1873) was a landScape painter, surveyor, cartographer, architect, and teacher. He was active from 1857 in New Orleans, where he was reported to have been making a chart of the Mississippi.

Persac cut figures of men and women out of contemporary publications and pasted them on his paintings and drawings. He would then paint them as well as the rest of the composition. Here, every figure through the first waiter on the left is a cut-out; the other two figures were drawn freehand. The earliest known painting of a Mississippi River steamboat, this is probably a memory picture recalling his wedding trip of 1851.

45 S. Barnard, *View along the East Battery, Charleston, South Carolina*, 1831
Oil on canvas, 60.3 × 89.5
Yale University Art Gallery, Mabel Brady Garvan Collection
Little is known of S. Barnard, except that he did three paintings of Charleston.

46 W.J. Bennett after G. Cooke, *Richmond from the Hill above the Waterworks*, 1834
Aquatint (hand colored), 25.1 × 17.13

The I.N. Phelps Stokes Collection, The New York Public Library
One of several fine prints by Bennett, this view encompasses a number of familiar landmarks in addition to the Capitol (1785–96). The Kanawha Canal, begun in 1785, flows alongside of the river. Just to the right of the Capitol is the Governor's Mansion (1811–13); the domed and columned building to the left of the Capitol is the City Hall (1814–16); and on the extreme left is the State Penitentiary (1797–1800), designed by Benjamin Latrobe.

47 C. Giroux, *Cotton Plantation*, c. 1850–65
Oil on canvas, 55.9 × 91.4
Museum of Fine Arts, Boston, M. and M. Karolik Collection
Nothing is known of the C. Giroux, whose signature appears in the lower left of this painting. A Charles Giroux had a studio at 90 Baronne Street in New Orleans in 1882 and 1883, but the color and paint suggest an earlier date. Another painting with the same signature is dated 1868.

48 Marie Adrien Persac, *The Olivier Plantation [near New Iberia], Louisiana*, 1861
Watercolor and collage, 46 × 58 (sight)
Louisiana State Museum, New Orleans
The plantation stood about 6 km. south-east of New Iberia at a now defunct railroad whistle-stop called Olivier. For Persac see the note to pl.44.

49 Harley after Harry Fenn, *A Garden in Florida*, c. 1872. From *Picturesque America* (1872–74)
Wood engraving, 22.6 × 16.1
Harry Fenn (1845–1911) was born in Richmond, England, and died in Montclair, New Jersey. He was commissioned to illustrate several of the regional pieces in *Picturesque America*.

50 David Johnson, *The Natural Bridge of Virginia*, 1860
Oil on canvas, 61 × 50.8
Collection of Jo Ann and Julian Ganz, Jr.
Jefferson purchased the Natural Bridge and adjoining land, and continually urged artists to paint it. The first image appeared in the Marquis de Chastellux's *Voyage en Amérique* (1786). Another version of Johnson's painting is in the collection of Reynolda House, Winston-Salem, N.C., and an engraving after it was issued by S.V. Hunt.

51 Albert Bierstadt, *The Bombardment of Fort Sumter*, 1862?
Oil on canvas, 66 × 167.6
Courtesy a Massachusetts Collector. Thanks to Bruce Grimleson
In the fall of 1861, Bierstadt and Emanuel Leutze, another Düsseldorf-trained painter, got a pass to visit the Civil War battlefields around Washington; but material for this painting probably came from the numerous eye-witness accounts of the battle which later appeared in New York newspapers.

52 William MacLeod, *Maryland Heights: Siege of Harper's Ferry*, 1863
Oil on canvas, 76.2 × 111.7
The Corcoran Gallery of Art, Washington, D.C.
Harper's Ferry is one of the most scenic spots in the United States. Thomas Jefferson first called attention to the spectacular landscape at the confluence of the Potomac and Shenadoah rivers, and MacLeod (1811–92), who had exhibited in New York City before moving to

Washington in 1857, probably knew it well. In this picture he has documented the Federal defensive works mounted to protect their armory.

53 Edward Lamson Henry, *The Old Westover Mansion*, 1869
Oil on panel, 28.6 × 39.4
The Corcoran Gallery of Art, Washington, D.C.
William Byrd II wrote in 1729, "In a year or 2 I intend to set about building a very good house." Westover is testimony to his taste and determination, and it is fortunate to have survived. It burned "to the ground" in 1748, then was burned again during the Civil War, yet it remains as an outstanding example of Colonial architecture in Virginia.

An inscription on the back of this picture indicates that it was painted after a sketch made in October, 1864, during General Grant's James River campaign of 1864–65. The sketch is in the New York State Museum, Albany, and a similar painting is in The Century Association, New York.

54 Unknown artist, *The "Belle Creole" at New Orleans*, c. 1845–1849
Oil on canvas, 122 × 182.9
The Corcoran Gallery of Art, Washington, D.C.
The artist of this delightful painting remains unknown; the initials on the box in the lower left hand corner may be his or hers. The *Belle Creole* was a sidewheel steamer of 447 tons, built in Cincinnati in 1845 and abandoned in 1852. The *Music* was a sidewheeler of 198 tons built at Jeffersonville, Indiana, in 1843 and abandoned in 1849, so the picture may be fairly accurately dated.

55 Edgar Degas, *The Cotton Office, New Orleans (Un Bureau de Coton à la Nouvelle-Orléans)*, 1872–73
Oil on canvas, 74 × 91.7
Musée des Beaux-Arts, Pau
Degas visited New Orleans at the invitation of his mother's family, who still lived in the Crescent City. Degas predicted that Manet would have seen "lovely things" in the brilliant New Orleans light, but that he "would not make any more of them" than himself. This grouping of relatives and customers in the cotton office is proof of the claim. The picture was shown in the second Impressionist exhibition in 1876.

56 Peter Rindisbacher, [*Captain W. Andrew Bulger saying Farewell at Fort McKay, Prairie du Chien, Wisconsin, on May 22, 1815*], c. 1823
Pen and watercolor, 35.5 × 60.6
Amon Carter Museum, Fort Worth, Texas
In 1822 Captain Bulger became governor of Red River Colony in Canada and met young Rindisbacher. He gave the artist a job as a clerk at Fort Garry and probably assisted him in finding scenes to paint. As Bulger prepared to leave the colony, he commissioned Rindisbacher to paint his previous departure from Fort MacKay. Rindisbacher had not witnessed the scene, but Bulger apparently selected one of the young artist's compositions that he liked and gave suitable instructions for its modification.

57 Unknown British officer, *View of Detroit*, 1794
Watercolor
Burton Historical Collection of the Detroit Public Library
Detroit was founded in 1701 when the French government established Fort Pontchartrain du

Detroit ("of the Strait"), and it was maintained as one of the three French strongholds through the center of the continent along with New Orleans and St Louis. It was turned over to the British in 1760 and then became a bastion against American expansion westward. This view was made during those post-Revolutionary Indian wars, before Detroit's capture by American troops in 1813.

58 John C. Wild, *Cincinnati: the Public Landing*, 1835
Watercolor, 45.7 × 63.5
The Cincinnati Historical Society
Wild (c. 1804–46) was a Swiss artist who, after spending considerable time in Paris, arrived in America c. 1830. He immediately set to drawing views of Philadelphia, which were lithographed by J.T. Bowen. By 1835, he had moved on to Cincinnati, where he did a number of watercolors, probably also intending them to be lithographed. Although none credited to Wild has been located, H.R. Robinson of New York City issued c. 1838 a colored lithograph of Cincinnati which is obviously copied from the present picture. Several merchants' signs are evident in the painting; others are shown in the print (New York Public Library). After a brief return to Philadelphia, Wild moved west again, to St Louis, where he did a number of views of that city and the Mississippi River, which were published as *Views of Saint Louis* and later expanded into *The Valley of the Mississippi Illustrated*.

59 Charles Alexandre Lesueur, *Tyawapatia Bottom or Commercetown [on the Mississippi in Missouri]*, April 13, 1826
Watercolor
Collection C.A. Lesueur, Muséum D'Histoire Naturelle, F76 Le Havre, No. 42084
Lesueur was well known as a naturalist when he arrived in the United States in 1816. Coming to serve as assistant to William Maclure, a geologist and philanthropist, Lesueur had been a member of a French expedition to Australia on which he and a friend had been credited with discovering more than 2,500 new species. He lived in Philadelphia for nine years, taking an active part in the proceedings of the American Philosophical Society and the Academy of Natural Sciences, and was a good friend of the Peales. He was the first to study the marine life of the Great Lakes region and contributed illustrations to John D. Godman's *American Natural History* (1826–28), and Thomas Say's *American Entomology* (1817–28). He was staying with Say at Harmony, Indiana, when Maximilian of Wied-Neuwied and Karl Bodmer passed through in 1833 (see the note to the illustration on p.37). He finally returned to France and became curator of the natural history museum at Le Havre.

Commerce, some 50 km. north of the confluence of the Mississippi and the Ohio, was a trading post as early as 1803.

60 Sarony & Major after Charles Sullivan, *Great Mound at Marietta, Ohio*. From Ephraim G. Squier and E.H. Davis, *Ancient Monuments of the Mississippi Valley* . . . Smithsonian Contributions to Knowledge, Vol. I (Washington, D.C., 1848)
Toned lithograph, 13.3 × 17.7
Squier, a journalist, and Davis, a doctor, both Ohio men, examined a great number of mounds, producing the first thorough survey of the subject; but they still believed – like William Cullen Bryant and many others – that

the mound-builders were a distant race, who had been replaced by the nomadic American Indians.

61 Edward Sachse, *View of St Louis from Lucas Place* (detail), c. 1860
Lithograph (hand colored), 48.1 × 79.4
The Chicago Historical Society

62 John Hazlehurst Boneval Latrobe, *Louisville (Upper Landing)*, 1832
Watercolor, 18.8 × 26
Amon Carter Museum, Fort Worth, Texas
Latrobe (1803–91) was born in Philadelphia and studied at Georgetown College, St Mary's College, and West Point, expecting to become an architect. He resigned from the Academy when he decided to take up law, and later worked as an attorney for the Baltimore and Ohio Railroad. He was an avid traveler and author, sketching wherever he went. He was the inventor of the small but efficient Latrobe stove for the fireplace and later served as a founder of the Maryland Historical Society and president of the Academy of Art.

63 After George Caleb Bingham, *The Jolly Flat Boat Men*, 1847
Colored line and mezzotint engraving, 47.4 × 60.6
Amon Carter Museum, Fort Worth, Texas
Bingham's original painting was selected by the American Art-Union as one of two pictures to be mezzotinted for its subscribers in 1847.

64 William Tylee Ranney, *Crossing the Ferry*, 1846
Oil on canvas, 74.9 × 101.6
The Thomas Gilcrease Institute of American History and Art, Tulsa
After studying drawing in Brooklyn, Ranney (1812–57) was attracted to the Texas frontier, where he helped in the fight for independence from Mexico. He returned east, established a studio in New York, and painted a number of scenes reminiscent of the country that he had seen. *Crossing the Ferry* is one of them, although it has often gone by other titles, such as *Pennsylvania Teamster*, *Going to the Mill*, and *Hauling Flour*. It was first exhibited at the American Art-Union in 1847.

65 Thomas Prichard Rossiter, *Opening of the Wilderness* (detail), c. 1858
Oil on canvas, 45.1 × 82.5
Museum of Fine Arts, Boston, M. and M. Karolik Collection
This picture probably dates from the famous Artists' Excursion sponsored by the Baltimore and Ohio Railroad in 1858. Because the track appears to be broad gauge, some have suggested that it may be the Erie, but it is virtually impossible to identify the roundhouse, so the scene might be anywhere along the route of any of the railroads that sponsored such trips in 1857 and 1858. Some art historians have detected "sinister" or "ominous and threatening" feelings about the picture: the locomotives (much larger than in the work of Rossiter's contemporaries) appear to be angry armored giants about to spring from their lair; and the sense of unease, they argue, is reinforced by the sharply pointed tree stumps, bare and dead trees, and harsh outcroppings of rock.

66 Karl Bodmer, *View of a Farm on the Prairies of Illinois*, 1833
Watercolor, 13.4 × 21.3
The InterNorth Art Foundation, Joslyn Art Museum, Omaha

67 Artist unknown, *Farm Residence of H.B. Kay's, Magnolia Tp., Putnam Co. Ill*. From *Atlas of the State of Illinois to which are added various General Maps Historical Statistics and Illustrations* (Chicago: Union Atlas Co., 1876)
Lithograph, 17.7 × 30.4
Amon Carter Museum, Fort Worth, Texas
A number of state atlases were published during the last quarter of the nineteenth century to document the phenomenal growth of the Midwest. This one is laced with large views of farms and homes all over the state.

68 Currier & Ives, *Chicago in Flames. Scene at Randolph Street Bridge*, 1871
Lithograph (hand colored), 8.8 × 12.8
Library of Congress, Washington, D.C.
One of the great disasters of modern times, the Chicago fire began in a barn in DeKoven Street on the evening of October 8, 1871, and spread rapidly. It burned all the next day and into the night, destroying more than 18,000 buildings, including the business center. Perhaps 300 persons were killed, 100,000 left homeless.

69 C. Rascher for Walsh & Co., *The Great Union Stock Yards of Chicago*, 1878
Color lithograph, 48.3 × 64.8
Library of Congress, Washington, D.C.

70 Ehrgott, Forbriger & Co., *Edmund Dexter's Residence, N.E. Corner of Fourth St. & Broadway, Cincinnati*, c. 1861–69
Chromolithograph, 40 × 51.4
Cincinnati Art Museum, Gift of Mrs William M. Chatfield

71 Karst after J. Douglas Woodward, *Superior Street, Cleveland, from Presbyterian Church*. From *Picturesque America* (1872–74)
Wood engraving, 22.5 × 15.5
Woodward (1848–1924) was born in Middlesex, England, and died in New Rochelle, New York.

72 Samuel Seymour, *Cliffs of Red Sandstone Near the Rocky Mts.*, c. 1820
Watercolor, 20.5 × 14.5
Beinecke Rare Book and Manuscript Library, Yale University
For Seymour and the Long expedition see above, pp.31–33. Most of his surviving paintings are in the Beinecke Library.

73 George Catlin, *St Louis From the River below* (detail), 1832–33
Oil on canvas, 49.2 × 68.1
National Museum of American Art (formerly National Collection of Fine Arts), Smithsonian Institution, Washington, D.C., Gift of Mrs Sarah Harrison
Catlin probably made this painting in St Louis during the summer of 1832. As he explained in *Letters and Notes*, the city was his "starting point, and place of deposit, to which I send from different quarters, my packages of paintings and Indian articles, minerals, fossils, &c., as I collect them . . ."

74 Beyer and Salathé after Karl Bodmer, *View of the Stone Walls. On the upper Missouri* (detail), 1840. From Maximilian, *Voyage* (see the note to the illustration on p.37)
Aquatint and etching, 30 × 43.9
Amon Carter Museum, Fort Worth, Texas

75 Worthington Whittredge, *Indian Encampment on the Platte River* (detail), 1870–72
Oil on canvas, 36.1 × 55.2

Collection of Jo Ann and Julian Ganz, Jr.

76 George Catlin, *White Cloud, Chief of the Tribe* [*Iowa*], 1844
Oil on canvas, 70.5 × 57.8
National Gallery of Art, Washington, D.C., Paul Mellon Collection
Catlin probably painted this portrait of the chief while he was in London in 1844. During their stay the Indians had breakfast with Disraeli, performed at the Vauxhall Gardens, and provided the live entertainment for Catlin's Indian Gallery until the fall. Catlin then took them on a tour of Ireland and Scotland, and in April, 1845, they were received in Paris by Louis Philippe.

77 George Catlin, *The Bull Dance, Mandan O-kee-pa Ceremony* (detail), *c.* 1832
Oil on canvas, 59 × 71.1
The Anschutz Collection. Photograph by Malcolm Varon
Catlin witnessed the Bull Dance in 1832. In addition to the men draped in buffalo skins, he observed two others ''painted entirely black with pounded charcoal and grease, whom they called the 'firmament or night,' and the numerous white spots which were dotted all over their bodies, they called 'stars.'''

78 Sarony, Major & Knapp after John Mix Stanley, *Herd of Bison, near Lake Jessie* [*North Dakota*], 1855. From *Reports of Explorations and Surveys . . . for a Railroad . . . to the Pacific Ocean* (1855–60), Vol. XII
Color lithograph, 14.7 × 22.7
Amon Carter Museum, Fort Worth, Texas
Stanley was the most prolific artist on the railroad surveys. He took up painting by the time he was twenty-one and had traveled throughout the Midwest by early 1846, when he joined a wagon train West and eventually accompanied American troops to California (see the note to Pl.109). By the time the government was looking for artists for the railroad surveys, Stanley, with his considerable experience in the West, was available and accompanied Isaac Stevens on the northern route.
Stanley recalled that he made this sketch from ''an elevation . . . whence, with a spyglass, he could see fifteen miles in any direction.'' Still he estimated that he ''saw not the limit of the herd.'' In his report, Stevens said that some members of the party estimated the bison to number half a million; he considered 200,000 a conservative figure. It is one of the few pictures to show such a great herd.

79 Alfred Jacob Miller, *Indians tantalizing a wounded Buffalo*, 1837
Watercolor, 21.4 × 34.7
Amon Carter Museum, Fort Worth, Texas
Miller witnessed many buffalo hunts during his 1837 trip to the Rockies. Of all his sketches of Indians, this is the only one that shows them laughing, something which few other artists observed or bothered to record.

80 Currier & Ives after Arthur Fitzwilliam Tait, *Life on the Prairie. The ''Buffalo Hunt,''* 1862
Toned lithograph (hand colored), 46.6 × 68.6
Amon Carter Museum, Fort Worth, Texas
One of America's great artists of sporting scenes, Tait (1819–1905) was born in Liverpool and attended the Royal Institute in Manchester. He went to New York in 1850 and worked as a painter and commission artist for various printing firms. His relationship with Currier & Ives, though prolific, was frequently strained because he would not permit any changes from painting to print.

81 Karl Bodmer, *Bellevue Agency – Post of Major Dougherty*, 1833
Watercolor, 16.5 × 24.1
The InterNorth Art Foundation, Joslyn Art Museum, Omaha
Bellevue became an active fur trading post during the 1820s and a government Indian agency and seat of missionary activities in the 1830s. It was a regular stop for travelers headed up the Missouri. As Nebraska began to grow and a site for the capital was designated in the 1850s, Omaha won out over Bellevue. A plate after this watercolor appears in Maximilian's book.

82 Karl Bodmer, *Mahchsi Karehde, Mandan Indian*, 1833–34
Watercolor, 42.9 × 30.5
The InterNorth Art Foundation, Joslyn Art Museum, Omaha
All of the white traders and explorers who came in contact with the Mandans were impressed with their courtesy, dignity, and spectacular ceremonies. Maximilian's general account of their appearance (*Travels*, 1843) describes Mahchsi Karehde: ''Their hair is parted transversely across the middle of the head, the front hair combed smoothly down, and generally divided into three flat bands, two of which hang down on the temples, and are generally plaited . . . Between these two singularly decorated plaits there is, in the centre of the forehead, a smooth flat lock reaching to the nose . . . The chief article of their dress is the ample buffalo robe, . . . which is often very elaborate and valuable. In dry weather these buffalo robes are worn with the hair inwards, and in rainy weather with the hairy side outwards. They are tanned on the fleshy side, and painted either white or reddish-brown, and ornamented with a transverse band of blue or white glass beads, and three large rosettes of the same beads, often of very tasteful patterns, at regular intervals. . . . Their leggins are . . . embroidered at the outer seam with stripes, one or two inches in breadth, of porcupine quills, of beautiful various colours, and often with blue and white beads, and long leathern fringes, which form at the ankle a thick bunch, which trails upon the ground. . . . Those men who have performed exploits wear, round the ankles, wolf's tail, or pieces of otter skin, which are lined with red cloth, and trail on the ground. In the summer, when the men are at home, and go about in state, they carry the fan of eagle's feathers in their hand.''
This watercolor of Mahchsi Karehde, paired with another Mandan, was engraved as pl.20 in Maximilian's book.

83 After Frederick Piercy, *Council Bluffs Ferry and group of Cotton-wood Trees.* From Piercy, *Route from Liverpool . . .* (1855)
Engraving, 25.5 × 17.6
Amon Carter Museum, Fort Worth, Texas
Piercy (1830–91) left Liverpool in March, 1853, commissioned by the Mormons to document the trail to Utah, to help Mormon missionaries in England to gain recruits for the new Zion. From New Orleans he traveled up the Mississippi River, sketching New Orleans, Baton Rouge, Natchez, Vicksburg, Memphis, and St Louis along the way. At Nauvoo he turned westward to Kanesville and on over what became known as the Great Platte River Road to Salt Lake City. A number of his watercolors exist in the Museum of Fine Arts, Boston, and the Missouri Historical Society.

84 After Frederick Piercy, *Entrance to Kanesville* (detail). From Piercy, *Route From Liverpool . . .* (1855)
Engraving, 16.5 × 24
Amon Carter Museum, Fort Worth, Texas
Kanesville, which became the town of Council Bluffs, Iowa, is located across the Missouri River from Omaha.

85 H.J. Toudy & Co. after Christian Inger, *View of Great Salt Lake City* (detail), 1867
Toned lithograph, 29.3 × 72.3
Amon Carter Museum, Fort Worth, Texas
This view looks south down the wide East Temple Street (later Main), flanked by irrigation ditches. On the right is Temple Square, where both the Temple (begun in 1853) and the Tabernacle (begun in 1864) are shown as completed. Across from the walled Temple Square to the left are the Tithing Office and Yard, the Church office, the Lion House (built in the mid-1850s for some of Brigham Young's wives), Young's office, and the Beehive House, his official residence.

86 Alfred Jacob Miller, *Fort Laramie* (detail), 1851
Oil on canvas, 45.7 × 68.6
The Thomas Gilcrease Institute of American History and Art, Tulsa
Miller continued to copy his Western sketches until his death in 1874, so there are a number of versions of this painting of the fort.

87 Alfred Jacob Miller, *Storm: Waiting for the Caravan*, 1858–60
Watercolor, 23.7 × 32.9
The Walters Art Gallery, Baltimore

88 Alfred Jacob Miller, *Indian Village, c.* 1850
Oil on canvas, 76.7 × 122.5
Amon Carter Museum, Fort Worth, Texas

89 Unknown artist, *The Independent Gold Hunter on his Way to California, c.* 1850
Lithograph, 31.4 × 21.2
Amon Carter Museum, Fort Worth, Texas
This was such a popular print that a number of publishers marketed versions of it, including Henry R. Robinson, and Nathaniel Currier and Kellogg & Comstock of Hartford and New York, whose prints are identical but with a different background than Robinson's. The version illustrated is Kellogg & Comstock's.

90 Charles C. Kuchel and Emil Dresel, *Scotts Bar and French Bar, On Scotts River, Siskiyou County, California. 1856.* From *Kuchel & Dresel's California Views* (San Francisco, 1858)
Toned lithograph, 40.5 × 69.9
Amon Carter Museum, Fort Worth, Texas
This unusual print was issued as part of Charles C. Kuchel's (1820–?) and Emil Dresel's series of views of towns in California.
The series was printed in San Francisco by Britton & Rey, the largest lithographic firm in California. Joseph Britton (1825–1901) was lured west in the 1849 Gold Rush. Frenchman Jacques Joseph Rey (1820–?) arrived in 1850. When Britton came down from the hills in 1852, unsuccessful in finding his fortune, he teamed up with Rey to form a partnership that lasted for years.

91 After Samuel Frank Marryat, *San Francisco* (detail), 1851
Colored lithograph, 41.9 × 64.5
Amon Carter Museum, Fort Worth, Texas
Printed in London by M. & N. Hanhart, this striking depiction of San Francisco provides a good view of the city's rapid expansion following the discovery of gold. By 1851 many of the tents and temporary structures of the first arrivals had given way to the raw and unfinished look of a boom town. Mexicans, Chinese, and Anglo-Americans mixed to form the city's polyglot population, some perhaps deserters from the many boats standing empty in the harbor.

Marryat (1826–55), the son of the famous novelist Frederick Marryat, visited California in 1850–53. He also wrote and illustrated *Mountains and Molehills, or Recollections of a Burnt Journal* (London, 1855).

92 Albert Bierstadt, *Emigrants crossing the Plains* (detail), 1867
Oil on canvas, 152.4 × 243.8
The National Cowboy Hall of Fame and Western Heritage Center, Oklahoma City
In 1863 Bierstadt and Ludlow set out from Atchison, Kansas, and were not disappointed in their adventure: they hunted and painted the buffalo, met Brigham Young, and had a meeting with the Goshoot Indians before they arrived at Lake Tahoe. They continued to San Francisco, where they made up a party to go to Yosemite (see pl.97). They returned by way of Mount Shasta and Oregon. Bierstadt had gathered fresh material from which some of his best pictures would come.

93 Carl William Hahn, *California Stage Coach Halt* (detail), 1875
Oil on canvas, 71.1 × 101.6
The Anschutz Collection. Photograph by James O. Milmoe
Carl William Hahn (1829–87) was born in Germany and trained in Dresden and Düsseldorf, where he became friends with Emanuel Leutze (best known for his painting, *Washington Crossing the Delaware*), and through him met a number of American artists also studying in Düsseldorf, including Charles Wimar, Eastman Johnson, Worthington Whittredge, and George Caleb Bingham. By the time he arrived in America in 1871, Hahn was a professional painter of some reputation. In June, 1872, he accompanied William Keith to San Francisco, where they shared studio space in the Mercantile Library Building. *California Stage Coach Halt* comes from this period. It shows a way station where the tired horses were exchanged for fresh ones and the travelers could stretch their legs.

94 William Endicott & Company after George V. Cooper, *Sacramento City Ca. From the Foot of J. Street, Showing I. J. & K. Sts. With the Sierra Nevada in the Distance, December 20, 1849* (detail), 1850
Color lithograph, 38.5 × 58.8
Amon Carter Museum, Fort Worth, Texas
John Sutter and his son employed a topographical engineer to survey the land between Sutter's Fort and the American and Sacramento rivers in the summer of 1848. By December, 1849, when Cooper (1810–78) arrived along with the first of the Forty-Niners, Sacramento was a bustling city, receiving supplies and more prospectors via the Sacramento River, shown in the foreground. At least one version of this view shows a hot-air balloon above the

town, suggesting that Cooper might have used it to gain his aerial perspective.

Cooper, who spent his career in New York City, traveled in California from 1849 to 1852 gathering sketches to illustrate J.M. Letts, *Pictorial View of California* (New York, 1853).

95 Charles C. Kuchel and Emil Dresel, *Los Angeles, Los Angeles County, Cal.* (detail), 1857. From *Kuchel & Dresel's California Views* (1858)
Toned lithograph, 40 × 58.8
Amon Carter Museum, Fort Worth, Texas
This is Los Angeles just before the establishment of the Butterfield Overland Stage Line from St Louis in 1858. A building boom followed and, with the subsequent arrival of the railroad, turned this picturesque adobe town into the largest American city on the Pacific coast.

The view is taken from a site south of Requem Street, looking north. The street on the left is Main, and the two-story building is the United States Hotel. On the right is Los Angeles Street; the long, low row of one-story adobe buildings housed various merchants. The two-story adobe structure at the north end was headquarters for Frémont while he was acting governor of California in 1847. The complete lithograph, like the others in Kuchel & Dresel's thirty-print series (see pl.90), has vignettes around the margin.

96 After Alfred E. Mathews, *F Street, Denver*, 1866. From *Pencil Sketches of Colorado, its Cities, Principal Towns and Mountain Scenery* (New York, 1866)
Toned lithograph, 22.8 × 40.5
Amon Carter Museum, Fort Worth, Texas
Mathews (1831–74) produced a number of views of the West after *Pencil Sketches of Colorado*. In addition to this view of F Street, that work contains pictures of Blake and Laramie streets as well as an overall view of Denver and Colorado Springs. Most of the rest of Mathews' work is devoted to natural scenery.

97 Albert Bierstadt, *Sunrise, Yosemite Valley*, date unknown
Oil on canvas, 92.2 × 132.8
Amon Carter Museum, Fort Worth, Texas

98 Currier & Ives, *Prairie Fires of the Great West*, 1871
Lithograph, 21.4 × 31.6
Amon Carter Museum, Fort Worth, Texas
Prairie fires, according to George Catlin, who painted them several times, formed "some of the most beautiful scenes that are to be witnessed in this country"; but, he continued, "There is yet another character of burning prairies . . . the war, or hell of fires! where the grass is seven or eight feet high . . . and the flames are driven forward by the hurricanes, which often sweep over the vast prairies of this denuded country . . . The fire . . . travels at an immense and frightful rate, and often destroys, on their fleetest horses, parties of Indians, who are so unlucky as to be overtaken by it."

99 Joseph Hubert Becker, *Snow Sheds on the Central Pacific Railroad in the Sierra Nevada Mountains, May 1869*, c. 1869
Oil on canvas, 48.2 × 66
The Thomas Gilcrease Institute of American History and Art, Tulsa
Soon after completion of the transcontinental railroad Frank Leslie sent Becker (1841–1910?) to picture events along the railroad for his

magazine, *Leslie's Illustrated*. Becker was on the first train that ran from Omaha straight through to San Francisco without changing at Promontory. The trip took eighty-one hours. He spent six weeks in California, making a special study of the Chinese, on Leslie's instructions. This painting, done after his return to New York, is the first made of the snow sheds on the Central Pacific and shows some of the Chinese who worked for the railroad.

100 Thomas Moran, *Cliffs of the Green River*, 1874
Oil on canvas, 68.8 × 115.2
Amon Carter Museum, Fort Worth, Texas
As he made his way northward in June, 1871, from the Union Pacific station at Corinne, Utah, to join Hayden's expedition outside Virginia City, Montana, Moran saw the spectacular cliffs of the Green River for the first time. He returned in August, 1872, with a commission from *Picturesque America* to record scenery along the western route of the transcontinental railroad. This view is a few miles north of the Union Pacific tracks near a station called Green River.

The painting was reviewed in the New York *Herald* on April 8, 1875: "The composition is remarkably picturesque, and the interest has been heightened by the introduction of an Indian guide and a cavalcade of white men. . . . Every touch of the brush displays knowledge which can only be fully appreciated by those who have seen the wild and picturesque regions which the artist so happily portrays."

When he returned to the Green River in 1879, Moran made several more sketches, and in the end he produced more than thirty paintings of the river and cliffs, which became something of an icon of the West to him, recalling his early days as an explorer-artist. The cliffs were also photographed by W.H. Jackson.

101 Thomas Moran, *Old Faithful*, 1873
Watercolor, 35.6 × 26
Private collection
Moran painted the now most famous geyser in the Yellowstone, Old Faithful – which Hayden called "one of the finest and most regular of all the geysers of the region" – for only one patron, the financier Jay Cooke.

102 J.T. Hammond, *Lazooing a Horse on the Prairie*, c. 1833. From *A Visit to Texas* (1834)
Engraving, 6.5 × 9.3
Amon Carter Museum, Fort Worth, Texas

103 VWB after W.J. Palmer, *Driving Cattle into a Corral in the Far West*. From *Harper's Weekly* (September 11, 1875)
Engraving, 31.4 × 49
Amon Carter Museum, Fort Worth, Texas
This image suggests that the Spanish practice of roping was not yet universal on the high plains.

104 Carl William Hahn, *Harvest Time* (detail), 1875
Oil on canvas, 91.4 × 177.8
The Fine Arts Museums of San Francisco, Gift of Mrs Harold R. McKinnon and Mrs Harry L. Brown
For Hahn and his time in California see the note to Pl.93.

105 John Russell Bartlett (attrib.), *Church at El Paso del Norte, Chihuahua*, c. 1851
Sepia wash, 22.8 × 28.5
The John Carter Brown Library, Providence, R.I.

Bartlett took up the job of commissioner of the boundary survey in August, 1850. He landed at Indianola, on the Texas coast, and set out to meet his Mexican counterpart at El Paso, the centuries-old settlement on the Rio Grande (see Pl. 115). He remained in the village – which was still officially in the Mexican province of Chihuahua – until the following summer.

Bartlett had begun his artistic training when, as a schoolboy of fourteen, he took lessons from an itinerant German artist. He continued the study, largely because of his interest in science, but in 1850 science and art were not so far apart. This view is reproduced in Bartlett, *Personal Narrative*, Vol. I. p. 189.

106 Samuel Emery Chamberlain, *General Wool crossing the Military Plaza, San Antonio*, c. 1856
Watercolor, 18.7 × 31.1
San Jacinto Museum of History, Houston
Chamberlain (1829–1908) joined General Wool in the fall of 1846. He returned to Boston in 1854, and in the calmness of the East Coast he vividly recalled – and enhanced – his wartime experiences in both words and pictures. There are two sets of Chamberlain's watercolors: the other, in the West Point Museum, is interspersed with his handwritten memoirs in the manner of an illuminated manuscript.

107 Edward Everett, *Mission of San José near San Antonio de Bexar*, 1846
Watercolor, 18.4 × 27.9
Amon Carter Museum, Fort Worth, Texas
Everett (1818–after 1900) was born in London and emigrated to the United States in 1840, settling in Quincy, Illinois. When the war with Mexico began, he accompanied General Wool and sketched several of the missions around San Antonio. San José was begun by Father Antonio Margil de Jesús in 1719.

The five known Everett watercolors are in the Amon Carter Museum. Four of them were published in the official report of Wool's expedition to Mexico: George W. Hughes, ''Report of the Secretary of War,'' *Sen. Ex. Doc. No. 32*, U.S. Cong., 31st Cong., 1st Sess.

108 Artist unknown, *March of the Caravan.* From Josiah Gregg, *Commerce on the Prairies* (1844)
Engraving, 5.5 × 14.2
Amon Carter Museum, Fort Worth, Texas
Gregg's book was immensely popular, going through fourteen printings from 1844 to 1933.

109 C.B. Graham after John Mix Stanley, *Mouth of Night Creek.* From W.H. Emory, *Notes of a Military Reconnoissance* (1848)
Lithograph, 10.4 × 17.1
Amon Carter Museum, Fort Worth, Texas
Stanley was a restless young artist who left a newly-established gallery in Cincinnati, where he had just opened his exhibition of 83 Indian portraits, and headed west. He joined Colonel S.C. Owen's wagon train, which included Dr Josiah Gregg and young Susan Magoffin, whose published diary of the venture became a classic. The group reached Santa Fe about the time American troops arrived, and Stanley joined Kearny as expedition artist.

The forty plates, including scenery, Indian portraits, natural history, Indian hieroglyphics, and botany, in Emory's *Notes* are apparently all Stanley's work. The document was published by both the House and the Senate. The House version (U.S. 30th Cong., 1st Sess., H.E.D. 41) is superior to the Senate version because some copies were apparently issued before the large map was ready.

110 After James W. Abert, *Pueblo de Santo Domingo.* From Abert, *Report of . . . New Mexico in the Years 1846–47*, in Emory, *Notes of a Military Reconnaissance*, 1848 (House of Representatives version)
Lithograph, 10.1 × 18.2
Amon Carter Museum, Fort Worth, Texas
The *Report* of Lieutenant Abert (1820–97) is bound in with some copies of Emory's *Notes*.

111 Richard H. Kern, ''*Robidoux's Pass, White Mountains, New Mexico*,'' 1848
Watercolor, 14.9 × 10.8
Amon Carter Museum, Fort Worth, Texas
Made after a November 27, 1848, trip through Hardscrabble Canyon, this is one of the most painterly of the early New Mexico pictures. Kern labeled it as Robidoux Pass, but I am indebted to Professor David Weber of Southern Methodist University for pointing out, in a manuscript on Kern that is now in progress, that it is more likely to be Hardscrabble Canyon.

112 Richard H. Kern, *La Parroquia, Santa Fe, New Mexico*, 1849
Watercolor, 10.1 × 14.6
Amon Carter Museum, Fort Worth, Texas

113 Richard H. Kern, *Valley of Taos, looking South, New Mexico*, 1849
Watercolor, 10.5 × 14.6
Amon Carter Museum, Fort Worth, Texas
The framework in the foreground is probably an elevated platform of the sort used by the Pueblo Indians for storing grain or corn out of the reach of animals.

114 John Russell Bartlett, *Ascent to the Quicksilver Mines, New Almaden, California*, c. 1851
Pencil and sepia wash, 44.4 × 32.3
The John Carter Brown Library, Providence, R.I.
This picture is included in Bartlett, *Personal Narrative*, Vol. II, p. 62.

115 John Russell Bartlett, *El Paso, Texas*, 1852
Pencil and sepia wash, 22.5 × 28.6
The John Carter Brown Library, Providence, R.I.
Bartlett's headquarters in El Paso was a large adobe house that belonged to James Magoffin. Soon after his arrival, he borrowed the entire house for a dinner and ball in honor of the Mexican commissioner and his officers. The leading citizens of El Paso dined at eight, had supper at midnight, and danced until dawn, when breakfast was served.

116 Artist unknown, *Mission Church of San Xavier del Bac* (detail). From *Reports of Explorations and Surveys . . . for a Railroad . . . to the Pacific Ocean* (1855–60), Vol. VII
Color lithograph, 20.9 × 28.5
Courtesy Amon Carter Museum, Fort Worth, Texas
The church was located ''in a truly miserable place consisting of from 80 to 100 huts of mud, poles, or straw,'' Bartlett recalled, ''the sole occupants of which are Pimo [sic] Indians, though generally called *Papagos*. In the midst of these hovels stands the largest and most beautiful church in Sonora.''

117 Worthington Whittredge, *Santa Fe*, July 20, 1866
Oil on canvas, 20.3 × 58.7
Yale University Art Gallery, Gift from the estate of William W. Farnam, BA 1866, MA 1869

118 John J. Young after Heinrich Balduin Möllhausen, *Chimney Peak* (detail), c. 1860. From Joseph C. Ives, *Report Upon the Colorado River of the West* (1861)
Lithograph, 14.6 × 22.2
Amon Carter Museum, Fort Worth, Texas
Möllhausen (1825–1905) arrived from Germany in 1849 and by 1854 had made two expeditions into the West and provided numerous illustrations for government publications as well as his own narratives.

119 J.J. Young after a sketch by H.B. Möllhausen, *Mohave Cañon* (detail), 1861. From Ives, *Report Upon the Colorado*
Lithograph, 14.3 × 22.2
Amon Carter Museum, Fort Worth, Texas
Of the ''profound chasm'' of the Mojave Canyon Ives wrote: ''A solemn stillness reigned in the darkening avenue broken only by the splash of the paddles or the cry of a solitary heron startled by our approach.''

120 Thomas Moran, *The Chasm of the Colorado*, 1873–74
Oil on canvas, 213.3 × 365.8
U.S. Department of the Interior, on loan to the National Museum of American Art (formerly National Collection of Fine Arts), Smithsonian Institution, Washington, D.C.
From his dozens of field sketches and watercolors, Moran produced this view from Powell's Plateau, one of the most magnificent paintings of the American West. For Moran and the Grand Canyon see above, p. 58.

121 José Cardero, *Funeral Pyre and Tombs of the Family of the present An-kay, Port Mulgrave*, 1792
Watercolor, 43 × 58
Museo Naval, Madrid
Malaspina had set out in 1789 to circumnavigate the globe. While in Peru he reassigned a cabin boy, José Cardero, as painter-cartographer for the expedition. Malaspina first called ''Pepi'' Cardero's drawings ''those of a simple amateur, not devoid of taste or artistic feeling,'' but by the time they reached the Northwest coast the amateur's work had improved and ultimately added a great deal to the knowledge that came out of the expedition. The ships returned to Spain in 1793.

122 Paul Kane, *Drying Salmon near Colville on the Columbia River* (detail), c. 1846
Watercolor, 14 × 23.5
Stark Museum of Art, Orange, Texas
Kane (1810–71) was born in Ireland, but moved to Canada at the age of eight. After a brief sojourn to study in Europe, he set out in 1845, with the support of several patrons, to spend the next three years traveling and sketching in the West.

123 Paul Kane, *Falls at Colville* (detail), c. 1848
Oil on canvas, 48.2 × 73.6
Royal Ontario Museum, Toronto
Observing the Chualpays' method of catching salmon, Kane was impressed by their concern for conservation. The ''Salmon Chief'' controlled the fishing, telling the Indians when they could fish and how much they could take. He agreed with Kane that more salmon could be taken, but pointed out that if they were, there would not be enough for the Indians upriver.

124 After Lieutenant (later Sir) Henry James Warre, *Fort Vancouver.* From Warre, *Sketches in North America and the Oregon Territory* (London: Dickinson & Co., 1848)

Toned lithograph (hand colored), 19 × 29.2
Amon Carter Museum, Fort Worth, Texas

125 After Henry James Warre, *Fall of the Peloos*. From Warre, *Sketches* (see Pl.124)
Toned lithograph (hand colored), 36.5 × 50.8
Amon Carter Museum, Fort Worth, Texas
The original drawing of the falls of the Palouse, along with eighty other sketches and watercolors by Warre (1819–98), is in the collection of the American Antiquarian Society, Worcester, Massachusetts.

126 John Mix Stanley, *Scene on the Columbia River* (detail), *c.* 1852
Oil on canvas, 43.5 × 53.6
Amon Carter Museum, Fort Worth, Texas
In 1849 Stanley displayed his Indian Gallery in several Eastern cities, then deposited it in

Washington in the Smithsonian Institution in the hope that Congress would purchase it. He was unsuccessful, and in 1865 a fire in the Smithsonian destroyed all but five of the paintings.

127 Paul Kane, *Mount St Helen's with smoke from the crater hovering in a peculiar form over the top of the mountain*, 1847
Watercolor, 20.5 × 34
Stark Museum of Art, Orange, Texas

128 John Mix Stanley, *Oregon City on the Willamette River* (detail), *c.* 1848
Oil on canvas, 66.3 × 100.3
Amon Carter Museum, Fort Worth, Texas
This painting, like Pl.126, probably resulted from Stanley's first trip to the Northwest in the summer of 1847.

129 After Grafton T. Brown, *City of Portland, Oregon* (detail), *c.* 1861
Toned lithograph, 48.4 × 74.9
Amon Carter Museum, Fort Worth, Texas
The founders of Portland rapidly sold lots to those who came west because of the California Gold Rush. This view, by a versatile black artist, is of the west bank. The surrounding vignettes show individual businesses, probably a way of selling advertising.

130 Carl William Hahn, *Looking down at Yosemite Valley from Glacier Point*, 1874
Oil on canvas, 69.2 × 116.8
California Historical Society, San Francisco/San Marino
For Hahn see the note to Pl.93.

Index

Figures in *italic* type indicate pages on which illustrations appear

ABERT, Lt James W.   41, 171, *171*, 173
Alaska   183, *183*
Alexander, Francis   *82*, 199(18)
Arkansas River   21, 32, 41, 170
American Turf Register and Sporting Magazine   34
Assiniboin Indians   *33*, 37, *37*
Audubon, John James   100–101, *100–101*, 126, 200(39)
Ayres, Thomas A.   58, *59*, 198(p.59)

BADGER, Daniel D. 91
Baltimore, Md.   48, 199(15)
Barlowe, Capt. Arthur   16
Barnard, S.   *106*
Barrow, Bennet H.   108
Bartlett, John Russell   43–44, *43*, 167, *167*, *174*, *174*, 175, *175*, 205(105, 115, 116)
Baton Rouge, La.   21, 203(83)
Beaumont, Gustave de   120
Becker, Joseph   *159*
Bellevue, Neb.   144, *144*
Benjamin, S. G. W.   200(24)
Bennett, William J.   48, *107*
Berthier, Louis-Alexandre   196(pp.26–27)
Bierstadt, Albert   52, 53–54, 58, *112–13*, 152, *152–53*, 156, *156–57*
Biloxi, Miss.: New   21, 98, *99*; Port   21
Bingham, George Caleb   52, 126, *127*, 204(93)
Birch, Thomas   48, 198(7)
Birch, William   31, 46, 70, *70*, 198(7)
Bird (later Bishop), Isabella L.   91, 155, 159, 163, 165
Blarenberghe, Louis Nicolas van   25, *26–27*, 196(pp.26–27)
Bloomington, Ill.   131
Bodmer, Karl   36–38, *37*, *38*, 39, *130*, 138, *139*, 144, *144–45*, 196–97(p.37, p.38)
Bomford, George   92
Boone (or Boon), Daniel   *28*, 29
Boqueta de Woiseri, J. L.   *103*, 200–201(41)
Borcke, Heros von   112
Boston, Mass.   20, 22, *24*, 25, 66, 67, 68–69, *68*, 72, *72–73*; Museum of Fine Arts   94, 95, *95*, 200(33)
Bowen, J. T.   202(58)

Bowles, Samuel   192
Bradford, William   19–20
Bright, Henry Arthur   134
Brissot de Warville, J. P.   71
Britton & Rey   203(90)
Browere, Alburtius del Orient   *80*, 199(16)
Brown, Grafton T.   *190–91*
Bryant, William Cullen   51–52, 64, *65*, 123
Bufford, J. H.   199(11)
Buffum, E. Gould   150
Bulger, Capt. Andrew W.   *119*, 201(56)
Burgis, William   21–22, *67*, 94

CABEZA DE VACA, Alvar Núñez   10
Caird, Sir James   131
California Illustrated Magazine   198(p.59)
Cambridge, Mass.   69; Harvard   94, *94*, 95
Cardero, José   183, *183*, 205(121)
Carver, Capt. Jonathan   23, *23*, 29
Castañeda, Pedro de   11–12
Catesby, Mark   22–23, 100, *100*, 200(38)
Catlin, George   34–36, *34–36*, 38, 94, 138, *138*, 140, 141, *141*, 200(32), 202(73), 204(98)
Catskill, N. Y.   80, *80*
Catskill Mountains   64, *65*, 80
Cerveau, Firmin   *102–03*
Chamberlain, Samuel E.   168, *168*, 205(106)
Charleston, S. C.   20, 22, 100–101, *100–101*, 106, *106*, 113
Chastellux, Marquis de   201(50)
Chateaubriand, François-René de   47, 71
Cheyenne, Wyo.   46, 163
Chicago, Ill.   *59*, 131, 132–33, *132–33*
Chittenden, George B.   56
Chugwater, Wyo.   55, *55*
Church, Frederic Edwin   52, 84, *84–85*
Cincinnati, O.   30, 36, 120, 121, *121*, 126, 134, *134*
Clark, William   30, 34, *34*, 38, 119; *and see* Lewis and Clark expedition
Cleveland, O.   134, 135, *135*
Coffin, Charles Carleton   114
Cole, Thomas   46, 47, 48–52, *49*, 64, *65*, 80, *81*, *82*
Colman, Samuel   52, 53, 88
Colorado River   58, 178, *178–81*
Columbia River   30, 184–85, *184–85*, 188
Columbus, Christopher   9–10, *10*, *11*
Colville, Wash.   *184–85*
Colville Indians   184–85, *184–85*
Commercetown (Commerce), Mo.   *122*, 202(59)

Cooke, G.   *107*
Cooper, George V.   *154*, 204(94)
Coronado, F. Vásquez de   11–12, 178
Council Bluff, Neb.   196(p.32)
Council Bluffs (Kanesville), Iowa   32, 146–47, *147*, 196(p.32), 203(84)
Council Bluffs Ferry, Iowa   *146*
Cree Indians   37, *37*
Crèvecoeur, Hector St John de   85
Crèvecoeur, Michel Guillaume Jean de   29, 83
Cropsey, Jasper F.   *2*, 96, *96–97*, 195(p.2), 200(35)
Crow, Thomas & Co.   200(26)
Currier & Ives   *86*, *132*, *143*, *158*

DAVIS, E. H.   *123*, 202(60)
de Bry, Theodor   *14*, *18*, 19
Degas, Edgar   116, *116–17*
Denver, Colo.   54, 138, 154, *155*, *155*
DeSmet, Fr P. J.   185
Detroit, Mich.   120, *120*
Dickens, Charles   74, 79, 129
Dodge, Maj. Gen. Grenville M.   158
Donner Lake, Nev.   154, 159
Dorchester Heights, Mass.   68–69, *68*
Doughty, Thomas   46
Dresel, Emil: *see* Kuchel
Dunton, John   66
Durand, Asher B.   49–52, *50*, *51*, 64, *65*, 200(34)

EAKINS, Thomas   60, *60*
Ehrgott, Forbriger & Co.   202(70)
Elliott, Henry Wood   55, 56
El Paso, Tex.   167, *167*, 175, *175*, 205(115)
Emerson, R. W.   52, 64
Emory, Lt (later Maj.) William H.   42, 43, 44, 171, *171*, 177, 205(109)
Endicott, William, & Co.   204(94)
Erie Canal   46, 74–75, *75*
Evans, Estwick   120
Everett, Edward   168, *169*, 205(107)

FENN, Harry   *110*, 201(49)
Filson, John   29
Flint, Timothy   105
Foote, Mary Hallock   174
Fort Caroline, Fla.   15
Fort Clark, N. D.   35, *37*, 38, 196(p.37)
Fort Laramie, Wyo.   40, 148, *148*
Fort McKenzie, Mont.   37, *37*, 38, 196(p.37)

Fort Pierre, S. D. 35
Fort Smith, Ark. 32, 44, 45
Fort Sumter, S. C. 53–54, 112–13, *112–13*
Fort Union, N. D. 34, 38
Fort Vancouver, Wash. 186, *186*
Fourdrinier, Pierre 200(40)
Franklin, Benjamin 119
Frémont, John C. 41–43, *41*, 152, 197(p.41), 204(95)
French Bar, Cal. *150–51*
Freneau, Philip 48

GENESEE VALLEY, N.Y. 48, *80*
Gifford, Sanford R. 52, 54–55, *55*, 56, 96, *96*, 200(34)
Giroux, C. *108*, 201(47)
Gold Rush 43, 150–51, *150–51*, 164, 190, 199(16), 204(94), 206(129)
Gordon, Peter 102, *102*
Grand Canyon 58, 178, *180–81*
Greeley, Horace 147, 156
Green River, Wyo. 57, 160, *160*, 204(100)
Gregg, Dr Josiah 170, *170*, 205(109)
Guadalupe Mountain, Tex. *43*
Gunnison, Capt. John W. 44, 45, 172

HAHN, Carl William 153, 156, *164–65*, *192*
Hammond, J. T. *162*
Harding, Chester *28*, 196(p.28)
Hariot, Thomas 16, 18
Harmony, Ind. 196(p.37), 202(59)
Harper's Ferry, W. Va. 48, 112, *113*
Harper's Weekly 162, 163, *163*, 198(p.59), 200(30)
Harris, John 198(3)
Harte, Bret 151
Harvard College 94, *94*, 95
Hastings, Lansford W. 191
Hatch Co. 200(27)
Havell, Robert, Jr. 200(39)
Hayden, Dr F. V. 54–55, 56, 57, 58, 160, 198(p.56)
Heade, Martin Johnson 52, *89*
Heap, George 22. *22*, 196–97(p.22)
Hennepin, Fr Louis 20, *21*, 195(p.21)
Henry, Edward Lamson 114, *114–15*
Hicks, Edward *83*, 199(20)
Hidatsa Indians *see* Minnetaree
Hilgard, E. W. 165
Hill, John 199(12, 13), 200(32)
Hoban, James 78, 199(14)
Hoffman, Charles Fenno 128
Holmes, William H. *56*, 198(p.56)
Homer, Winslow 60, 92, *92–93*
Hornor, Thomas *76–77*, 199(13)
Hudson River *26–27*, 46, 68, *69*, 75, *75*, 80, *80*, 88, 89, 95, *96–97*, 97
Hunt, S. V. 201(50)
Hutchings, James Mason 198(p.59)

INGER, Christian *147*
Inness, George 86, *86–87*
Iowa Indians *140*, 141
Irving, Washington 66, 126, 127
Ives, Lt Joseph C. 58, 178, 205(119)

JACKSON, William Henry 55, 56, 57, 160 198(p.55, p.56), 204(100)
James, Edwin 137; *and see* Long expedition
Jefferson, Thomas 29–30, 31, 47–48, 61, 106, 107, 110, 123, 199(14), 201(50)
Jeffreys, Thomas 195–96(p.22)
Jesse (Jessie), Lake, N.D. *142*
Johnson, David *111*
Johnson, Eastman 204(93)
Joliet and Marquette expedition 20

KANE, Paul 96, 184, *184–85*, 187, 188–89, *189*, 205(122)

Kanesville (Council Bluffs), Iowa 146–47, *147*, 203(84)
Kearny, Col. (later Gen.) Stephen Watts 42, 171
Keith, William 204(93)
Kellogg & Comstock 203(89)
Kemble, Frances Anne 106
Kendall, George W. 169
Kensett, John Frederick 52, *53*, 54
Kern, Benjamin and Edward 42–43
Kern, Richard H. 42–43, 45, 172, *172–73*
King, Mrs Aurelia 132
Kipling, Rudyard 133
Kuchel, Charles C., and Emil Dresel *150–51*, *155*, 204(95)

LANDER, Col. Frederick West 53
Lane, Fitz Hugh 52, *52*, 53
Laramie, Wyo. 158; *and see* Fort Laramie
La Salle, Robert Cavalier, Sieur de 20
Latrobe, Benjamin 78, *78*, 201(46)
Latrobe, John H. B. *126*, 202(62)
Laudonnière, René de 14, 15, *15*, 19
Le Bouteaux, J.-B. M. 21, *99*
Le Moyne de Morgues, Jacques 14–16, *14*, *15*, *18*, 19
L'Enfant, Pierre *26–27*, 78
Leslie, Frank 204(99)
Lesueur, Charles Alexandre 122, *122*, 196(p.37), 202(59)
Letts, J. M. 204(94)
Leutze, Emanuel 201(51), 204(93)
Levinge, Capt. (later Sir) Richard George Augustus 104, *104*, 201(43)
Lewis, James Otto 196(p.28)
Lewis, Meriwether 30, *30*; *and see* Lewis and Clark expedition
Lewis and Clark expedition 30–31, 32, 38, 160, 196(p.32)
Lisiansky, Urey 183
Lockport, N.Y. *74–75*, 75
Long, Maj. Stephen H. 31–32, *31*, 196(p.31)
Long expedition 31–33, *31*, *32*, *33*, 38, 137, *137*, 196(p.31)
Los Angeles, Cal. 154, *155*
Louisville, Ky. 30, 100, 126, *126*
Lowell Offering 93
Ludlow, Fitz Hugh 152, 156, 204(92)

MACLEOD, William *113*, 201(52)
Maclure, William 202(59)
Magoffin, James 205(115)
Magoffin, Susan 205(109)
Malaspina, Alejandro 183, 205(121)
Mandan Indians 30, 35–36, *35*, *36*, 38, *38*, 141, *141*, 144, *145*, 197(p.38), 203(82)
Marcy, Col. Randolph B. 45
Marietta, O. 123, *123*
Marryat, Capt. Frederick 86, 95, 124, 204(91)
Marryat, Samuel Frank *151*, 204(91)
Marston, James B. *72–73*
Martineau, Harriet 121, 129
Martyr, Peter 9
Mather, Cotton 20
Matthews, Alfred E. *155*, 204(96)
McAllister, Gen. Robert 114
Melville, Herman 93
Meneghelli, Enrico 95, 200(33)
Memphis, Tenn. 203(83)
Menghelli, Enrico 95, 200(33)
Mexican boundary survey 42–44, *43*, 174, *174*, 175
Miller, Alfred Jacob 39–40, *39*, *40*, *143*, 148, *148–49*
Minnetaree (Hidatsa) Indians 30, 38
Mississippi River 20, 21, *23*, 32, 53, 54, 105, 109, 124, *124–25*, 126, 127, 128, *138*, 201(44)
Missouri River 21, 30, 32, *32*, 34, 126,

138–39, *139*, 146, *146*
Mojave Canyon 178, *179*
Möllhausen, Heinrich Balduin 178, *178*, *179*, 205(118)
Moran, Thomas 55–59, *57*, 164, *164–65*, 178, *180–81*
Mostaert, Jan 10–13, *12–13*, 195(pp.12–13)
Mount, William Sidney 52
Mount Desert Island, Me. 96, *96*
Mount St Helens, Wash. 188–89, *188–89*
Munson, William Giles 92, *92*, 200(29)

NARRAGANSETT BAY, R.I. *89*
Natchez, Miss. 21, 203(83)
Natural Bridge of Virginia 30, 110, *111*
New Almaden, Cal. 174, *174*
New Amsterdam 66, *67*
New Orleans, La. 21, 25, 39, 102, *103*, 116, *116–17*, 201(44), 203(83)
New York City 20, 21, 22, 59, 66, *67*, 68, 71, *71*, 75, *76–77*, 90–91, *90–91*, 97, *97*
Niagara Falls *2*, 20, *21*, 39, 84–85, *84–85*, 195(p.21), 196(p.37)

O'FALLON, Major Benjamin 38, 196(p.31)
Ohio River 29, 32, 126, *126*
Olivier Plantation, La. 108, *109*
Omaha, Neb. 46, 144, 203(81)
Oregon City, Ore. 190–91, *190*
Oregon Trail 40, 43, 138, 146, 148, 152–53, *152–53*, 190; *and see* Parkman
Otis, Bass *41*, 197(p.41)
Owen, Col. S. C. 205(109)

PACIFIC RAILROAD SURVEY 44–46, *44–45*, *142*, 175, *175*
Palmer, Frances F. 86, 199(22)
Palmer, Joel 191
Palmer, W. J. *163*
Palouse (Peloos) River 187, *187*
Parke, Lt John G. 44
Parkman, Francis 142, 148, 152, 153
Pawnee Indians *31*, 153
Peale, Charles Willson *30*, *31*, 32, 38, 196(p.30, p.31), 202(59)
Peale, Titian Ramsay 31–33, *32*, 38, 202(59)
Pecos River *43*
Pelham, Henry 196(p.24)
Penn, Thomas 22, 196(p.22)
Persac, Marie Adrien 104, *105*, 108, *109*, 201(44)
Philadelphia, Pa. 20, 22, *22*, 31, 32, 34, 38, 46, 59, 70–71, *70*, 90, *91*, 202(58)
Phyfe, Duncan 71, *71*, 198(8)
Picturesque America 96, 110, *110*, 135, *135*, 201(49), 204(100)
Piegan Indians 37, *37*
Piercy, Frederick 146–47, *146*, *147*, 203(83)
Pierie, Lt William 68, 198(4)
Pike, Lt Zebulon M. 31, 38
Pittsburgh, Pa. 30
Platte River 32, *33*, 40, 46, 54, 138, *139*, 148
Portland, Ore. 190, *190–91*
Port Mulgrave (Yakutat Bay) 183, *183*
Powell, Col. John Wesley 58, 160, 178
Prairie du Chien, Wis. 34, 119, *119*
Preuss, Charles *41*, 42–43
Pyramid Lake, Nev. *41*

RAILROADS 86–87, *86–87*, 90, 128, 129, *129*; Baltimore & Ohio 202(62, 65); transcontinental 42–43, 44–46, *44–45*, 158–59, *158–59*. See also Pacific Railroad Survey
Ranney, William Tylee *128*, 202(64)
Rascher, Charles 202(69)
Reck, Baron von 200(40)
Red River 21, 41, 104, *104*

Remick, Christian 196(p.24)
Remington, Frederic 162
Revere, Paul *24*, 196(p.24)
Richmond, Va. 106, 107, *107*
Rindisbacher, Peter 33–34, *33*, 119, *119*
Roanoke Island, N.C. (colony) 16, 18–19, *62–63*, 98
Robinson, Henry R. 202(58), 203(89)
Rocky Mountains 32, *33*, 38, 39, *44–45*; *and see* Wind River Mountains
Rooker, Michael Angelo 23, *23*
Rosenthal, Max *91*, 200(28)
Rossiter, Thomas Prichard 128, *129*
Rush, Benjamin 47
Ruskin, John 55, 199(21)
Russell, Charles M. 162
Russell, William Howard 109, 113
Ruxton, George Frederick 173, 177

SACHSE, Edward, & Co. *78–79*, *124–25*, 199(15)
Sacramento, Cal. 46, 150, 154, *154*, 204(94)
St Anthony, Falls of 23, *23*, 29
St Augustine, Fla. 110, *110*
St Louis, Mo. 30, 32, 34, 36, 38, 39, 59, 124, *124–25*, 128, 138, *138*, 203(83)
Salt Lake City, Utah 146, 147, *146–47*, 158
San Antonio, Tex. 167, 168–69, *168–69*
San Francisco, Cal. 150, *151*, 154, 204(92, 93)
Sangre de Cristo Mountains 172
Santa Fe, N.M. 42, 54, 138, 170, 172, *172*, 173, 176–77, *176–77*, 205(109)
Santo Domingo, N.M. 171, *171*
San Xavier del Bac, Ariz. *175*
Sarony & Major 202(60)
Sarony, Major & Knapp 203(78)
Savannah, Ga. 102, *102–03*
Say, Dr Thomas 32, 196(p.31, p.37), 202(59)
Scotts Bar, Cal. *150–51*
Scranton, Pa. *87*
Secoton 16, *99*
Serres, Dominic *69*, 198(5)

Seymour, Samuel 31–33, *31*, *33*, 38, *137*, 198(7)
Sierra Nevada Mountains *154*, 159, *159*
Simpson, Lt James H. 171, 172
Sioux Indians 33, 35, *35*, 153
Smith, John Rubens *71*, 198(8)
Smith, William Loughton 107
Sohon, Gustavus *44–45*, 197(pp.44–45)
Springfield, Ill. 131
Squier, E. G. *123*, 202(60)
Stanley, John Mix 42, *142*, 171, *171*, 188, *188*, *191*, 197(pp.44–45), 203(78), 205(109), 206(126)
Staten Island, N.Y. *96–97*, 200(35)
steamboats 75, 104–05, *104–05*, 116, 120, *121*, 124, *124–25*, 144, 178, *178–79*, *190–91*; *Yellowstone* 34, 35, 36, 138, *138*
Stevens, Isaac I. 44, 203(78)
Stewart, Capt. William Drummond 39–40, *39*, 197(p.39, p.40)
Strickland, William 70, *70*
Sturges, Jonathan 198(1)
Sullivan, Charles 202(60)

TAIT, Arthur F. *143*, 203(80)
Taos, N.M. 173, *173*
Tattersall, George *74*, 199(10)
Thoreau, Henry David 87
Thorpe, Thomas Bangs 109
Tocqueville, Alexis de 122
Toudy, H. J., & Co. 203(85)
Trollope, Anthony 124
Trollope, Mrs Frances 75, 79, 89, 116
Trumbull, John 46
Tuckerman, Henry T. 49
Turner, J. M. W. 49, 199(21)
Twain, Mark 105, 126, 127, 153, 154
Tyawapatia Bottom, Mo. *122*

VANCOUVER, Wash. 186, *186*
Vicksburg, Miss. 203(83)
Vinckeboons, Jan *67*
Virgin, Rio 58

A Visit to Texas 162, *162*
"A Visit to the States" 133

WALL, William Guy 75
Walter, Thomas Ustick 78, *78–79*
Warre, Lt (later Sir) Henry James 186, *186–87*
Washington, D.C. 78–79, *78–79*
Westover, Va. 114, *114–15*
West Point, N.Y. *26–27*, 94, *94*, 95, 171, 202(62)
Whipple, Lt Amiel W. 44
White, John 16–19, *17*, 98, *99*
Whiting, William Henry Chase 43
Whitman, Walt 97
Whitney, Eli 92, 108
Whittredge, Thomas Worthington 52–55 *passim*, 138, 139, *139*, 176, *176–77*, 200(34), 204(93)
Wied-Neuwied, Maximilian, Prince of 36–38, *37*, 39, 138, 144, 196(p.37); quoted 69, 72, 75, 80, 131, 138, 139, 144, 197(p.38), 203(82)
Wild, John Caspar *121*, 200(58)
Wilkes, Cdr Charles 41, 186
Willis, Nathaniel P. 198(6)
Wiman, Charles 204(93)
Wind River Mountains 39–40, *39*, *149*
Woods, John 126
Woodward, J. Douglas *135*, 202(71)

YELLOWSTONE (Park) 55, 56–58, *57*, 160, *161*; *Grand Canyon of the Yellowstone* (Moran) 55, *57*, 58
Yorktown, Va. (battle) 25, *26–27*, 196(pp.26–27)
Yosemite, Cal. 58, *59*, 156, *156–57*, 192, *192*, 204(92)
Young, John J. 205(118, 119)

ZUÑI INDIANS 11